THE NEW DEVELOPMENT

The New Development Politics
The Age of Empire Building and New Social Movements

JAMES PETRAS

ASHGATE

Published by
Ashgate Publishing Limited
Gower House
Croft Road
Aldershot
Hants GU11 3HR
England

Ashgate Publishing Company
Suite 420
101 Cherry Street
Burlington, VT 05401-4405
USA

Ashgate website: http://www.ashgate.com

British Library Cataloguing in Publication Data
Petras, James, 1937-
   The new development politics : the age of empire building
   and new social movements
   1.Imperialism 2.Globalization 3.Social movements - Latin
   America 4.United States - Foreign economic relations -
   Latin America 5.Latin America - Foreign economic relations
   - United States 6.Latin America - Social conditions - 1982-
   I.Title
   325.3'2

Library of Congress Control Number: 2002117153

ISBN 0 7546 3539 2 (Hbk)
ISBN 0 7546 3540 6 (Pbk)

Printed and bound by MPG Books Ltd, Bodmin, Cornwall.

Contents

Chapter 1

Imperialism and Empire-building in the Twenty-first Century

Introduction

This chapter looks at one of a number of over-optimistic postmodern analyses of the capitalist world economy from which imperialism, economic crisis, the state, class and class struggle have all been purged. The analysis in question is provided by Michael Hardt and Antonio Negri in *Empire* (2000). Unfortunately, this book is having considerable impact in certain intellectual circles on the political left, influencing the way world developments are understood. According to its authors, as a result of new science and technology, global capitalism now functions as an autonomous 'empire', ruled only by the market and the multinational corporation. Against this celebratory interpretation of capitalism today, it is argued in this chapter that the role of the imperial state *vis-à-vis* capitalist reproduction has been underestimated, and, conversely, that the economic impact of innovation, science and technology on capitalist productivity has been over-estimated. Not only is the imperial state still important to an understanding of the dynamics of world development today, it is also central to the study of agrarian transformation as well as to the role of peasants and workers in this process.

Like so many others in the postmodern mould, this book seeks to persuade the reader that we all live in 'new' times; that it represents what can only be termed the intellectual synthesis and political nadir of postmodern theoretical analysis. In this respect, it does for international relations and global capitalism what previous postmodern texts have done for national, local, regional or village relations and conflicts. Just as these studies have expelled class and class struggle from our understanding of the dynamics of the agrarian grass-roots, so Hardt and Negri seek to expunge imperialism from the way the world economy is reproduced, banishing this important concept to the epistemological black hole of 'post-history'. As such, the book has profound implications for the study of peasants and workers, their reasons for and roles in rural mobilizations, and the whole issue of capitalist transition (and within this the agrarian question) in the so-called Third World.

These implications can be stated simply. If there is no imperialism, then capitalism itself cannot be said to give rise to contradictions (which manifest themselves in imperial rivalries), nor can it be said to carry within itself the seeds of its own demise (and thus possess an alternative to its historically specific forms of property, production, and exchange). The concept of systemic transition is thus swept off the political agenda and, with it, emancipation of various kinds, not least that of peasants and workers operating at the margins of existence. Although the subject of imperialism, and whether or not this concept continues to be applicable to the global capitalist system, seems to be far removed from the everyday reality of the peasant in a Third World village, the opposite is the case. Therefore, not only is the debate about the presence/absence of imperialism still relevant to the study of agrarian grass-roots transformation, but the impact/effects on the latter context of imperialism could be said to form an epistemological dimension missing from much recent discussion about the peasantry, Marxist and non-Marxist alike. This has not always been the case: the imperialism/agriculture/peasantry link has a long history in the political debates of the left, and it is necessary only to mention the work of Rosa Luxemburg and Nicolai Bukharin (1972) and Lenin (1950) for this to be clear. For all these reasons, and also because the book will assuredly become fashionable as an 'analysis' of globalization, the arguments put forward by Hardt and Negri merit close scrutiny. Accordingly, this chapter is organized into four parts: the first three deal with the macrolevel implications of *Empire* (Hardt and Negri, 2000) while the fourth part examines the way in which the microlevel is theorized.

The argument in Part I is that, far from being superseded by the overseas expansion of capital, the imperial states have grown and become essential components of the world political economy. Hardt and Negri's concept of 'empire' mystifies the role of the imperial state, thus undermining an essential adversary, in the front lines of the defence of the privileges and power of the multinational corporations. Part II examines and challenges the claim made by Hardt and Negri about the existence of a 'new capitalist epoch' based on a purported information revolution. In this regard it is clear that the innovations in the early and middle twentieth century were far more significant sources of economy-wide productivity improvement than the electronic, computerized information systems of the late twentieth century. Part III suggests that, instead of empire, the current situation corresponds to a new form of imperialism, while Part IV considers the related questions of the microlevel structure and the kind of agency to which empire gives rise. The analysis informing *Empire* (Hardt and Negri, 2000), it is argued, follows what is now the well-worn path of postmodern theory. Not only do Hardt and Negri replace the notion of 'class' with that of the 'subaltern', they also conflate the latter with what is termed a 'new proletariat'. The resulting category exhibits all the characteristics that Negri in his earlier autonomist phase attributed to the 'subproletariat', a 'marginal subject' of the capitalist development project.

Empire or Imperialism?

Empire (Hardt and Negri, 2000) is a strange book. At a time when the United States is the only superpower, when almost 50 per cent of the five hundred biggest multinationals are US-owned and headquartered, and Washington lead a war of intervention against the peasants and workers of Afghanistan and Iraq – after previous wars of intervention against peasants and workers in the Balkans, Central

America (Panama), the Caribbean (Grenada) and proxy wars in Colombia (Plan Colombia) and earlier Angola, Mozambique, Nicaragua – the authors of this widely praised book tell us that imperialism is a thing of the past. They argue that empire is a post-imperialist phenomenon in which power is dispersed and that no single nation can control the empire. More than this, their view is that empire is a positive advance in world history: 'The thing [sic] we call Empire is actually an enormous historical improvement over the international system and imperialism.' After 413 pages of text and 57 pages of notes the best the authors can do in discussing empire is to tell us that: 'In this smooth space [?] of Empire there is no place of power – it is everywhere and nowhere. Empire is an Ou-Topia or really a non-place' (Hardt and Negri, 2000: 190). Without providing us with a clear notion of the agents of empire, or of its dynamic in the real existing imperial states and their corporations, we are told that the empire is imperial but not imperialist, that the US Constitution is imperial and not imperialist. From this they deduce (and we learn) that it is imperial because (in contrast to imperialism's project always to spread its power linearly in closed spaces and invade, destroy and subsume subject countries within its sovereignty) 'the US constitutional project is constructed on the model of re-articulating an open space and reinventing incessantly diverse and singular networks across an unbounded terrain. The contemporary idea of Empire is born through the global expansion of the internal US constitutional project' (Hardt and Negri, 2000: 182). In other words, this celebration of empire is also a celebration of US constitutionalism (the idea to be exact) that is a model for 'democratizing' the empire. The study disposes of classes and class conflict (and with them peasants and labourers) as outdated and imprecise concepts, and substitutes the notion of 'biopolitical production multitudes' – a term which is never clearly delineated and is without any historical or empirical specificity. Apart from 'multitudes' there are no designated agencies for the announced but unspecified 'revolution'. The program of this novel revolution is not very different from that embraced by welfare state social democrats.

Much has been written about the 'sweep of the book' and 'its theoretical grandeur'. Unsurprisingly, the postmodern theorist Frederic Jameson (Hardt's colleague at Duke University) calls it 'the first great new theoretical synthesis of the new Millennium' ('Globalization and Political Strategy', 2000). Hyperbole aside, few literary reviewers have commented on the book's lack of historical and empirical evidence to buttress the authors' innumerable and unsubstantiated assertions. They argue early on that the intellectual origins of the US revolution can be traced to Spinoza and Machiavelli; Rousseau and Locke are given short shrift, despite their greater immediate relevance. Extended and tendentious discussions of sovereignty are interspersed with reductionist assertions, which either collapse or omit numerous variations. For example, in their discussion of totalitarianism and the nation state Hardt and Negri argue:

If Nazi Germany is the ideal type of the transformation of modern sovereignty into national sovereignty and of the articulation in its capitalist form, Stalinist Russia is the ideal type of the transmission of popular interest and the cruel logics that follow from it into a project of national modernization, mobilizing for its own purposes the productive forces that yearn for liberation from capitalism. (Hardt and Negri, 2000: 110)

I have quoted extensively in order to illustrate the confused, illogical, unhistorical nature of the authors' broad and vacuous generalizations. What empirical or historical basis is there for claiming Nazi Germany is the 'ideal type'? National sovereignty pre-existed the Nazis and continues after its demise in non-totalitarian settings. If Stalin's Russia embodied 'popular interest', why should anyone seek to be liberated from it? The 'cruel logic' of 'popular interests' is stuff from the *ancien régime* – hardly the basis for orienting the 'multitudes' that the writers describe as being the new agents for democratizing the world. Precisely where workers and peasants feature in all this (except as part of the socio-economically amorphous multitudes), what kind of agency they will undertake, and with what aims, remains unclear.

The authors engage in what George Saboul (personal conversation, July 4, 1976, Algiers) once referred to as the 'vacuum cleaner' approach to history: a little bit of ancient history, a smattering of the exegesis of elementary political theory, a plus and minus evaluation of postmodernism, a celebration of US constitutionalism, a brief synopsis of colonialism and post-colonialism. These discursive forays provide an intellectual gloss for the core argument dealing with the contemporary world: the disappearance of imperialism; the obsolescence of imperial states, nation states (and boundaries) and the ascendancy of an ill-defined empire, globalization, and supranational governing bodies, apparently resembling the United Nations. Drawn into this conceptual black hole along with imperialism and class is the role of peasants and workers as agents of historical transformation.

Imperialism-is-US

Let us start with an assertion made by Hardt and Negri regarding the decline of the nation or imperial state. Their argument for a stateless empire exaggerates the autonomy of capital vis-à-vis the state, and parrots the false propositions of the free market ideologues who argue that the 'world market' is supreme and acceptable politically precisely because it operates independently of any specific national interest. Contrary to the view of Hardt and Negri, however, in the contemporary world, the national state, in both its imperial and neocolonial form, has expanded its activity. Far from being an anachronism, the state has become a central element in the world economy and within nation states. But the activities of the state vary according to their class character and whether they are imperial or neocolonial states. In recent years the centrality of the imperial state has been evident in all the fundamental areas of politico–economic, cultural and economic activity that buttress the position of the imperial powers, particularly the US.

Over the past decades several major financial and economic crises have occurred in various regions of the world. In each instance, the imperial states, particularly the US, have intervened to save the multinational corporation, and avoid the collapse of the financial system. For example, in 1994, when Mexican finances were on the verge of collapse, the then US president, Clinton, intervened to dispatch US$20 billion to the Mexican state to bail out US investors and stabilize the peso. Similarly, during the Asian crisis of 1998, the US and European governments approved an International Monetary Fund (IMF) and World Bank (WB) multibillion dollar bail-out in exchange for opening their economies, particularly that of South Korea, to foreign takeovers of basic industries. In the Brazilian crisis of 1999 and the present Argentine crisis, Washington has pressured the IMF to bail-out the regimes. Within the US itself, the threatened bankruptcy of a major international investment bank led to Federal Reserve (the US central bank) intervention, pressuring a private bank bail-out. With greater frequency and with greater resources, therefore, the imperial state has played a dominant role in crisis management, saving major investors from bankruptcy, propping up insolvent multinational corporations and preventing the collapse of currencies. More than ever these corporations and the so-called global economy depend on the constant and massive intervention by imperial states to manage the crisis, and secure benefits (buyouts of local enterprises).

Much the same is true of national debt in general, and that of the US farming and agribusiness sector in particular. The 1970s and 1980s were boom times for US farmers, as the then-USSR made large grain purchases. This was a period when markets were relatively secure and US farmers, who had guaranteed outlets, expanded production, bought more land and machinery and borrowed heavily. US banks were happy to lend money, because markets were buoyant and land prices were high. In the 1980s, however, agricultural commodity prices fell, as US President Carter embargoed further grain sales to the USSR following its presence in Afghanistan. Bank collateral declined in value and farmers, together with the banks that had lent them money, were technically bankrupt. To avert this domestic debt crisis, and to help the US agribusiness enterprises affected, the US state turned increasingly to export subsidies.

Historically and currently, competition between rival imperial powers, economic enterprises and multinational corporations has been spearheaded essentially by rival imperial states. This is particularly true where agriculture is concerned. For example, in 1989 the European states threatened to ban meat imports from the US, on the grounds that growth-inducing hormone treatment of livestock constituted a health risk. This would have blocked US exports worth US$140 million, and the US government threatened to retaliate by preventing imports of European meat worth US$100 million. A common feature of this inter-imperial rivalry surfaces in the form of disputes over what are regarded as trade-distorting price supports. During the late 1980s, for example, the US operated an Export Enhancement Programme (EEP) in an attempt to dispose of grain surpluses and simultaneously win new markets or recapture old ones. Both the Canadian and European states responded not by reducing grain production, but by matching US subsidies. Currently, the US imperial state is leading the fight to open European markets to US beef and US exports of bananas from South and Central America, while the Japanese and the European states negotiate with the US to increase the quota on a series of exports (including steel, textiles, and so on). Trade and markets are largely defined by state-to-state agreements, and the supposedly autonomous and spontaneous process of globalization is not only a product of the growth of the multinational corporations, but largely an artifice of these state-to-state agreements. Accordingly, the situation is one in which competition between capitals is mediated, influenced, and directed by the state; markets do not transcend the state, but operate within state-defined boundaries.

The state plays a pervasive and profound role in the conquest of overseas markets and the protection of local markets. To begin with, the state provides indirect and direct subsidies to export sectors. In the US, agricultural exports receive both indirect subvention, in the form of subsidized water and electrical power, and direct subsidies in the form of tax relief. Secondly, the imperial state, via the International Financial Institutions (IFIs), pressures loan recipient states in the Third World, through conditionality agreements, to lower or eliminate trade barriers, privatize and denationalize enterprises, thus permitting US, European and Japanese multinational corporations to penetrate markets and buy into or purchase local enterprises. In short, globalization would not exist were it not for state intervention, nor would the markets remain open were it not for imperial state military and electoral intervention, politico-economic threats or pressure and recruitment of local clients.

Imperialism takes many forms, but pursues similar goals: the conquest of markets, the penetration of competitors and the protection of home markets. The US has erected an elaborate set of trade barriers in a wide range of product areas of strategic importance: auto imports are limited by quotas, as are sugar, textiles, and steel. A multiplicity of non-traditional constraints and informal agreements limit export countries from entering US markets – all negotiated on a state-to-state basis. In many cases, in its dealings with neo-colonial regimes like Brazil under Cardoso, the US state rejected reciprocity, instead demanding and securing the liberalization of the information industry, while restricting Brazilian steel exports on the bogus pretext of 'anti-dumping' charges.

All major internationally binding trade agreements, liberalizing trade and establishing new trade regulations, are negotiated by the states, enforced by the states and subject to state modifications. Thus, for example, the General Agreement on Tariffs and Trade (GATT), the World Trade Organization (WTO), and the Lomé Convention, which established the trade rules and framework for global trading networks, were all formulated by the states. In addition, bilateral as well as regional multilateral trade pacts, such as the European Union (EU), the North American Free Trade Area (NAFTA) and the Latin American Free Trade Area (LAFTA) are initiated by the state to open new markets for the multinationals. The imperial state operates in synergy with its multinational corporation. The 'expansion in markets' which Negri and Hardt perceive as spontaneous and unguided has nothing to do with multinational corporations superseding anachronistic states; on the contrary, most movements of capital to new markets depend on the state intervening to eliminate barriers and, in some cases, destabilizing nationalist regimes.

The same is true of investment agreements, protection, subsidies and adjudication. New multilateral as well as bilateral investment agreements are formulated at the state level, with the agreement and active participation of the multinational corporations. The reason is clear: the multinational corporations want state participation to guarantee that their capital will not be expropriated, subject to 'discriminatory' taxes or restricted in remitting profits. The state is, to put it bluntly, the enforcer of investment guarantees, a crucial element in corporate investment expansion. In many cases, the imperial states use their representatives in the IFI to impose new investment codes as conditions for 'stabilization' or development loans. The imperial states within the European Union impose powerful protection barriers for their agricultural products. Both the US and the EU subsidize agriculture heavily, with low rates for electricity and water use. New technology research and development is heavily financed by the state, and the results are then turned over to the multinationals for marketing. At each stage prior to, during and after the expansion of the multinational corporations overseas into the international market, the state is deeply involved. Moreover, where national enterprises are non-competitive, the imperial states invent pretexts to protect them from more efficient producers. Thus, for example, Japan protects its rice producers, even though their production is ten times more costly for consumers to purchase. The US provides huge subsidies to agribusiness exporters in the form of research. cheap water rates and loans tied to the purchase of US grain exports, while the EU subsidizes the formation of its high technology industries.

What might be termed 'statism' or 'neostatism' is central to the global expansion of the multinational corporations located in the imperial states. The state has grown, its reach has extended and its activities have expanded; in short, its role in the international economy is essential to the reproduction of the capitalist system. Thus, it is unfortunate that the doctrine and rhetoric of free markets promoted by conservative ideologues has been consumed by those who should know better – the 'globalist Left'. While Hardt and Negri write about the declining role of the state, the political right worldwide has been active in promoting state activity to further the interests of the multinational corporations. Similarly, while Hardt and Negri write about the 'globalization' of markets, the multinational corporations from the imperial countries and their states carve up the markets, enlarging their spheres of influence, domination and control. Above all, the imperial state is not simply an economic institution; the overseas expansion of the multinational corporations is heavily dependent on the military and political role of the imperial state.

The overseas expansion of the multinational corporations has been made possible by the military–political expansion of Euro-American imperialism via NATO and surrogate armies in Southern Africa, Latin America, and Asia. In Russia (the former USSR) and Eastern Europe, client regimes have been sponsored and supported by the imperial states, laying the groundwork for the takeover of a vast array of strategic industries, energy sources, and so on. The US imperial state's triumph over the USSR provided the impetus for dismantling the welfare states in Europe and what pretended to be a welfare state in the US. The Euro-American wars in the Gulf and Balkans consolidated the imperial states' dominance and extended their influence over dissident states. The destabilization of the former communist regimes, the destructive wars against nationalist and socialist regimes in Southern Africa, Latin America and elsewhere, opened these regimes to neo-liberal policy prescriptions. Military expansion was organized within the state apparatus that accompanied and promoted the overseas expansion of multinational corporations.

So-called globalization grew out of the barrel of a gun – a gun wielded, pointed and fired by the imperial state. To protect overseas capital, the US and the EU created a new NATO doctrine which legitimates offensive wars outside of Europe against any country that threatens their vital economic interests (that is, the multinational corporations). NATO has been expanded to incorporate new client states in Eastern Europe, and new 'peace associates' among the Baltic states and the former republics of the USSR (Georgia, Kazakstan, and so on). In other words, the imperial state/military alliances incorporate more states, involving more state apparatuses than before, to ensure the safe passage of European and US multinational corporations into their countries and the easy flow of profits back to their headquarters in the US and Western Europe. The argument about a stateless, classless empire without imperialism is based, in short, on the notion of a world market dominated by multinational corporations that 'must eventually overcome imperialism and destroy the barriers between inside and outside' (2000: 234). These 'global' multinational corporations have turned the nations and imperial states into anachronisms.

Theorizing from Facts to Fiats

Hardt and Negri provide no data on the internal organization of the multinational corporations, no analysis of the decision-making structure and no discussion of their relations with states. Theorizing by fiat is a convenient way of evading inconvenient empirical studies. In essence, the argument advanced is based on a number of unsubstantiated assumptions, of which the first is that multinational corporations are global enterprises that have no specific location in any particular nation state. According to Hardt and Negri, such enterprises form the core of a new world economy divorced from national controls, and they are part of a new world ruling class. This assumption in turn is based on the fact that large-scale corporations operate in a number of countries, they are mobile and they have the power to evade both taxes and regulations (particularly those protecting the workers or peasants they employ) in many national jurisdictions. There are several conceptual and empirical problems with this assumption.

First, the fact that multinational corporations operate in many countries does not detract from the fact that the headquarters, where most of the strategic decisions, directors and profits are concentrated, are located in the US, the EU and Japan. Second, mobility is based on strategic decisions taken by directors in the headquarters in the imperial centres. These decisions depend on the political and economic conditions created by the imperial state and its representatives in the IFIs. Mobility is contingent on interstate relations. Third, evasion of taxes and regulations is possible because of deliberate policies in the imperial states and their multinational banks. Non-enforcement of laws against transfers of illicit earnings from the neo-colonial countries to the imperial countries is a form of state activity favouring large-scale transfers of wealth that strengthen external accounts. The flouting of neo-colonial state regulations on the part of multinational corporations is part of a broader set of power relations that are themselves anchored in the relationships between imperial and neo-colonial states.

The second assumption informing Hardt and Negri's analysis is that the old nation state governments have been superseded by a new world government, made up of the heads of the IFI, the WTO and the heads of the multinational corporations (Hardt and Negri, 2000: 326). This is an argument based on a superficial discussion of epiphenomena, rather than a deeper analytical view of the structure of power. While it is true that in a great many geographical locations the IFIs make many important decisions affecting significant economic and social sectors, these decisions and the decision makers are closely linked to the imperial states and the multinational corporations that influence them. All top IFI officials are appointed by their national/imperial governments, and all the crucial policy guidelines that dictate their loans and lending conditions are set by the finance, treasury and economy ministers of the imperial states. The vast majority of funds for the IFIs themselves come from the imperial states. Representation on the executive board of the IFI is based on the proportion of funding provided by the imperial states. The IMF and the WB have always been led by individuals from the US or the EU. The vision Hardt and Negri have of IFI power is based on a perception of derived power and not on its source in the imperial states. What they miss, therefore, is the degree to which international power is based in the imperial states not on supra-national entities. The latter concept grossly overestimates the autonomy of the IFIs and consequently underestimates their subordination to the imperial states. The real significance of the IFIs is how they magnify, extend and deepen the power of the imperial states, and how – because of this – they become terrain for competition between rival imperial states. Far from superseding the old states, therefore, the IFIs have strengthened their positions.

Globalization theorists like Hardt and Negri like to write of an 'imperial system' as opposed to imperialist states (Hardt and Negri, 2000: Preface), as if one could not exist without the other. The 'system' has no 'centre', since all states have lost their special significance before the all-powerful multinational corporations that dominate markets. Systems approaches fail to recognize the class and institutional power of nationally owned and directed banks and industries. Even more worryingly, system theorists fail to connect the structures, operations, legal codes and linkages that exist between imperial states, the multinational corporations and their offspring in the IFI's, together with the vast reach of their power and concentration of profits, interest, rents and royalties in the imperialist countries. The 'system' is in fact derived from and sustained by the combined forces of the imperial state and its multinational corporations. To abstract from the specificities of ownership and state power in order to describe an imperial system is to lose sight of the basic contradictions and conflicts, the interstate imperial rivalries and the class struggles for state power.

The Sweet Smell of (Scientific/Technological) Success?

One of the more common arguments made by globalization theorists like Hardt and Negri is that an information revolution has taken place, a process that has eliminated state borders and transformed capitalism (a 'new epoch'), by providing a new impetus to the development of the productive forces (Hardt and Negri, 2000: 145). The claims that information technologies have revolutionized economies and thus created a new global economy in which nation states and national economies have become superfluous is extremely dubious. Moreover, the US population census provides another explanation for the higher productivity figures – the five million illegal immigrants who have flooded the US labour market in the 1990s. Since productivity is measured by the output per estimated worker, the five million uncounted workers inflate the productivity data. If the five million are included the productivity figures would deflate.

According to Hardt and Negri, we are living in a New Economy that has superseded the Old Economy of manufacturing, mining, agriculture and social services (Hardt and Negri, 2000: 3–21). Thanks to the third scientific technological revolution, therefore, Hardt and Negri maintain that we are living in a totally new epoch, nothing less than a completely new form of capitalism. According to the globalization theorists, the market creates new efficiencies produced by the new technologies and ensures high growth. If nothing else, the recession of late certainly refutes the claims of the New Economy ideologues: the business cycle continues to operate and, moreover, the cycle is particularly accentuated by the highly speculative nature of the New Economy. As it turns out, the New Economy demonstrates all the features of a volatile speculative economy, driven by exorbitant claims of high returns. In the absence of profits, or even revenues, it turns out that much of what was touted as a New Economy was a colossal financial swindle, where the high returns to the early investors led to financial ruin to the later investors.

Unfortunately for the authors of this book, detailed empirical studies on the economy of the 1990s have effectively refuted the argument that information technology (IT), fibreoptics and biotechnology inaugurated a 'new epoch of capitalism' by revolutionizing the forces of production. Japan, which early on 'robotized' its factories and engineered and applied many of the new IT products, has been stagnant (an average annual growth of about 1 per cent for the past eleven years) and entering a deep recession in 2001. The US manufacturing sector has been in negative growth since the end of August 2000, a situation that has continued to the time of this writing (2003) – the longest period of negative growth on record since the end of the Second World War. The recession is expected to continue for an uncertain period – estimates run from one to three years. The IT growth rates were negative throughout 2001. The prospect for an early recovery is poor, as negative savings rates and huge deficits, inhibit domestic or export powered growth. As structural and cyclical crises coincide, it is highly likely that the recession will continue for some time ahead. The recession totally undermines the IT ideologues who declared that the New Economy had made the business cycle obsolete. In fact, the IT companies have been the hardest hit in the current downturn, over 80 per cent of the dot.coms being affected.

With the decline of the information economy and its stock valuations, it becomes clear that the 'information revolution' is not the transcendent force defining the economies of the major imperial states, let alone defining a new world order. The fact that most people have computers and browse and that some firms have better control over their inventories, does not mean that power has shifted beyond the nation state. Claims made by publicists about the information revolution ring hollow, particularly as the investors in the world stock markets move funds toward the real economy, and away from the high technology firms which show no profits and increasing losses.

Paul Strassman (*Financial Times*, June 28, 2001), a leading critic of IT ideologues, produced a study of three thousand European companies, which demonstrates that no relationship exists between investment in computers and profitability. Thus the three basic claims of the IT revolution, that it has put to rest the business cycle, has generated a sustained productivity revolution and produces high profits, are not in accordance with reality. In fact, the systemic irrationalities of capitalism have been amplified by the IT bubble: the business cycle operates in full force, productivity tends to stagnation and there is a tendency for the rate of profit to decline.

Another article by Robert Gordon (1999), which analyzes the increase in productivity over the 1995–1999 period, raises serious doubts about the claims made by Hardt and Negri concerning the existence of a 'new epoch'. He argues that almost 70 per cent of the improvement in productivity can be accounted for by improved measurements of inflation (lower estimates of inflation necessarily mean higher growth of real output, thus productivity) and the response of productivity to the exceptionally rapid output growth of the three and a half year period. Thus, only 30 per cent of the 1 per cent increase in productivity (or 0.3 per cent) during the 1995–1999 period can be attributed to computerization in the so-called information revolution. Some revolution! According to Gordon's longitudinal study of technical progress covering the years 1950–1996 (see Chapter 5 for more details), the period of maximum technical progress as manifested in annual multifactor productivity growth was in the period between 1950 and 1964, when it reached approximately 1.8 per cent. The period of lowest multifactor productivity growth in this century was from 1988–1996, approximately 0.5 per cent!

The 'new efficiencies' promised did not overcome the logic of the capitalist business cycle. What was optimistically categorized as 'just in time production' was premised on the stable and continuous growth of demand. The recession of 2000–2002, and the sudden decline in demand, led both to an accumulation of inventories among producers and sellers, and to the resultant lay-offs. Cash-flow problems, increased indebtedness and bankruptcies characteristic of the Old Economy reappeared with a vengeance. It is clear that the so-called New Economy does not transcend the propensity of capitalism towards crisis. To the contrary – it is more vulnerable and has fewer resources to fall back on since most of its cash flow depends on speculative expectations of continuously high returns. The sharp

The New Development Politics

decline in commercial advertising earnings on web sites and the saturation of the computer market has led to a structural crisis for producers of both hardware and software, leading to a giant shakedown in the industry: the stocks have tumbled to a fraction of their former, exorbitant paper value, and the major internet companies are struggling to survive, let alone define the nature of a 'new capitalist epoch'.

The New Imperialism: An Alternative to 'Empire'

The current global supremacy of the US and Europe is built on three unstable and increasingly unsustainable supports. One of these is a highly vulnerable and speculative sector prone to great volatility and entering into deep recession. The second is the high level of transfers of profits, interest payments and royalties from their respective colonized areas. In the case of Latin America alone over US$700 billion was transferred as payments to Europe and US banks and multinationals from 1990–1998. The third support underpinning the 'empire' is political power (including the power to print money to cover deficits) and the security that the state provides foreign nationals who transfer funds, including billions illicitly secured from their home countries. Political power and the security of the imperial states depend on the acquiescence or consent of strategic economic sectors that are vulnerable to free market competition by rival imperial and non-imperial countries. The problem for European–US rulers is, in short, how to manage their empires in the face of a growing recession, a deflated IT sector and rising unemployment in economic sectors which are not competitive in the world market.

As many have pointed out, neo-liberalism was always a myth: the imperial states have never completely opened their markets, eliminated all subsidies or failed to intervene to prop up or protect strategic economic sectors, either for political or social reasons. Neo-liberal imperialism always meant selective openness to selective countries over specified time periods in selective product areas. Markets were opened by the US government to products produced by US affiliates in overseas countries. 'Free trade' in the imperial country was not based on economic, but political criteria. On the other hand European–US policymakers and their employees in the IMF–WB preached 'market fundamentalism' to the Third World: elimination of all trade barriers, subsidies and regulations for all products and services in all sectors. Imperial states' selective free market practices allowed their multinationals to capitalize on market opportunities in target countries practising market fundamentalism while protecting domestic economic sectors which included important political constituencies. Conflict erupted when the two imperial rivals, the US and Europe (both selective free marketeers) attempted to pry open the others' markets while protecting important political constituencies.

With the advent of the triple crises of recession, speculative collapse and intensified competition, the imperial countries have resorted to increased state intervention in a multiplicity of sectors: agricultural and other state subsidies – US$30 billion in the US in 2001; interfering in trade relations to impose quotas on imports (President Bush's commitment to the US steel industry); intensified exploitation of the Third World to increase the flow of profits, interests and trading advantages (the US proposal for the 'Free Trade of the Americas') and war – military Keynesianism (as in the 2002 US attack on Afghanistan). State-managed trade that combines protection of home markets and aggressive intervention to secure monopoly market advantages and investment profits defines the content of neo-mercantilist imperialism. Neo-liberal imperialism, with its free market rhetoric and selective opening of markets, is being replaced by a neo-mercantilism that looks toward greater monopolization of regional trading zones, greater unilateral political decisions to maximize trade advantages and protection of domestic producers, and a greater reliance on military strategies, all to deepen control over crisis-ridden neo-liberal economies run by discredited clients and to increase military Keynesianism. Just as the US was the leader in developing its neo-liberal empire and Europe was a follower region, so with regard to the transition to a neo-mercantilist empire the US plays a leading role. Of equal importance is the fact that the US state will dictate the rules and regulations that govern trade, investment and patent laws that will reign throughout the Americas. This will enable the US government to be in a position to combine protectionism at home, European exclusion from Latin America, and free markets within Latin America.

Mercantilist imperialism, in which the imperial state combines protectionism at home, monopolies abroad, and free trade within the empire, is thus the chosen strategy for maintaining the empire and sustaining domestic political support, at a terrible cost to Latin America and to the dismay of its European competitors. In pursuit of the neo-mercantilist empire, Washington must increasingly rely on unilateral decisions and policy making. By its monopolistic nature, neo-mercantilism depends on excluding competitor allies and maximizing trade advantages via unilateral state decisions. Hardt and Negri notwithstanding, the terrorist attacks in New York and Washington led Washington to bomb Afghanistan in the best imperialist tradition, even as conditions on world markets were deteriorating. The alliance-building strategy, particularly with the European Union, has not modified Washington's pursuit of hegemony. On the contrary, the alliance is built on European Union subordination to US military command and monopolization of all decisions pertaining to the war, even to a greater extent than was the case in Kosovo. What was striking in the early phases of the US military intervention was the degree to which its war demands were totally accepted by the European Union, Russia, China and some Middle Eastern Arab regimes without any explicit quid pro quo. Needless to say, the Afghan intervention and the powerful role of the imperial state in defining the issues, alliances and political circumstances for market transactions hammers another nail in the coffin of stateless empires and strengthens the argument for a theory of a new mercantilist style of imperialism. The war in Afghanistan led to vast increases in military expenditures (US$100 billion), greater protectionism and military threats on all sides. Imperialism and empire are indeed doing well – only the 'multitudes' (that is, peasants and workers) are suffering, a situation which raises two additional questions: do peasants and workers react against the empire and, if so, how and as what?

The Empire of the Subaltern?

When defining the configurations of power, Hardt and Negri operate at such a rarified level of abstraction that they obscure the most significant variations in types of regime, state and class. As a result, their conceptualization of socio-economic change hovers uneasily in an epistemological penumbra, being either non-existent or wholly unconvincing. It comes as no surprise, therefore, that, given their postmodernist sensibility, change stems from the agency not of class but of the now fashionable and ubiquitous category of the 'subaltern'. It is tempting to search Negri's earlier writings for theoretical elements that prefigure his present position on imperialism. In the light of the celebration of 'marginality' by postmodernists such as Foucault and varieties of post-colonial/subaltern analysis (for example, Mallon, 1994), it is significant that from the early 1970s onwards Negri in *Autonomia* (Red Notes, 1979) embarked on a search for a new political class able to operate outside and against the Italian party system. In the absence of mass support from the northern industrial working class – which continued steadfastly to support the PCI (Italian Communist Party) – those allocated this role by *Autonomia* were the déclassé 'marginals', composed of unemployed youth (migrants from rural areas in southern Italy), women and self-employed in the urban informal sector ('off-the-books' workers) – or precisely those categories subsequently lionized by much postmodern theory as potentially/actually the rural and/or urban 'empowered'.

This earlier perception in *Autonomia* does indeed permeate *Empire*, which informs us that 'the new proletariat ... appears as a constituent power ... a new proletariat and not a new industrial working class ... all those whose labour is exploited by capital, the entire cooperating multitude' (Hardt and Negri, 2000: 402). The same point is made earlier in the book (Hardt and Negri, 2000: 52ff.), where Hardt and Negri state: 'Our point ... is that all of these diverse forms of labour are in some way subject to capitalist discipline and capitalist relations of production. This fact of being within capital and sustaining capital is what defines the proletariat as a class.' The presence of the words 'capitalist relations of production' notwithstanding, it is clear that the proletariat is not defined in terms of property relations. Rather, it is defined merely by the fact of being part of the same economic circuit as capital, in which capacity it yields a portion of surplus to the latter. Not only is this definition unMarxist, but a feudal landowning class that yield a portion of surplus labour to an emergent bourgeoisie could also be said to form part of the proletariat!

Empire, therefore, inherits the dubious proposition from *Autonomia* that a 'refusal' of capitalist work (and work discipline) necessarily translates into a progressive politics that, it is inferred, prefigures socialism or something like it. It is clear from an earlier text that Negri was prepared to accept the 'subjective side' of grass-roots agency without enquiring too closely as to how this was constructed, by whom, or in what political direction it was going. In short, existing ideology/ideologies were (wrongly) identified for Negri over a decade ago as liberating simply because it/they were what a subject engaged in struggle happened to believe. Moreover, such views were regarded as evidence for the fact that the subject concerned was 'virtually independent' of capitalist relations of production. The difficulty with this 'refusal of capitalist work' argument is that – like postmodernists such as Scott and those associated with the Subaltern Studies project – it assumes any/all 'discourse-against' is politically progressive simply by virtue of being 'discourse-against'. No allowance is made either for the presence of capitalist agents/agency/ideology or for the existence of a regressive/reactionary ideology among the working-class elements – false consciousness, in other words – within the very broad ranks of the subaltern.

Like the catch-all category of the 'subaltern', therefore, the term 'new proletariat' embraces 'subjects' whose class position is not just different, but antagonistic and whose agency is accordingly designed to achieve what are mutually irreconcilable political ends. Thus, for example, in support of the view that peasants generally are 'uprooted from their fields and villages and thrown into the burning forge of world production' (Hardt and Negri, 2000: 247) the authors invoke the work of James Scott on peasant resistance against capitalism (see p. 455, note 16), forgetting (or perhaps not knowing) that the latter's analytical approach has been heavily criticized for conflating not only rich, middle and poor peasants but also agency aimed at capitalism (for example, poor peasants opposed to low wages) with that targeted at socialism (for example, rich peasants opposed to land reform). In keeping with their enthusiasm for subalternism, Hardt and Negri categorize 'subaltern nationalism' as 'progressive' (Hardt and Negri, 2000: 105ff.). The inference here is that the struggles waged by the 'multitudes' at the periphery of 'empire' are *ipso facto* progressive.

Just how flimsy this claim is can be seen in the following statement: '[t]he nation appears progressive ... insofar as it poses the commonality of a potential community. Part of the "modernizing" effects of the nation in subordinated countries has been the unification of diverse populations, breaking down religious, ethnic, cultural, and linguistic barriers.' One is left wondering what planet Hardt and Negri were living on during the past decade (1991–2001). The global situation after the fall of the Berlin Wall in 1989 has been exactly the opposite of that which they describe, namely, one in which the 'other' of modernization has been the unleashing of rival nationalisms, culturalisms, religions and ethnicities, all of which have gone to war in order to sustain their specific kind of 'difference'. Hardt and Negri try to get round this problem by claiming that contemporary fundamentalisms are not backwards looking (Hardt and Negri, 2000: 149), an extremely dubious view justified in the following manner: 'The antimodern thrust that defines fundamentalisms might be better understood ... not as a premodern but as a postmodern project.' The antinomic and thus unsustainable character of this claim is something they recognize almost immediately, but are nevertheless unable to explain, let alone escape from. ('This marriage between postmodernism and fundamentalism is certainly an odd coupling considering that postmodernist and fundamentalist discourses stand in most respects in polar opposition: hybridity versus purity, difference versus identity, mobility versus stasis.') Because they equate postmodernism with a chronological transcendence of modernity, Hardt and Negri find it difficult to reconcile what is clearly a traditional discourse with a temporal 'going-beyond'. Not surprisingly, the solution – that the very identities invoked by postmodernism are no different from those defended by a backward looking fundamentalism (hybridity means different purities, identity means plurality of difference) – eludes them.

Conclusion

The concept of empire informing the analysis by Hardt and Negri resembles nothing so much as the world systems approach. Instead of core, semiperiphery and periphery, however, they write of 'empire' and 'multitudes' – in the process subsuming peasants and workers under the catch-all category of 'subaltern'. This kind of simplistic abstraction of the world economy and its relations of power subordinates the dynamic of class relations to a static distribution of market forces and shares. The abstract categories that they use obscure fundamental differences in class interests between nations in each category, differences that determine how market shares are distributed, the ownership of property and living standards, as well as differences between dynamic and stagnant countries. In short, their analysis erases class distinctions as these are reproduced by capital in more developed industrial countries and by less developed agrarian contexts in erstwhile colonies. More fundamentally, by looking at market positions, Hardt and Negri overlook the critical role of the state in preserving and challenging the relationship between states and economies and reconfiguring the world economy.

After reading *Empire* it is no surprise that reviewers for *Time* and *The New York Times* welcomed the book. In line with general 'globaloney' theory, *Empire* argues that globalization is a progressive movement in history, a position that requires the abolition of imperialism by intellectual fiat and that systemic alternatives are located within an amorphous multitude lacking both structural cohesion and political organization necessary for contemporary revolutionary struggles. The book's citation of potted quotes from a sweeping array of thinkers provides the formal trappings for a celebration of US constitutionalism at a time when its leaders were bombing Afghanistan (and its peasants and workers) into the stone age, after sending Iraq and Yugoslavia (plus their peasants and workers) into the iron age. *Empire* provides a sweeping synthesis of the intellectual froth about globalization, postmodernism, postmarxism, posthistory, all held together by a series of unsubstantiated arguments and assumptions that seriously violate economic and historical realities. The *Empire* thesis of post-imperialism is not novel; neither is it a great theory. It does not explain much about the real world. Rather, it is a wordy exercise devoid of critical intelligence. Those who have encountered farmyard dunghills in the course of their fieldwork research in rural areas will need no reminding as to what, precisely, is the true fragrance of imperialism. It is a pity, therefore, that where the latter is concerned, Hardt and Negri appear to have lost their sense of smell.

Chapter 2

The US Offensive in Latin America: Golpes, Retreat and Radicalization

Introduction

The current worldwide US political and military offensive is manifest in Latin America in multiple contexts, using a variety of tactics (military and political) and instruments. It is directed toward propping up decaying clients, destabilizing independent regimes, pressuring the centre-left parties to move to the right and destroying or isolating the burgeoning popular mass movements challenging the US empire and its client regimes. In this chapter we start by discussing the particular forms of the US offensive in each country and then we explore the specific and general reasons for the offensive in contemporary Latin America. This discussion will provide the bases for the theoretical analysis of the specific nature of the 'new imperialism' that informs the current offensive and its impact on the centre-left electoral parties and the radical socio-political movements. In the concluding section we will discuss the political alternatives in the context of the US offensive and the new imperialism.

Military–Political Offensive: Diverse Approaches, Singular Goal

The most striking aspect of the US military–political offensive in Latin America is the diverse tactics utilized to establish or consolidate client regimes and defeat popular socio-political movements opposed to imperial domination.

The focus of high-intensity US intervention is in Colombia and Venezuela. In both countries, Washington has high stakes, involving political, economic and ideological interests as well as geopolitical considerations. Both countries face both the Caribbean and the Andean countries – as well as Brazil. Therefore, the emergence of a revolutionary regime in Colombia or the stabilization of a nationalist regime in Venezuela could inspire similar transformations in the adjoining regions and undermine US control via its client regimes. Moreover, significant political changes could affect US control over oil production and supply from Venezuela and Colombia and also pressure Mexico and Ecuador to back off from the privatization process.

Washington, at all costs, wants to maintain a secure supply of oil in the current period of threats and war against the Gulf oil producers, namely Iraq and Iran, and in the face of an increasingly vulnerable Saudi Arabia. Socio-political transformations in Colombia and Venezuela could lead to an integration pact with revolutionary Cuba, thus destroying Washington's forty-year-old embargo and creating a viable alternative to the US-sponsored Free Trade Agreement of the Americas (FTAA; ALCA in Spanish).

Washington has adopted different strategies to the two countries. To defeat the popular insurgency in Colombia, it has embraced a 'total war' strategy. In Venezuela it includes a combined civil political–economic destabilization strategy culminating in a military coup. Washington's counter-insurgency strategy in Colombia operated under cover of an anti-narcotics campaign, to justify the accelerated military build-up. The anti-narcotics campaigns centered on regions where the FARC (Revolutionary Armed Forces) was strongest, while virtually ignoring the areas controlled by paramilitary clients of the Colombian Armed Forces. The political and military advance of the FARC in the late 1990s forced the Colombian government to the negotiating table and increased its dependence on the US for military aid and advisors. In the US (and in Colombia) the 'peace negotiations' were seen as a temporary tactic to forestall a full-scale FARC assault on the urban centers of power and a time period in which to build the military capability of the Colombian Armed Forces and strengthen and extend the scope and depth of US military influence on the military–paramilitary forces and military strategy. The government peace negotiators also hoped to entice or split the FARC by offering them an electoral option, as was done in Central America (El Salvador and Guatemala). The FARC, cognizant of the brutal assassination of leftist political activists (4000–5000) in the mid to late 1980s and of the abject failure of the Central American guerrillas-turned-electoral-politicians to bring about any meaningful social changes, refused to surrender. They insisted on basic reforms of state structures and the economy as preconditions for any durable peace settlement. These proposals for democratic and socio-economic reforms were totally unacceptable to the US and the Pastrana regime, which were moving in the opposite direction toward greater militarization of political life and liberalization of the economy.

Throughout the period of peace negotiations, the US and President Pastrana combined peace rhetoric with funding and promotion of paramilitary groups (via the Colombian military) involved in the capture and destruction of villages and towns, displacing millions of peasants and trade unionists and killing thousands of peasants suspected of having leftist sympathies. The idea was to isolate the FARC within the demilitarized zone, train, arm and mass troops on the borders, carry on high technology electronic surveys to identify strategic targets and then abruptly break off negotiations and blitz the region with a land and air attack, capturing or killing the FARC leaders and demoralizing the fleeing insurgents. Needless to say the tactics failed. The guerrillas continue to be active out of the peace zone, they strengthened their forces within the demilitarized zone and suffered no serious losses when Pastrana broke off peace negotiations.

The US has made Colombia the test case for its politico-military offensive in Latin America. This is, first of all, because the FARC is the most powerful anti-imperialist formation challenging for state power. Second, it borders Venezuela and is perceived as an ally of President Chavez. Defeating the FARC allows Washington to encircle and increase the external pressure on Venezuela and reinforce the internal destabilization campaign.

As the political base of Pastrana eroded due to the prolonged recession and social cutbacks resulting from the huge military budget, the US escalated its military support. The entire Colombian economy is now subordinated to the US military strategy and the military strategy is directed by a scorched-earth total-war policy. This means that all Colombian civilian and economic considerations are secondary to Washington's primary interests in 'winning the war' against the FARC.

Given the strength and experience of the FARC and the formidable strategic capacity of its leader, Manual Marulanda, and his general staff, the US–Colombian war promises to be a prolonged and bloody outcome, in which there is likely to be a continuous major escalation of US intervention, increased use of paramilitary terror and greater indiscriminate bombing of civilian targets. None the less a military victory by the US is very doubtful: the end result may be nearer to Vietnam than Afghanistan.

The first signs that Washington's offensive may have a boomerang effect are visible in Colombia. Less than two weeks after the US pressured President Pastrana to end the peace talks and declare the demilitarized area a war zone, the first general to lead troops into the zone resigned. He publically declared that military victory was impossible. The immediate cause for his resignation was the FARC's destruction of a bridge leading into the former demilitarized zone under the General's direct command. The successful FARC military offensive following the end of the peace talks led the US Ambassador to Colombia to admit that Plan Colombia was a failure.

In contrast to the scorched-earth military strategy in Colombia, the US is implementing a civil military approach to overthrowing president Chavez in Venezuela. Chavez is a liberal nationalist: he has followed a fairly orthodox domestic economic policy while pursuing an independent nationalist foreign policy. US strategy is multi-phased and combines media–civic–economic attacks with efforts to provoke fissures in the military, culminating in a military coup.

The first phase of this struggle is to destabilize the economy via closely coordinated actions with client business and professional groups and corrupt right-wing trade union bosses. The purpose is to mobilize public opposition and focus mass-media attention on the instability of the country, inhibiting investment from less politicized capitalists, who are fearful of declining profits in a conflictual situation. The mass media engages in a systematic propaganda campaign to overthrow the Chavez regime, advocating a violent seizure of power. Government and public protests against the subversive behaviour of the mass media allows Washington to orchestrate an international campaign against 'violations of free speech', particularly via the US-influenced Inter-American Press Association. The second phase of the Bush Administration's strategy was to move from destabilization directly toward a military coup. This involved two steps. The first is to mobilize US intelligence assets, retired officials and those labelled 'dissident' among the active military officers from the more reactionary branches of the military – in the case of Venezuela, the air force and navy. The idea was to force a political discussion in the military command, provoke other like-minded officials to come out in defense of the expelled officers and to reinforce the mass media – a business message of 'instability' and the imminent 'fall of Chavez', thus further stimulating capital flight. The second step was to organize authoritarian navy and air force officials to put pressure on the army – the main bulwark of Chavez support – to gain adherents, neutralize apolitical officers and isolate Chavez loyalists. Washington's two-step approach culminated in a military coup with active US military support, in which a 'transitional civic–military junta' ruled for one day before it was overthrown.

Linked with its internal strategy, based on its Venezuelan clients, Washington has implemented an 'external strategy'. US Secretary of State Powell has publically denounced Chavez as an authoritarian and both he and the IMF have publically stated their support for a 'transitional government' – a clear and obvious signal of US support for the internal golpistas. US Special Forces now operate in Ecuador, Colombia, Peru, Panama, Afghanistan, Yemen, Philippines, Georgia, Uzbekistan and other Central Asian client states. It is more than likely that, in the event of a coup attempt, the Pentagon will send tactical operatives and political advisers to 'guide the coup' and ensure that the appropriate configuration of civilian personalities emerges for propaganda purposes.

The dangers that face the Venezuelan regime is that in Washington's 'war of political attrition', where daily propaganda barrages and provocative actions abound, Chavez cannot depend on constant mass mobilizations. He must actually implement immediate radical redistributive socio-economic policies to sustain mass commitments and active organized support. The US-orchestrated offensive is geared to creating permanent tension as a psychological weapon to exhaust popular support and undermine army morale.

Chavez's independent foreign policy is what antagonizes the US. This includes his opposition to Plan Colombia, criticism of the US war in Afghanistan and worldwide imperial offensive, his cordial relations with Iraq, Libya, Iran and Cuba and his refusal to allow the US to colonize Venezuelan airspace. His foreign policy has not been complemented by a series of comprehensive socio-economic reforms affecting the welfare of millions of his unemployed and poorly paid supporters living in the slums and shanty towns.

US efforts to overthrow Chavez are based on his refusal, in early October, to back Washington's worldwide imperial offensive – the so-called 'antiterrorist campaign'. Close advisers to President Chavez informed me that a delegation of high officials from Washington visited Chavez and bluntly informed him that he would 'pay a high price for his opposition to President Bush'. Shortly thereafter the local business federation and trade union bosses launched their campaigns – even though President Chavez had introduced a very modest tax reform (mostly affecting foreign oil companies), a compensated land purchase plan and had privatized the major publically owned electrical enterprise company in Caracas.

Clearly Chavez attempts to ride two horses, an independent foreign policy and liberal reform domestic policy makers, and this makes him very vulnerable to the US-designed coup strategy. US imperial tactics in Venezuela differ substantially from Colombia, largely because in one case it is defending a client state against a popular insurgency and in the other trying to create a civilian movement to provoke a coup. Strategically, however, the political outcome is the same: to consolidate a client regime that will subordinate the country to the neo-mercantilist empire embodied in the FTAA, and to become willing vassals in policing the Latin American empire and perhaps supplying mercenaries for new overseas wars.

Argentina is the third country in which Washington is intervening. Following the mass popular uprising of 19/20 December 2001 and the fall of five client 'Presidents', Washington began to work through a multi-phased strategy which was designed to continue the transfer of billions of dollars in assets to US companies, prejudice European competitors and secure a privileged position in the Argentine political and economic system. The collapse of the client regime of De la Rua and the weakness of the Duhalde regime in 'imposing' a return to the *status quo ante* (the popular uprising) has led Washington to turn to unconditional civilian clients (ex-President Menem and ex-Minister of Economy Murphy) and the military intelligence apparatus – relatively intact since the days of the bloody dictatorship.

Washington's problem with the Duhalde regime was not his rectification of populist measures (he has agreed to partial debt payments, has sworn unconditional support of the US global offensive, proposes to limit spending). The US problem was that Duhalde could not forcefully fulfil his commitments to the IMF and Wall Street. The popular movements are growing in size and activity and they are more organized and radical. In their assemblies they are raising fundamental issues as well as immediate concerns. Their demands include repudiating the foreign debt, nationalizing the banks and strategic economic sectors and redistributing income – in a word repudiating the 'neo-liberal model', at a time when the US is seeking to extend and deepen its control via the neo-mercantilist FTAA.

There is little doubt that the Duhalde regime was prepared to meet most of the demands of the IMF, but Duhalde lacks the power to implement the whole austerity package and bail-out of the banks in the time frame and under the conditions that Washington and the IMF demand. Each concession to the IMF – like budget cuts – ignites more demonstrations among teachers and public employees; the bail-out of the foreign banks requires the continued confiscation of private savings; slashing provincial budget provokes greater unemployment, hunger and revolts. The Duhalde regime has already increased the level of repression and unleashed street thugs, but the movements still proliferate and the thin veneer of legitimacy of Duhalde's regime is dissolving. CIA Director Tenet has already pointed out US 'preoccupation' with instability in Argentina – meaning popular mobilizations. US assets in the Argentine intelligence apparatus are floating trial balloons, evaluating the response to rumours of a military coup. These tentative, exploratory moves are designed to secure a consensus among the military, financial and economic elites – together with US and European, especially Spanish, bankers and multinationals. The US and European mass media have begun to resonate with Washington's evolving strategy, writing of the 'chaos', 'breakdown' and 'chronic instability' of the civilian regime.

Washington is pointing toward a civic–military regime if or when Duhalde resigns. Washington's strategy is to decapitate the popular opposition. It can be summarized as the Triple M, a regime configured with ex-President Menem, ex-Minister of Economy Murphy and the military. Their lack of any social support among the middle and urban poor means that regime would be a 'regime of force': designed to drive the middle class to the wall, into a massive exodus via a brutal reduction in living standards to meet foreign debt obligations.

In summary, Washington worked on two tracks: on the one hand pressuring Duhalde to conform with its demands by assuming full executive powers and on the other hand preparing the conditions for a new more right-wing authoritarian civic–military client regime.

The reversion to client–military dictatorships with a civic facade provides the Bush Administration with the ideological fig leaf of 'defending democracy and free markets'. The US mass media can embellish this and any variety of related motifs.

Washington's militarization strategy is also evident in Ecuador, Bolivia and Paraguay, where client regimes, stripped of any popular legitimacy, hold onto power and impose Washington's neo-mercantilist formulas (free markets in Latin America and protectionism and subsidies in the US).

In Brazil and Mexico, Washington relies heavily on political and diplomatic instruments. In the case of Mexico, Washington had direct entrée to the Fox Administration in economic policy and a virtual agent in the ex-Foreign Minister Jorge Castañeda. The goal of Mexican subordination to US neo-mercantilism was not in question, as Fox and Castañeda were in total agreement. What is in question was the effectiveness of the regime in implementing US policy. Fox's effort to convert southern Mexico and Central America into one big US assembly plant, tourist and petroleum center (Puebla–Panama Plan) has run into substantial opposition. The massive shift of US capital to cheaper labour in China has provoked large-scale unemployment in the Mexican border towns. The so-called 'reciprocal benefits' of integration are glaringly absent. US dumping of corn and other agricultural commodities has devastated Mexican farmers and peasants. The US takeover of all sectors of Mexican economy (finance, telecommunications, services, and so on) led to massive outflows of profits and royalty payments. In foreign affairs, Washington's influence had never been greater, as Castañeda crudely mouthed the policies of the US Defense Department and CIA, declaring unconditional support for US policy in Afghanistan and any future military interventions, and grossly intervening in Cuban internal politics and provoking the worst incident in Cuban–Mexican diplomatic relations in recent history. Castañeda's crude anti-Cuban interventions on behalf of Washington backfired, with the great majority of the Mexican political class calling for his censure or resignation. Yet, it is clear that the mere presence of such an unabashed promoter of US policy like Castañeda in the Fox Administration was indicative of Washington's aggressive conquest of space in the Mexican political system. The powerful presence of US multinational corporations and banks and numerous regional and local client politicians facilitates the recolonization of Mexico against an increasingly restive and impoverished labour force.

In Brazil, the US has been active in both the political and economic sphere: its backing of Cardoso produced unprecedented results, the virtual sell-off of the principal public telecommunications, financial, natural resource, and commercial sectors. More significantly, the link-up between US and European capital and Brazilian media empires and big business sectors has had a powerful influence on the political class and on shaping electoral politics. This power bloc has succeeded in turning centre-left electoral politicians to the right in order to secure the media access and financial support needed to win national elections. US hegemony over Brazil is a political process. Influence moves through local and regional power brokers and national media monopolies. The US offensive's most recent 'conquest' is the leadership of the so-called Worker's Party (PT) and in particular its presidential candidate Inacio Lula da Silva. In response to the US offensive, Lula selected a millionaire textile magnate from the right-wing Liberal Party as his vice presidential candidate. He has tried to ingratiate himself by seeking a meeting with Bush, declared loyalty to the IMF and pledged to honour the foreign debt and to continue the privatization policy. The right turn of Lula and the Worker's Party means that all major electoral parties remain within the US orbit and guarantee uncontested US hegemony over the political class.

In summary, the US imperial offensive has adopted a variety of tactics and approaches in different countries in a variety of politico-military contexts. While giving greater primacy to military intervention and military coups (always with some sort of civilian facade) in countries such as Columbia and Venezuela, Washington continues to instrumentalize its political and diplomatic clients and 'turn' its political adversaries.

The strategic goal of constructing a neo-mercantilist empire faces a great variety of political, social and military obstacles, particularly evident in Columbia, Venezuela and Argentina. In other words, the imperial projection of power is far from realization; it is enmeshed in a series of conflictual relations and in a context where the past socio-economic failures of the empire do not create a favourable terrain for easy advance, or provide any justification for assuming an inevitable victory. On the contrary, the current imperial offensive is, in part, the result of severe setbacks in recent years and the growth of opponents among previous supporters in the middle class in some countries.

The Decline of Empire: The Basis of the Imperial Offensive

The US political and military offensive in Latin America is part of a worldwide campaign to reverse a deterioration of political influence and economic dominance and to extend and consolidate its imperial power via a combination of military bases and client political regimes. Beginning on 7 October 2001 with the massive bombing, and subsequent occupation of Afghanistan, Washington proceeded to establish a puppet regime, completely dependent on US military power. Satellite building extended to Central Asia, where Washington abruptly brushed aside the Russian links and established military bases and client–patron relations with the regimes. Similar processes of military interventions, base occupations and client–patron relations were established with rulers in the Philippines, Yemen and Georgia. In Latin America prior to 7 October 2001, the US already had established military bases in Ecuador, Peru, Aruba, El Salvador and Northern Brazil. Significantly, the location of the new bases was accompanied by extensive and direct operational roles in financing, training and directing the counter-insurgency operations of the Colombian military and paramilitary forces fighting the popular insurgency.

Two points are important to note. First, part of this expansion of US power is directed to counter the advances of popular movements and anti-imperialist regimes. Second, the offensive seeks not only to regain lost influence, but to establish new strategic centers of power in order to impose an unchallenged worldwide empire. In the case of Latin America, both processes are underway: a concerted imperial effort to defeat popular challenges to imperial rule and the establishment of a more exclusive, exploitative and repressive neo-mercantile empire than existed during the so-called 'neo-liberal' period.

The immediate purpose of the US military–political offensive in Latin America is to regain dominance in a region where its client regimes are discredited and weakening and where the imperial multilateral economic institutions are losing their capacity to control macroeconomic policy due to mass opposition.

Essentially a long-term US military presence has a political purpose: to prop up discredited regimes, to replace weak client regimes with more authoritarian civil–military juntas and to overthrow independent national governments that refuse to follow Washington's policies.

That US client regimes are weakening is evident in the failed liberal economic model, the vertical decline in popularity registered in the public opinion polls, the escalating flight of local capital and, most important, in some countries the increasing belligerency of robust mass popular movements directed at challenging regime authority, if not state power.

Colombia

The most powerful and organized challenge to the satellite-building project of the empire is in Colombia. Popular opposition to the civil–military regime is found in a powerful multisectoral agricultural movement (including farmers, peasants and rural workers), prejudiced by cuts in Government credits, its door open to cheap US food imports and the low price of its export commodities. The opposition includes militant trade union struggles, particularly of the oil, public employee, and agricultural and industrial unions. The most significant opposition, however, is found in the most powerful and well-organized guerrilla movement in recent Latin American history. The FARC and the smaller National Liberation Army (ELN) include over 20 000 combatants. The main thrust of the counter-insurgency experts is to direct the paramilitary death squads to forcibly evict hundreds of thousands of peasants, sympathetic to the guerrillas, from the countryside and to assassinate progressive urban slum dwellers, student activists, human rights workers and trade union leaders. Paramilitary violence is directed at isolating the guerrillas from their natural mass base and their source of food and recruits so that the Armed Forces can engage the guerrillas directly.

The scope and depth of military violence – 40,000 civilians killed in the 1990s – suggests the degree to which the guerrillas were and are deeply rooted among the working and peasant population. The guerrillas control, or are influential, in half of the rural municipalities of the country and have not suffered any significant defeats, despite frequent military extermination campaigns. On the contrary, the guerrillas are active less than fifty miles from the capital Bogota, control major highways and dominate a vast swathe of the countryside. While engaged in mobile, rather than positional warfare, the insurgents have, in effect, established a system of dual power in several regions of the country. Moreover, the insurgents have the advantage of knowledge of the terrain, proximity to local people and a strategically superior leadership that more than compensates for the technological and numerical superiority of the US-directed, mostly conscript army.

The massive infusion of US arms and officials is directed toward bolstering the regime and preventing its deterioration or collapse in the face of the two-year recession, the civil discontent and the guerrilla onslaught.

Venezuela

In Venezuela, the Chavez regime has challenged US foreign policy in several vital regions. In the Middle East, the Gulf State and North Africa the Chavez government strengthened OPEC and visited Iraq, Iran and Libya, thus breaking the US boycott. In South Asia, Chavez opposed US military intervention (the 'response to terror is not more terror'). In Latin America he opposed Plan Colombia and the US counter-insurgency military strategy, banned US spy planes from flying in Venezuelan airspace, rejected immediate implementation of FTAA, developed close ties with Cuba, and offered to mediate the dispute between the guerrillas and the regime in Colombia. In more general terms, Chavez has strengthened OPEC and revitalized its decision-making capacity and, above all, refused to submit to the Bush–Rumsfeld crusade to establish world dominance. The latter position led the US to temporarily withdraw its Ambassador and to send a high delegation of State Department officials to threaten Chavez in a style more reminiscent of the Mafia than career diplomats. Chavez's independent foreign policy is a sharp reversal from the previous corrupt client regimes that echoed US international policy.

Argentina

The third country that has witnessed a sharp decline in US influence is Argentina. The collapse of the De La Rua regime and its entourage of ministers in the tow of foreign bankers and Euro-US controlled multilateral banks, started bells ringing in Washington. The installation of the Duhalde clique and his concessions to Washington and the IMF has not pacified Washington because his regime is perceived to be unstable and unable to effectively put an end to mass mobilizations.

The most significant political fact is that most of the middle class has turned against neo-liberalism and its overseas promoters, and reject all local politicians associated with them. Unlike the 1976 coup, in which the US and the Generals, were able to blame the left for the 'disorder' and 'violence', in 2002 it was the pro-US liberal right-wing regimes which confiscated middle-class savings, lowering living standards, and violently repressed middle-class assemblies and pot-banging marches. A US-backed civic military coup would take place in a political vacuum with virtually no social basis of support and dependent exclusively on violent repression against the entirety of civil society organizations. The absolute political discredit of US client politicians like ex-President Menem, and ex-Minister (Minister for 15 days) Murphy and the genocidal military commanders, means that Washington faced a most unfavourable correlation of socio-political forces either now or in the immediate future. In this context Washington's most likely strategy will be to call on newly elected President Kirchner to take even more severe repressive measures as a means of demobilizing opposition in order to comply with the conditions of foreign bankers, with the promise of new IMF loans. Another possible scenario would be new elections in which a new version of a centre-left coalition comes to power and Washington resorts to a strategy of political attrition, undermining investments, loans, and so on in order to provoke discontent and thus launch the military coup in a context of chaos and failed policies.

In this context a race is taking place, between the mass movements and Washington to see who can fill the space of the disintegrating civilian right. The US has the arms of the state but not the social base. The mass movements have popular support but no organized national leadership in a position to bid for state power.

Other Latin American countries

Colombia, Venezuela and Argentina clearly express the centres of declining US influence and power. However, alternative forces are advancing in several other Latin American countries. There are clear signs that client regimes in Paraguay (Macchi), Bolivia (Sanchez de Losado), Ecuador (Garcia), Peru (Toledo) are discredited and have little public support in implementing Washington's agenda. Moreover, there are powerful multisectoral mass movements in the first three of the above countries that have demonstrated their capacity for direct action in blocking some of the most retrograde legislation. While these movements are powerful, their strength resides in particular regions and social classes (peasants) and they are prone to negotiate limited agreements (never implemented by the regime, thus precipitating a new round of mobilizations and confrontations).

Analysing Washington's political influence in Brazil is very complex. On the one hand the centre-right pro-US Cardoso regime lost much of its public support, except among the overseas bankers and local elites, thus weakening US hegemony. On the other hand the left has been severely weakened by the right-turn of the leadership of the Worker's Party and its newly elected President Inacio Lula Da Silva. The alliance with the right-wing Liberal Party and their embrace of most of the neo-liberal agenda, provides the US with a win-win situation. The right turn will alienate many rank and file Worker's Party voters and perhaps split the party, causing it to lose future elections. The Worker's Party – Liberal victory, will not adversely affect basic US interests. The incognito is the extent to which the Luld regime's right turn will result in a regrouping of the left in which powerful social movements (Landless Workers, small farmers, urban and housing movements), the radical leftist parties (PSTU, PcdoB, and so on) and the left dissidents of the Worker's Party can join forces. Independently of the electoral parties, there is a powerful and growing current of nationalist and anti-imperialist opinion, which is strongly opposed to the FTAA and the economic policies promoted by the US and Europe that have led to a decade of economic stagnation. Moreover, the Brazilian military is not a reliable ally of the Pentagon, as there is a strong, historically rooted, nationalist current that may resist further US intervention.

In summary, it would be a mistake to attribute the current US military–political offensive exclusively to global factors. The US counter-offensive predates 9/11 and 10/7 and Plan Columbia was initiated almost two years earlier. The imperial offensive in Latin America certainly received a greater ideological and military impetus from the events in the last half of 2001, but equally important was the advance of the popular movements and the extension of anti-imperialist, anti-liberal sentiment to substantial sectors of the middle class in some of the major countries. The complex interaction of declining influence in Latin America and in the Gulf states, combined with the competition from Europe, has dramatically changed Washington's conception of empire.

The New Imperialism: From Neo-liberalism to Neo-mercantilism

Argentina is a dramatic illustration of the 'failed regimes' within the US neo-liberal empire in Latin America but they are pervasive everywhere. Neo-liberalism, as an imperial strategy for capturing control over markets, national enterprises and natural resource, seems to be reaching its end point. This does not mean the end of imperialism. What is taking place is a greater degree of imperial state control over the economies and circuits of capital and commodities. Washington's FTAA is precisely a blueprint of a neo-mercantilist empire, in which the US establishes the legal framework for consolidating a privileged position in Latin American markets and economy over and against its European/Japanese competitors.

Neo-mercantilist empires are essentially based on unilateral state decisions (rejecting consultation) and military supremacy, both designed to impose policies on international, regional and national competitors. Given the weakness of the neo-liberal client states in containing popular insurgency, the neo-mercantilist imperial state opts for greater use of force and the militarization of politics. Against the economic gains in Latin America of its European allies the new mercantilism seeks to limit future losses by tying Latin America closer to the US.

The transition from neo-liberal to a neo-mercantilist empire is not an abrupt shift, the new imperialism still carries many of the characteristics of the past: the US still imports far more commodities than it did thirty years ago, and it will continue to be import-dependent into the foreseeable future. But increasingly Washington is moving toward import controls, quotas and tariffs to protect non-competitive local industries, from steel to shrimps.

Also, many US exports have been subsidized and protection has to some degree always existed, even at the height of the neo-liberal empire. The real question is the degree and, more important, the direction of state-subsidized trade. The US has vastly increased its agricultural subsidies, and, because of the over-valued dollar, moved to impose steel tariffs costing overseas exporters nearly US$10 billion in lost revenues. Europe will retaliate; the Latin American clients will not, especially those committed to FTAA.

Finally, as the US moves to a state-directed trade and investment empire in Latin America it will retain its neo-liberal rhetoric while implementing its statist strategy, thus disorienting superficial commentators. Several factors lead to a coincidence between neo-mercantilism and increased militarization.

- The blatant asymmetry of trade relations – the US protects and subsidizes its industry but demands 'free trade' for Latin America – leads to trade imbalances, for example, which can only be enforced and sustained by force.
- Neo-mercantilism degrades and alienates sectors of the local middle class, farmers and urban business, thus narrowing the political base of its local client regime.
- The increased role of the imperial state directly politicizes opposition to the state.
- Neo-mercantilism undermines local employment in industries and public sector social services, swelling the ranks of the un- and underemployed and enlarging the base for mass direct action.
- The imperial state's pressure on client states to meet foreign debt payments eliminates most revenue to finance local social services or capital projects, undermining professional employment and infrastructure development.

In summary, the transition to a neo-mercantilist economy requires greater exploitation and domination. The global 'antiterrorist' ideology used to justify greater US militarization in Latin America is a propaganda ploy: the economic bases for militarization are rooted in the transition to the new imperialism.

The US Offensive: Impact on the Left

The current US imperial offensive has had a differential impact on left formations in Latin America. In general, we can say that the electoral parties have bent to the right and the socio-political movements have been radicalized. The offensive has not only affected political alignments and strategies, but also economic programs.

Let us start with the negative side – those sectors of the left that, as a result of US intervention, threats, pressure and propaganda, have moved to the right. The two most prominent cases are the Sandinista Party (FSLN) in Nicaragua and the

Workers Party in Brazil. In both cases there was a gradual shift to the centre over the past decade. In the presidential election in Nicaragua in 2001, Daniel Ortega chose a neo-liberal vice presidential candidate and after 9/11 endorsed the US bombing of Afghanistan, its worldwide military offensive, the FTAA, payment of the foreign debt and orthodox neo-liberal policies. To no avail: Washington and the US ambassador intervened in the election favouring the conventional liberal candidate and issued threats to the electorate if it voted for the recycled guerilla turned liberal. Ortega lost the election alienating militants and the left, without securing the support of the business elite. In Brazil, the Worker's Party leadership has evolved from a socialist to social-democratic and more recently, neo-liberal program. While the party still has a strong minority of left-social democrats and a contingent of Marxist intellectuals, its present orientation is to move to the centre-right in securing alliances with the conservative Liberal Party and the PMDB (the Brazilian Democratic Movement Party). As the party leader moves to the right, the titular leader, Lula, assumes more of the characteristics of an authoritarian caudillo, more interested in winning positions of power than in reforming or changing the socio-economic system. Lula and his cohort in the leadership have taken both symbolic and substantive measures to ensure Washington of their willingness to be obedient clients: they promise to guarantee debt payments, defend the privatized enterprises, and encourage US foreign investors. On a symbolic level Lula's selection of a millionaire textile mogul, hostile to militant trade unions, homosexuals and the Landless Workers' Movement (MST) and favourable to the FTAA suggests that the Worker's Party is still moving to the right. Lula praised Kissinger, arch-proponent of imperial wars and the WTO, during his recent visit to Sao Paulo. Lula has visited Washington to assure the White House of his full support for its global 'antiterrorist campaign'. The PT's more accentuated move to the right after 9/11 suggests that, Washington's pressure accelerated a process which was already in place as a result of internal party politics. In Mexico, the Revolutionary Democratic Party (PRD)'s vote in favour of legislation (along with the two other major rightist parties), prejudicing the Zapatista-led Indian communities – in fact, all Indian communities – is indicative of the conciliatory policies of the current leadership. The refusal of the current party leader to denounce the Mexican Foreign Minister's provocative pronouncements and actions against Cuba is indicative that some sectors of the PRD may be competing with the National Action Party (PAN) to be Washington's favourite client in the Mexican senate.

In conclusion, the US offensive has had a significant impact in pushing most centre-left electoral parties to the right. In most cases, however, this right turn was already under way: the pressure accelerated the process and perhaps pushed these parties much further to the right than was anticipated.

In contrast, the US political and military offensive and the big push to impose FTAA has increased the scope, depth and radicalization of many of the region's socio-political movements. In Colombia US pressure to break off the peace negotiations and militarize the neutral zone has led to a major successful counter-offensive by the guerrillas, closer collaboration between the FARC and the ELN and a sharp deterioration of the economy, including petroleum flows, power, energy and water supplies, due to guerrilla attacks. Moreover, under conditions of warfare and class confrontation, the programmatic demands of the insurgency are likely to radicalize. At least in the first phase the US–Colombian offensive has led to several tactical defeats and, outside of capturing a few isolated towns in the demilitarized zone, it has led to significant losses among the US-Colombian military sponsored paramilitary death squads.

In Argentina, Duhalde's attempt to pacify the US on debt payments, offering a vote against Cuba, IMF compliance, and so on, heightened opposition and radicalized demands. The former disparate opposition groups and classes attempted to coalesce into an effective coalition. National unity meetings were attended by thousands and the pot-banging demonstrations by the middle class continue in tandem with major road blockages by the unemployed. But unity was never achieved, the economy continues to sink toward negative growth. The mass of the middle class with their funds still confiscated are aware that US and European bankers and their Argentine clients were able to send to the US, Europe and Uruguay close to US$40 billion before their bank accounts were frozen. The result is a powerful and conscious rejection of the existing political class. The US offensive has had the effect of isolating its political clients. It has had no effect in dampening or neutralizing the popular upsurge. While the Duhalde regime backs the US offensive, it is socially impotent and politically isolated, unable to implement any significant policies. More significantly, Washington does not possess stable interlocutors in the presidential mansion; the Duhalde regime may not last out its term.

In Venezuela the US offensive has successfully mobilized the business elite (FEDECAMARAS), the religious hierarchy and the trade union bosses in large-scale demonstrations with the hope of provoking a military coup and the replacement of Chavez by a loyal client. On the other hand, Chavez has responded by encouraging mass mobilizations by his supporters among the urban poor and dissident trade unionists. He also retains the loyalty of the army commanders. US intervention has radicalized Chavez speeches and he has given signals that he may introduce more substantive socio-economic changes favouring the poor.

The confrontations are leading to a greater social polarization between the rich upper class and affluent middle class on the one hand and the impoverished middle class and urban and rural poor on the other. Washington's offensive has polarized the country and radicalized the political and social demands on both sides: the business and wealthy classes are openly supporting a military solution to re-impose a client regime reversing Chavez's independent foreign policy; the poor are calling on Chavez to take the gloves off in his treatment of the foreign directed opposition and to implement a radical redistributive program. Chavez, so far, is maintaining an increasingly untenable 'middle ground' – resisting the attempts of the right to overthrow him, calling on mass mobilizations to support the constitutional regime, maintaining his independent foreign policy, but without clearly embarking on a clearly delineated social transformative process.

In Mexico, Brazil, Bolivia, Ecuador, Paraguay, the US has secured the endorsement of its worldwide offensive from the client regimes. But, in the process, the regimes themselves are increasingly isolated and ineffective instruments of US policy within Latin America. Moreover, below the regime level, there is little support for any US military campaign that supports the killer economic policies and relies on the oppressive military forces that have a long history of massacring popular movements.

Washington does secure favourable international alignments among most of the regimes in international forums by threats and vote buying, but it has lost ideological hegemony throughout the region, except in some elite intellectual circles and among conformist non-government organizations (NGOs). In contrast, the road blockages multiply; from the highways of Patagonia to the country roads of Bolivia and the jungles of Colombia: 'they' do not pass. The US secures the pledges of the peon Presidents but, increasingly, the presidential palaces and congressional buildings are encircled by protestors, while the smell of burning tyres filters through the barbed wire and past the grim faces of heavily armed soldiers. The US offensive has intimidated or co-opted opportunist politicians precisely at the moment in which the mass electorate is abandoning them.

Conclusion

It is clear that we are entering a period of a US political–military offensive, military coups (or attempted coups) mass direct action, political polarization and new forms of social representation. There are no uniform results; the gains and losses resulting from the US offensive cannot be measured by counting the votes of presidents and the assent of loyal generals. The advancing social movements and popular insurgency have unmasked the imperial plunder and have toppled client regimes, but consequential political outcomes are still to come.

The social conflicts and military engagements take place on a continent-wide basis; client presidents rise and fall, new replacements are imposed. Movements and parties grow and then face decisive challenges: to compromise or go for power. The failures and limitations of reformist programs have once again put socialism on the agenda.

A new generation has emerged which did not experience the political defeats and terror of the 1960s and 1970s, but certainly has experienced the hunger, poverty, unemployment and political corruption of the 1990s. None of the emerging militant movements or popular insurgencies has experienced a historical defeat in this decade. The movements, with temporary ups and downs, are still on an upward trajectory. However, no outcome is inevitable or predetermined: conscious organization, political clarity, and audacious human intervention is necessary to counter the current imperial offensive and to turn it into a historic defeat and beyond that into a successful socialist revolution.

Chapter 3

Dirty Money: The Foundation of US Growth and Empire

There is a consensus among US Congressional Investigators, former bankers and international banking experts that US and European banks launder between US$500 billion and US$1 trillion of dirty money annually, half of which is laundered by US banks alone. Senator Levin summarizes this record: 'Estimates are that US$500 billion to US$1 trillion of international criminal proceeds are moved internationally and deposited into bank accounts annually. It is estimated half of that money comes to the United States.'

Over the decade of the 1990s, between US$2.5 and US$5 trillion criminal proceeds are laundered by US banks and circulate in the US financial circuits. Senator Levin's statement however, only covers criminal proceeds, according to US laws. It does not include illegal transfers and capital flows from corrupt political leaders, and tax evasion by overseas businesses. A leading US scholar, Raymond Baker, an expert on international finance associated with the prestigious Brookings Institute, estimates:

> the flow of corrupt money out of developing [Third World] and transitional [ex-Communist] economies into Western coffers at $20 to $40 billion a year and the flow stemming from mispriced trade at $80 billion a year or more. My lowest estimate is a $100 billion per year by these two means we facilitated a trillion dollars in the decade, at least half to the United States. Including other elements of illegal flight capital would produce much higher figures. (Baker, 1999: 85)

The Brookings expert did not include illegal shifts of real estate and securities titles, wire fraud, and so on.

In other words, an incomplete figure of dirty money (laundered criminal and corrupt money) flowing into US coffers during the 1990s amounted to between US$3 and US$5.5 trillion. This is not the complete picture, but it gives us a basis on which to estimate the significance of the 'dirty money factor' in evaluating the US economy. In the first place, it is clear the combined laundered and dirty money flows cover part of the US deficit in its balance of merchandise trade, which ranges in the hundreds of billions annually. As it stands, the US trade deficit is close to US$300 billion. Without the dirty money the US economy external accounts would be totally unsustainable, living standards would plummet, the dollar would weaken, the available investment and loan capital would shrink and Washington would not be able to sustain its global empire. The importance of laundered money is forecast to increase. Former private banker Antonio Geraldi, in testimony before the Senate Subcommittee, projects significant growth in US bank laundering: 'The forecasters also predict the amounts laundered in the trillions of dollars and growing disproportionately to legitimate funds.' The US$500 billion of criminal and dirty money flowing into and through the major US banks far exceeds the net revenues of all the IT companies in the US, not to speak of their profits. These yearly inflows surpass all the net transfers by the major US oil producers, military industries and aircraft manufacturers. The biggest US banks, Bank of America, J.P. Morgan, Chase Manhattan and particularly Citibank, derive a high percentage of their banking profits from serving these criminal and dirty money accounts. The big US banks and key institutions sustain US global power via their money laundering and managing of illegally obtained overseas funds.

US Banks and The Dirty Money Empire

Washington and the mass media have portrayed the US in the forefront of the struggle against narco-trafficking, drug laundering and political corruption: the image is of clean white hands fighting dirty money from the Third World (or the ex-Communist countries). The truth is exactly the opposite. US banks have developed a highly elaborate set of policies for transferring illicit funds to the US, investing those funds in legitimate businesses or in US government bonds and legitimating them. The US Congress has held numerous hearings, provided detailed exposés of the illicit practices of the banks, passed several laws and called for stiffer enforcement by any number of public regulators and private bankers. Yet the biggest banks continue their practices, the sums of dirty money grow exponentially, because both the state and the banks have neither the will nor the interest to put an end to the practices that provide high profits and buttress an otherwise fragile empire.

The first thing to note about the money laundering business, whether criminal or corrupt, is that it is carried out by the most important banks in the US. Second, the practices of bank officials involved in money laundering have the backing and encouragement of the highest levels of the banking institutions; these are not isolated cases of loose cannons. This is clear in the case of Citibank's laundering of the US$200 million account of Raul Salinas (brother of Mexico's ex-president). When Salinas was arrested and his large-scale theft of government funds was exposed, his private bank manager at Citibank, Amy Elliott, told her colleagues that 'this goes in the very, very top of the corporation, this was known ... on the very top. We are little pawns in this whole thing' (Baker, 1999: 35).

Citibank, the biggest money launderer, is the biggest bank in the US, with 180,000 employees worldwide operating in one hundred countries, with US$700 billion in known assets and over US$100 billion in client assets in private banks (secret accounts) operating private banking offices in thirty countries, which is the largest global presence of any US private bank. It is important to clarify what is meant by 'private bank'.

Private banking is a sector that caters for extremely wealthy clients (US$1 million deposits and up). The big banks charge customers a fee for managing their assets and for providing the specialized services of the private banks. Private bank (PB) services go beyond the routine banking services and include investment guidance, estate planning, tax assistance, offshore accounts, and complicated schemes designed to secure the confidentiality of financial transactions. The attractiveness of the PBs for money laundering is that they sell secrecy to the dirty money clients. There are two methods that big banks use to launder money: via private banks and via corresponding banking. PBs routinely use code names for accounts, concentration accounts (concentration accounts co-mingle bank funds with client funds, which cut off paper trails for billions of dollars of wire transfers) that disguise the movement of client funds, and offshore private investment corporations (PIC) located in countries with strict secrecy laws (Cayman Islands, Bahamas, and so on).

For example, in the case of Raul Salinas, PB personnel at Citibank helped Salinas transfer US$90 to US$100 million out of Mexico in a manner that effectively disguised the funds' sources and destination, thus breaking the paper trail (Baker, 1999: 11–35). In routine fashion, Citibank set up a dummy offshore corporation, provided Salinas with a secret code name, provided an alias for a third-party intermediary who deposited the money in a Citibank account in Mexico, and transferred the money in a concentration account to New York where it was then moved to Switzerland and London.

The PICs are designed by the big banks for the purpose of holding and hiding personal assets. The nominal officers, trustees and shareholders of these shell corporations are themselves shells corporations controlled by the PB. The PIC then becomes the holder of the various bank and investment accounts and the ownership of the private bank clients is buried in the records of so-called jurisdiction, such as the Cayman Islands. Private bankers of the big banks like Citibank keep pre-packaged PICs on the shelf awaiting activation when a private bank client wants one. The system works like Russian Matryoshka dolls, shells within shells within shells, which in the end can be impenetrable to a legal process.

The complicity of the state in big bank money laundering is evident when one reviews the historic record. Big bank money laundering has been investigated, audited, criticized and subject to legislation; the banks have written procedures to comply. Yet banks like Citibank and the other big ten banks ignore the procedures and laws and the government ignores the non-compliance. Over the last twenty years, big bank laundering of criminal funds and looted funds has increased geometrically, dwarfing in size and rates of profit the activities in the formal economy. Estimates by experts place the rate of return in the PB market between 20 and 25 per cent annually. Congressional investigations revealed that Citibank provided 'services' for four political swindlers, moving US$380 million: Raul Salinas, US$80 to US$100 million; Asif Ali Zardari (husband of the former Prime Minister of Pakistan) in excess of US$40 million; El Hadj Omar Bongo (Dictator of Gabon since 1967) in excess of US$130 million; Abacha sons of General Abacha ex-Dictator of Nigeria in excess of US$110 million (Baker, 1999: 935–939). In all cases, Citibank violated all of its own procedures and government guidelines: there was no client profile (review of client background), determination of the source of the funds, nor of any violations of country laws from which the money accrued. On the contrary, the bank facilitated the outflow in its prepackaged format: shell corporations were established, code names were provided, funds were moved through concentration accounts, the funds were invested in legitimate businesses or in US bonds. In none of these cases – or thousands of others – was due diligence practiced by the banks (under due diligence a private bank is obligated by law to take steps to ensure that it does not facilitate money laundering). In none of these cases were the top banking officials brought to court and tried. Even after arrest of their clients, Citibank continued to provide services, including the movement of funds to secret accounts and the provision of loans.

Correspondent Banks: The Second Track

The second and related route which the big banks use to launder hundreds of billions of dollars in dirty money is through correspondent banking (CB). CB is the provision of banking services by one bank to another bank. It is a highly profitable and significant sector of big banking. In jurisdictions like the US where the banks have no physical presence it enables overseas banks to conduct business and provide services for their customers, including drug dealers and others engaged in criminal activity. A bank that is licensed in a foreign country and has no office in the US for its customers attracts and retains wealthy criminal clients interested in laundering money in the US. Instead of exposing itself to US controls and incurring the high costs of locating to the US, the bank will open a correspondent account with an existing US bank. By establishing such a relationship, the foreign bank (called a respondent) and through it, its criminal customers, receive many or all of the services offered by the correspondent US banks. Today, all the big US banks have established multiple correspondent relationships throughout the world so they may engage in international financial transactions for themselves and their clients in places where they have a physical presence. Many of the largest US and European banks located in the financial centres of the world serve as correspondents for thousands of other banks. Most of the offshore banks laundering billions for criminal clients have accounts in the US. All the big banks specializing in international fund transfer are called money centre banks; some of the biggest process up to a trillion dollars in wire transfers a day. Through June 1999, the top five correspondent bank holding companies in the US held correspondent account balances exceeding US$17 billion; the total correspondent balances of the seventy-five largest US correspondent banks was US$34.9 billion. For the billionaire criminals an important feature of correspondent relationships is that they provide access to international transfer systems that facilitate the rapid transfer of funds across international boundaries and within countries. The most recent estimates (1998) are that sixty offshore jurisdictions around the world licensed about 4000 offshore banks that control approximately US$5 trillion in assets.

One of the major sources of impoverishment and crises in Africa, Asia, Latin America, Russia and the other countries of the ex-USSR and Eastern Europe, is the pillage of the economy and the hundreds of billions of dollars that are transferred out of the country via the correspondent banking system and the private banking system linked to the biggest banks in the US and Europe. Russia alone has seen over US$200 billion illegally transferred in the course of the 1990s. The massive shift of capital from these countries to US and European banks has generated mass impoverishment and economic instability and crises. This, in turn, has made them increasingly vulnerable to pressure from the IMF and WB to liberalize their banking and financial systems, leading to further flight and deregulation. As a result, there is greater corruption and more overseas transfers via private banks, as the senate reports demonstrate.

The increasing polarization of the world is embedded in this organized system of criminal and corrupt financial transactions. While speculation and foreign debt payments play a role in undermining living standards in the crises regions, the multi-trillion dollar money laundering and bank servicing of corrupt officials is a much more significant factor, sustaining Western prosperity, US empire building and financial stability. The scale, scope and time frame of transfers and money laundering, the centrality of the biggest banking enterprises and the complicity of the governments, strongly suggests that the dynamics of growth and stagnation, empire and recolonization are intimately related to a new form of capitalism built around pillage, criminality, corruption and complicity.

Chapter 4

The Centrality of the State

Introduction

One of the most pervasive and insidious myths of our times is the idea that we live in a world without nation states.[1] Nothing could be further from the truth. In all regions of the world the state, whether imperial, capitalist, or neo-colonial, has been strengthened, its activities expanded, its intervention in the economy and civil society ubiquitous. The state in the imperialist nations, what we call the imperial state, is particularly active in concentrating power within the nation and projecting it overseas in a great variety of institutions, economic and political circumstances, and establishing vast spheres of influence and domination. The US imperial state leads the way, followed by the EU led by Germany and France and Japan. The power of the imperial state is extended to international financial institutions (IFIs) such the International Monetary Fund (IMF), the World Bank (WB), the Asian Bank (AB) and the World Trade Organization (WTO). The imperial states provide most of the funds, appoint the IFI leaders and hold them accountable for implementing policies that favour the multinational corporations (MNC) of their respective countries. The advocates of a world without nation states, or globalization theorists, fail to understand that the IFIs are not a higher or new form of government beyond the nation state, but institutions who derive their power from the imperial states.

This chapter starts by discussing and criticizing the unsubstantiated arguments of the globalist theorists and then details and discusses the significance of the state in the contemporary world, regional and local economies.[2] The final part of the chapter presents an explanation of the reasons for the growth of statism in the neo-liberal economies of the world.

The Myth of a World without Nation States

The advocates of the thesis of a 'world without nation states' – what we will call 'globalism' – start from a set of very dubious assumptions. There are nuanced variations and nuances on the theme, with some arguing that the nation state is an anachronism, others that it is declining, and others still that it is no longer a reality. While these arguments continue to provoke debate, more significant is the shared assumptions that inform globalist theorizing. These questionable assumptions include the following.

The Role of the Multinational Corporations

Multinational corporations are global corporations that have no specific location in any particular nation state. They form a new world economy divorced from national controls and are part of a new world ruling class. This assumption is based on the fact that large-scale corporations operate in a number of countries, they are mobile and they have the power to evade taxes and regulations in many national jurisdictions. There are several conceptual and empirical problems with this assumption.

First, the fact that multinational corporations operate in many countries does not detract from the fact that the headquarters in which most of the strategic decisions, directors and profits are concentrated are located in the US, the EU and Japan (Doremus, et al., 1998: Ch. 5).

Second, mobility is based on strategic decisions taken by directors in the headquarters in the imperial centres. These decisions depend on the political and economic conditions created by the imperial state and its representatives in the IFIs. Mobility is contingent on inter-state relations.

Third, evasion of taxes and regulations is possible because of deliberate policies in the imperial states and their multinational banks.[3] Non-enforcement of laws against transfers of illicit earnings from the neo-colonial countries to the imperial states is a form of state activity favouring large-scale concentration of wealth that strengthens the external accounts of the imperial economies. The flouting of neo-colonial state regulations by the multinational corporations is part of a broader set of power relations anchored in the imperial, neo-colonial state relations.

The Power of the IFI

The old nation state governments have been superseded by a new world government, made up of the heads of the IFIs, the WTO and the CEOs of the multinational corporations. This is an argument that is based on a superficial discussion of epiphenomena rather than a deeper analysis of the power structure. While it is true that IFIs make many important decisions in a great many geographical locations affecting significant economic and social sectors, these decisions and the decision-makers are closely linked to the imperial states and the multinational corporations that influence them. All of the top IFI officials are appointed by their national/imperial governments. All their crucial policy guidelines on loans and conditions for lending are set by the finance, treasury and economy ministers of the imperial states. The bulk of IFI funds come from the imperial states, representation on the executive board of the IFI is based on the proportion of funding by the imperial states. The IMF and the WB have always been led by individuals from the US or the EU.[4]

The globalist vision of IFI power is based on derived power, not its source in the imperial states. In this sense, international power is based in the imperial states, not in supranational entities. To focus on the latter is to grossly overestimate the autonomy of the IFIs and to underestimate their subordination to the imperial states.

The real significance of the IFIs is how they magnify, extend and deepen the power of the imperial states and how they constitute a terrain for competition between rival imperial states. Far from superseding the old states, the IFIs have strengthened their position.

Information Revolution

One of the common arguments of globalists is that an information revolution has eliminated state borders and created a new global economy. Globalists argue that a new technological revolution has transformed capitalism by providing a new impetus to the development of the productive forces. The claims that information technologies have revolutionized economies and thus created a new global economy in which nation states and national economies have become superfluous is extremely dubious.

A comparison of productivity growth in the US from the 1950s onwards fails to support the globalist argument. Between 1953 and 1973, before the so-called information revolution, US productivity grew an average of 2.6 per cent but, with the introduction of computers, productivity growth between 1972 and 1995 was less than half of this (Wolf, 1999: 10). Even in the misperceived boom period of 1995–1999, productivity growth was 2.2 per cent below the pre-computer period. Japan, which makes the most extensive use of computers and robots, has witnessed a decade of stagnation and crises. Between 2000 and 2001 the information sector went into a deep crisis; tens of thousands lost their jobs; hundreds of firms went bankrupt and the value of stocks dropped by some 80 percent. The speculative bubble that defined the 'information economy' burst. Moreover, the major source of productivity growth claimed by the globalists was in the area of computer manufacture. Studies have shown that computer use in offices is directed more toward personal use than for exchanging information and ideas; it is estimated that up to 60 per cent of computer time is spent in activity unrelated to the enterprise. Computer manufacturers account for 1.2 per cent of the US economy and less than 5 per cent of capital stock (Wolf, 1999: 10).

Moreover, the US population census provides another explanation for the higher productivity figures: the five million US workers, mostly illegal immigrants, who flooded the US labour market in the 1990s. Given that productivity is measured by the output per estimated worker, the five million uncounted workers inflate the productivity data. If the five million were included, productivity figures would deflate to below 2 per cent.

With the decline of the information economy and its stock valuations it becomes clear that the information revolution is not the transcendent force that defines the economies of the major imperial states, let alone configuring a new world order. The fact that most people have computers and browse, and that some firms have better control over their inventories, does not mean that power has shifted beyond the nation state. Publicist claims about the 'information revolution' ring hollow as the investors in the world stock markets shift funds toward the real economy and away from the fictitious high technology firms that show no profits and increasing losses.

The New Economy

Related to the previous assumption, globalists argue that we are living in a New Economy that has superseded the Old Economy of manufacturing, mining, agriculture and social services. According to the globalists the market creates real democracy in which ordinary people make choices about their future, and the new efficiencies produced by the new technologies ensure high growth. The recession of late 2000–2001 certainly refutes the claims of the New Economy ideologues: the business cycle continues to operate and, moreover, the cycle is particularly accentuated by the highly speculative nature of the New Economy. As it turns out, the New Economy demonstrates all the features of a volatile, speculative economy, driven by exorbitant claims of high returns. In the absence of profits, or even revenues, it turns out that much of what was touted as a New Economy was a colossal financial swindle where the high returns to the early investors led later investors to financial ruin.

The new efficiencies promised by the New Economy publicists could not resist the logic of the capitalist business cycle. 'Just in time production' was premised on a stable and continuous growth of demand: the recession of 2001, the sudden decline in demand, led to an accumulation of inventories among producers and sellers, and resultant lay-offs. Cash-flow problems, increased indebtedness and bankruptcies, characteristic of the Old Economy.

It is clear that the so-called New Economy does not transcend capitalist crisis. In fact it is more vulnerable and has fewer resources to fall back on since most of its cash flow depends on speculative expectations of continuous high returns. The sharp decline in commercial advertising earnings on the websites and the saturation of the computer market has led to a structural crisis for producers of hardware and software, leading to a giant shake-down in the industry; the exorbitant paper value of the stocks has tumbled and the major internet companies are struggling to survive, let alone define the nature of a New Economy.

The Imperial System

Some globalists like Antonio Negri (2001) write of an 'imperial system' as opposed to imperialist states, as if one could exist without the other. The 'system' has no centre since all states have lost their special significance before the all-powerful multinational corporations that dominate markets. This systems approach fails to recognize the class and institutional power of nationally owned and directed banks and industries. Even more problematic is that systems theorists fail to link the structures, operations, legal codes and linkages among imperial states, the multinational corporations and their offspring in the IFIs. The vast reach of their power concentrates on profits, interest, rents and royalties in the imperialist countries. The 'system' is derived from, and is sustained by, the combined forces of the imperial states and their multinational corporations. To abstract from the specificities of ownership and state power in order to describe an imperial system is to lose sight of the basic contradictions and conflicts, the inter-state imperial rivalries and the popular struggles for state power. The chimera of 'stateless empires' contains the same problems as the notion of a 'world without nation states': it exaggerates the autonomy of capital from the state and reproduces the false propositions of the 'free market ideologues' who argue that the market (or, in the words of Negri, the 'collectivist capitalist') dominates the imperialist system.

The World System Approach

Globalists operate at such a high level of abstraction in defining the configurations of power that they amalgamate the most significant variations in regimes, states, and class configurations. As a result, they do not have a very convincing conception of socio-economic change. The most egregious misconception is in the world system approach,[5] with its categories of 'core', or 'centre', and 'semi-periphery' and 'periphery'. This type of simplistic abstract stratification of the world economy and power subordinates the dynamic of class relations to a static distribution of market shares. The abstract categories obscure fundamental differences in class interests between nations in each category, differences that determine how market shares are distributed within nations, the ownership of property, living standards, as well as differences between dynamic and stagnant countries. More fundamentally, by looking at market positions, globalists overlook the role of the state in preserving and challenging the relationship between states and economies and in reconfiguring the world economy.

The Centrality of the State

In the contemporary world the nation state, in both its imperial and neo-colonial form, has multiplied and expanded its activity. Far from being an anachronism, the state has become a central element in the world economy and within nation states. However, the activities of state vary according to their class character, whether they are imperial or neo-colonial states.

Imperial States and Crisis Management

In recent years the centrality of the imperial state (Petras and Morley, 1980) has been evidenced in the fundamental areas of political, cultural and economic activity that buttress the position of the imperial powers, particularly the US.

Since 1990, several major financial and economic crises have occurred in various regions of the world. In each instance, the imperial states, particularly the US state, have intervened to save the multinational corporations, and avoid the collapse of financial systems. For example, in 1994, when the Mexican financial system was on the verge of collapse, US President Clinton intervened to dispatch US$20 billion to the Mexican state to bail out US investors and stabilize the peso. In the second instance, during the Asian crisis of 1998, the US and European governments approved an IMF–WB multi-billion dollar bail-out in exchange for opening the economies, particularly South Korea, to foreign takeovers of basic industries. In the Brazilian crisis of 1999 and the Argentine crisis of 2001, Washington pressured the IFIs to bail-out the regimes. Within the US the threatened bankruptcy of a major international investment bank led to Federal Reserve (central bank) intervention, pressuring a private bank bail-out. In a word, with greater frequency and with greater resources the imperial state has played a dominant role in crisis management, saving major investors from bankruptcy, propping up insolvent multinational corporations and preventing the collapse of currencies. More than ever the multinational corporations and the so-called global economy depend on the constant massive intervention of imperial states to manage the crisis, and secure benefits (buyouts of local enterprises).

Inter-imperialist Competition

The competition between rival imperial powers, and multinational corporations has been essentially spearheaded by rival imperial states. For example, the US imperial state is leading the fight to open European markets to US beef and US exports of bananas from South and Central America, while the Japanese and the European states negotiate with the US to increase the quota on a series of exports, including steel and textiles. Trade and the markets are largely defined by state-to-state agreements. 'Globalization' is not only a product of multinational corporation growth but is largely an artifice of state-to-state agreements. The competition between capitalist terms is mediated, influenced and directed by the state, the markets do not transcend the state but operate within state-defined boundaries.

Conquest of Markets

The state plays a pervasive and profound role in the conquest of overseas markets and the protection of local markets. In the first instance, the state provides indirect and direct subsidies to export sectors.[6] In the US, agricultural exports receive subsidized water and electrical power, and export subsidies in the form of tax relief. Second, the imperial state via IFI pressures loan recipient states in the Third World to lower or eliminate trade barriers, privatize and denationalize enterprises through conditionality agreements. This allows US, EU and Japanese multinational corporations to penetrate markets and buy local enterprises. Most exports are financed by agencies of the state. So-called globalization would not exist if it were not for state intervention; nor would the markets remain open if it were not for imperial state military and electoral intervention, political–economic threats or pressure and recruitment of local clients. Imperialism takes many forms but pursues similar goals: the conquest of Third World markets, the penetration of competitors' economies and the protection of home markets. The US, Europe and Japan have elaborate sets of trade barriers in a wide range of product areas of strategic importance: auto imports are limited by quotas, as are sugar, textiles, steel, and so on.[7] There is a multiplicity of non-traditional constraints and informal agreements that limit export countries from entering US markets – all negotiated on a state-to-state basis. In many cases, in its dealings with neo-colonial regimes like Brazil under Cardoso, the US state rejects reciprocity, demanding and securing the liberalization of the information industry while restricting Brazilian steel exports, on the bogus pretext of 'anti-dumping' charges.

Trade Agreements

All the major economic agreements, liberalizing trade and establishing new investment regulations, are negotiated by the states, enforced by the states and subject to state modifications. GATT, WTO, Lomé, and so on, which established the trade rules and framework for 'global trading networks' were formulated by the states. In addition, bilateral as well as regional multilateral trade pacts, such as NAFTA, LAFTA, are initiated by the imperial state to open new markets for their multinationals. The imperial state operates in synergy with its multinational corporation. The expansion in markets has nothing to do with multinational corporations superseding anachronistic states. On the contrary, most movements of capital to new markets depend on the state intervening to knock down barriers and, in some cases, destabilize nationalist regimes.

Investment Agreements

The new multilateral and bilateral investment agreements are formulated at the state level with the agreement and active participation of the multinational corporations. The reason is clear: the multinational corporations want state participation to guarantee that their capital will not be expropriated, subject to discriminatory taxes, or restricted in remitting profits. The state is the enforcer of investment guarantees, a crucial element in corporate investment expansion. In many cases, the imperial states use their representative in the IFIs to impose new investment codes as conditions for stabilization or development loans.

Protection, Subsidies and Adjudication

The imperial states of the EU impose powerful protective barriers for their agricultural products. The US and the EU heavily subsidize agriculture with low rates for electricity and water use. Research and development of new technology is heavily financed by the state and then turned over to the multinationals. At each stage prior to, during and after the expansion of multinational corporations in the international market, the state is deeply implicated. Moreover, where national enterprises are non-competitive, the imperial states invent pretexts to protect them from more efficient producers. Japan protects its rice producers, even though their price is ten times more costly to consumers. The US provides huge subsidies to agribusiness California exporters in the form of research, cheap water rates and loans tied to the purchase of US grain exports. The EU subsidizes the formation of its high technology industries and agriculture.

Statism or neo-statism is the centrepiece of multinational global expansion. The state has grown, its reach has been expanded, and its role in the international economy is essential. The empty rhetoric of 'free markets' promoted by conservative ideologues has been consumed and parroted by the globalists on the left. While the left talks abut the declining role of the state, the right has been active in promoting state activity to further the interests of the multinational corporations. While the Left talks of the 'globalization' of markets, the multinational corporations penetrate and carve up the markets, enlarging their spheres of domination and control. The imperial state, in this context, is not simply an economic institution; the overseas expansion of the multinational corporations is heavily dependent on the military and political role of the imperial state.

Expansion of Political and Military Power of the Imperial State

The overseas expansion of the multinational corporations has been made possible by the military–political expansion of Euro-American imperialism via NATO and surrogate armies in Southern Africa, Latin America, and Asia. In Russia (the former USSR) and Eastern Europe, client regimes have been sponsored and supported by the imperial states, laying the groundwork for the takeover of a vast array of strategic industries, energy sources, and so on. The triumph of the US imperial state over the USSR provided the impetus for dismantling the welfare states in Europe and what pretended to be a welfare state in the US. The Euro-American wars in the Gulf and Balkans consolidated the imperial states' dominance and extended their influence over dissident states. The destabilization of the former Communist regimes, the destructive wars against nationalist regimes in Southern Africa, Latin America and elsewhere opened these regions to neo-liberal policy prescriptions. Imperial military expansion directly related to state military apparatuses accompanied and promoted multinational corporate overseas expansion. So-called globalization grew out of the barrel of a gun – an imperial state gun. To further protect overseas capital, the US and the EU have created a new NATO doctrine that legitimates offensive wars, inside and outside of Europe against any country that threatens vital economic interests (their multinational corporations).[8] NATO has been expanded to incorporate new client states in Eastern Europe, and new 'peace associates' among the Baltic states and the former republics of the USSR (Georgia, Kazahkstan, and so on). In other words the imperial state military alliances incorporate more states, involving more armed state apparatuses than before – to ensure the safe passage of Euro–US multinational corporations into their countries and the easy flow of profits back to their headquarters in the US and Western Europe.

The State and the Mass Media

While the mass media and its political–cultural apparatus crosses more borders than ever, ownership and control is highly concentrated in the hands of US and European multinationals. The message is increasingly homogenous, and the source and inspiration is closely coordinated with policymakers in Washington, Berlin,

London, and so on. Global flows, imperial controls – these are the essence of the mass media today. The mass media multinational corporations look to the imperial states and officials to set the political line and define the parameters for discussion, while they reap the profits.

To conclude, the imperial states, far from being superseded by the overseas expansion of capital, have grown and become essential components of the configurations of the world political economy. Globalists mystify the role of the imperial state, an essential adversary, in the front lines of defence of the privileges and power of the multinational corporations.

While a few globalist writers might concede the importance of the imperial state, they would argue that the recolonized states are withering away before the global corporations that undermine their capacity to make decisions and regulate national economies.

Recolonized States: The State as Terrain for Struggle

The starting point for any discussion of Third World states is historical: most of them developed socio-economic policies contrary to the IMF and WB prescriptions throughout the period between 1945 and 1975. The basic reason had little to do with the existence or not of the USSR. The main reason was the social classes, political alliances and ideology that directed TWS policy and pressure from the mass movements. Throughout this thirty-year period, the imperial states, such as the US, pressured Third World states to liberalize their economies and privatize public enterprises. Most of these states resisted these imperial pressures (now dubbed globalization). Two basic changes took place which altered this scenario: imperialist powers led by the US launched a military offensive, utilizing mercenary client military–political forces in Southern Africa, Central and South America and Asia to destroy the economies and topple nationalist and socialist regimes which rejected the liberal program. The second change was the ascendancy in the Third World of a new transnational capitalist class (TCC) (including top political functionaries) linked to international financial circuits, with overseas bank accounts and investments and largely engaged in export markets. This TCC, sharing the neo-liberal program of the imperial powers, became the dominant class in Third World states and proceeded to implement policies privileging the interests of the imperial powers. The dynamic interplay between TCC and the imperial powers produced what is mistakenly described as globalization. What emerged is the recolonization of the Third World via the pivotal role of the TCC in Third World states.

Third World states are described by globalization theorists as powerless, lacking the attributes of a state and incapable of resisting the forces of globalization. There are several problems with this view:

- It places all Third World states under the same rubric, failing to distinguish those who, in the past, possessed different attributes from the contemporary neo-colonial states.

- It fails to take account of the fact that Third World states were active agents in developing the policies that facilitated economic liberalization.
- Globalization theorists cannot account for the variations in Third World state policy with regard to the liberal and neo-liberal agenda of the imperial powers.
- Globalists overlook the importance of the new class configuration that has gained ascendancy within the state and pushes the neo-liberal agenda.
- Globalists understate the scope and depth of state intervention in the neo-liberal world order, equating a weak state with the absence of a social welfare state. In fact, the neo-colonial state is as active, regulatory and interventionist as the populist or welfare state, but its activity, rules and intervention is directed to serve different class interests – those of the transnational capitalist class.

While the recolonized state acts on behalf of foreign capitalists, bankers and states, it requires and retains substantial resources and consequential attributes that enable it to fulfil its mission. In fact, without a strong (recolonized) state, the imperial goals would be imperilled. Strength is measured in this context by the capacity of state actors and institutions to carry out fundamental structural changes and ensure their stabilization against the majority of the popular social movements, trade unions and political parties. While the recolonized state appears weak before the demands of the IFIs, it is strong in translating those demands into national policies. In fact, the concept of the weak state is of dubious value, since the recolonized state shares the policies of the imperial state and is made up of the associates of the multinational corporations and therefore cannot be conceived of as capitulating to the IFIs or being dominated by these so-called 'global forces'.

The centrality of the recolonized state in the liberal counter-revolution is evident in several inter-related policy areas.

Privatization

The recolonized state, in consultation with IFIs, implements the neo-liberal agenda by, among other things. the privatization of strategic and lucrative public enterprises. Privatization requires intensive state intervention including the making of political alliances, repression of trade unions and/or firing of militant workers, socializing the debts of the enterprises, securing the advice of overseas investment banks in organizing the sale, intervening to ensure that favoured buyers have purchasing advantages, and eliminating any rate or price controls if the public enterprise operated with fixed fees.

Structural Adjustment Policies

Essentially Structural Adjustment Policies (SAPs) mean far more than mere economic 'adjustment', and 'structural' refers to class power, wealth and control (Veltmeyer, Petras and Vieux, 1997: Ch. 3). In this case, the state is extremely important and active since SAPs involve changing property ownership (from public to private, from national to private), imposing regressive taxes (increasing VAT against progressive taxation on the rich and foreign capital), concentrating income and property (regressive wage policies, freezing minimum wages, promoting agro-business at the expense of peasant agriculture), lowering tariff barriers (bankrupting national producers, allowing multinational corporations greater shares of local markets, and so on), lowering social expenditures for health and education and increasing subsidies for exporters. The SAP is a strategy for, and by, the ruling class TCC and foreign capital, and against the great majority of local producers, workers and peasants. It increases inequality and poverty. To implement SAPs requires a strong state willing to persist against the opposition of the majority, an ideologically committed state willing to shed its historical role as an independent entity and to reject the idea of popular sovereignty in order to implement policies via authoritarian means, by executive decree.

Who speaks of a neo-liberal regime speaks for a powerful state that imposes and implements its policies.

Flexibility of Labour

This is a euphemism for concentrating power in the hands of the employers and the recolonized state. The new so-called Labour and Pension Reforms refer to policies that increase the powers of employers to hire workers on precarious contracts and fire them with little or no severance pay. It represents the subjection of labour to capital: workers are excluded from any voice in hours or days worked, safety or health conditions. The precarious contracts give workers no job security as employment is based on short-term contracts without benefits such as vacations and pensions. The privatization of pension funds put billions of dollars in the hands of private investment houses that receive exorbitant management fees and access to funds for speculation and fraud, enriching the few and threatening the retirement income of millions. Implementing the regressive labour and pension legislation requires a strong state that can intervene against the popular sectors of civil society, and repress and resist strong trade union protests. Enforcement requires consolidating support among the capitalist class, and securing backing from the IFIs, which is readily available. A weak state would not be able to resist the pressures of the popular classes; it would make concessions. A strong state would ignore the protests and proceed to implement the regressive labour and pension legislation.

In examining the most important policies pursued by the recolonized state it is clear that the scope and depth of state intervention is as strong as ever. The main difference is in the socio-economic direction of state activism and intervention: liberal neo-statism involves intervention to transfer wealth and property to the private rich, especially foreign capital. The state has not deregulated the economy; it has established new rules governing incomes policy, pensions, labour relations, import–export policies, the flow of capital and so on. The new rules favouring the TCC and foreign capital require a new regulatory regime in which representatives of the new ruling class replace populists and nationalists.

In the dismantling of the previous regulatory regime and social economy, and the construction of the new liberal economy and society, the recolonized state plays an essential activist and interventionist role, albeit one operating under the dominance of the imperial state.

Why the State Plays a Central Role

The imperial powers and the TCC in the Third World have a much more realistic and pragmatic understanding regarding the centrality of the state, whether imperial or recolonized, than the so-called globalist theorists who purport to be on the left. While the publicists of the ruling class mouth the globalist rhetoric, in practice they work to strengthen and extend the power of the state. This is because it is required for the expansion and survival of their interests. There are several reasons why the state continues to play an essential role in the contemporary world.

Volatility of Markets

The contemporary world economy is profoundly influenced by financial sectors and speculative activity that is highly volatile and constantly requires state intervention to prevent periodic financial crises in particular regions from spreading throughout the world economy. Stock market speculators in the imperial countries are highly dependent on interest rates fixed by central banks. To prevent the collapse of financial and banking systems, state intervention is often required to restructure bad loans. This has been the case, for example, in Japan, South Korea and Russia, not to speak of the US itself. Stagnating economies depend on state intervention to stimulate growth as in Japan and China. The examples could be multiplied, but the point is that increasing movements of speculative capital have multiplied and increased the role of the state in trying to stabilize the anarchy of the market, with whatever resources can be mobilized from whatever sources are available.

Financial Deregulation

Decreased state control over financial transactions has increased the role of state intervention in bailing out crisis-ridden financial systems and enterprises. The lack of capital controls and free convertibility has allowed for speculation on currencies and massive outflows of capital in panic conditions. The state has intervened by supporting currencies, letting the currency float and/or tightening lending by raising interest rates. The frequency and increasing intensity of crises has turned the state from a police to a firefighter role – putting out the fire of financial conflagrations.

Inter-imperial Competition

Imperial states have increasingly taken part in the struggle for market shares, each defending its own multinational corporations; the recolonized states are active in promoting joint ventures between their transnational capitalist enterprises and the multinational corporations. The states have negotiated quotas on imports, taken competitors to the WTO, organized boycotts to strengthen their multinational corporations at the expense of rivals. The US imperial state has fought for its cattle exporters against the EU, threatening boycotts and retaliatory measures; it has limited imports of agricultural products from sugar-producing tropical countries. In a word, competition among national multinational corporations has been converted into inter-state conflicts with the state itself as the final arbiter. Given shrinking markets and growing recession, we can expect greater state intervention and protection, not less.

The Scope and Depth of the Transformations

No single multinational corporation, or group of multinational corporations, by itself or themselves have the power and authority to transform the economic and social structures, allowing capital to flow *en masse* in overseas markets. The state created the shell within which capital flows and established the rules of the game that guide overseas expansion. Given the fragility of these structures the state must continuously intervene in bailing out capital, propping up recolonized regimes, and so on.

Buttressing the IFIs

Since the IFIs depend directly on the imperial states for their leaders, programs and priorities, the support of the imperial states is essential in allowing the IFIs to continue to intervene in the recolonized states. Funding of the IFIs depends on the imperial states. Without it they have no leverage and no authority in enforcing their prescriptions. To the degree that IFIs serve to link the imperial and recolonized states, their position as a power centre is derived from the imperial centres. For these reasons, the state continues and will continue to be essential in the world political economy. Far from being a residual power derived from the past the continuing relevance of the state is structurally built into the contemporary imperial system.

Conclusion

The globalization paradigm fails to explain the central role played by the state in the political economy of world development. Likewise, the notion of an imperial system has no meaning unless we understand the activities of the imperial state and the multiplicity of roles it plays in opening markets for the expansion of its multinational corporations.

The fundamental theoretical point is that the current configuration of power in the world economy is not based on 'stateless' or 'global' corporations, but on multinational corporations working closely with their imperial states. IFIs, like the WB and IMF, do not form a new global state, but derive their power and funding from the imperial states. Imperialism and not globalization is the key concept to understanding inter-state conflicts and inter-corporate competition. The imperial state and the multinational corporations do not constitute polarities: there is a fundamental synergy between neo-statism and neo-liberalism. Contrary to neo-liberal free market ideology, in today's world, policymakers in both the imperial and recolonized states pick winners and losers through incentives, subsidies, and tariffs resulting in the expansion of specific big capitalist groupings, and the decline of small and medium-sized firms as well as large firms without close ties to the regime.

The debate among bourgeois economists is whether the large-scale, long-term intervention and bail-out of multinational corporations is a 'moral hazard', meaning whether the knowledge held by corporate directors of a state bail-out encourages 'reckless speculation'. The New Economy economists set aside their free market ideology when faced with a crises and look to the state for financial resources to stave off bankruptcy. On the other hand, fundamentalist neo-liberals argue that profits are earned on the basis of investment risks and, therefore, if the state eliminates the risk it undermines the market's efficient allocation of resources, and promotes destructive speculation.

The basic problem with globalization theory is that it looks at epiphenomena – the overseas expansion of national corporations – and fails to take account of their ties to the headquarters of the global corporations that buy and sell globally, but whose strategic decisions on technology and investment is controlled from the national headquarters in the imperial state. These corporations are multinational in form, but national in content, particularly vis-à-vis the close ties between the headquarters of the multinational corporation with the senior officials of the imperial state.

The globalist notion of a new 'global regime' based on the supremacy of the IFIs is based on a superficial extrapolation of the activities of the IMF and WB from the larger imperial state networks and matrix in which they form a subordinate part. As a result, globalist theorists inflate the power of the IFIs and deflate the powers of the state, particularly that of the imperial states. Globalists further compound their errors by confusing a shift in state activism from welfare to corporate subsidies as a 'decline of the state' or a 'weakening of the state'. As we have argued, the recolonized state is very active, interventionist and strong in implementing the neo-liberal agenda. In writing off 'the state' because the welfare state has been eclipsed by the neo-liberal state, globalists obscure one of the most important terrains from struggle.

As we have argued, the state potentially retains great resources, capacity and a strategic position between producers and the world economy. The question thus becomes not one of globalizing the struggle, but of transforming the class nature of the state, reconfiguring its relation to the multinational corporations, and the TCC. This means the class struggle within the nation for state power is essential in securing economic resources – technological research centres, means of production, land, and so on – for redistributing wealth and recreating national markets. The multiple and profound activities that the recolonized and imperial state performs for the multinational corporations and the TCC indicates that it is a site of resources, power and activities that can transform and improve the lives of working people. The ideology of decline or disappearance of state is a mystification designed to divert popular movements to the secondary institutions that derive their power from the state.

The internationalism of left-wing globalists is event specific – G-8 Summits, meetings of the IMF, the WB and the WTO, and so on, where large conglomerates of groups meet, protest and disperse. While the publicity value is fine, these activities do not challenge the foundations and structures of imperial and neo-colonial power. Internationalism has strength only in so far as the national political movements are powerful, where oppressed classes have state power and can intervene in support of their comrades abroad. Strong national movements build powerful international solidarity.

Notes

1 The most prominent theorists of this view are Ignacio Ramonet and Bernard Cassen of *Le Monde Diplomatique* and their disciples in ATTAC.
2 For a more extended critique of globalization theory see Petras and Veltmeyer (2000) and Petras (2000).
3 'Private Banking and Money Laundering: A Case Study of Opportunities and Vulnerabilities', Hearings Before the Permanent Sub-Committee on Investigations of the Committee on Governmental Affairs, United States Senate, One Hundred Sixth Congress, November 9-10, 1999. Also 'Report on Correspondent Banking: A Gateway to Money Laundering', Minority Staff of the US Senate Permanent Subcommittee on Investigations, Feb. 2001.
4 Washington appoints the head of the WB, Europe the director of the IMF. At the recent selection of the IMI head, the US tried to impose one of its own, but the Europeans eventually won out, but not before they were forced to alter their nominee.
5 Refer to Immanuel Wallerstein's yearly production.
6 In the year 2000 US Export–Import financed more than US$15 billion in US export sales. Currently, the US ranks seventh among countries subsidising exports behind Japan, France, Germany, The Netherlands, Canada and South Korea (*Financial Times*, 6 March, 2001: 4).
7 Both the United States and the EU manipulate 'anti-dumping' regulations to protect uncompetitive industries from more efficient producers (*Financial Times*, 6 March, 2001: 8).
8 'The Strategic Concept of the Atlantic Alliance', NATO Summit Meeting, 23–24 April, 1999. Ratified by the Heads of State in Washington.

Chapter 5

The Myth of the Third
Scientific–Technological Revolution

Introduction

The 1990s was a decade in which the most influential writers, journalists and academics wrote, spoke and polemicized about two overriding themes: globalization and the New Economy based on the growth of information technology (IT), the biotechnical and telecommunications 'revolution'. The expansion of capital into the ex-Communist countries, the neo-liberal conquest of formerly protectionist Third World economies and the widespread privatization of public enterprises, North and South, led many authors to write of the global dominance of capital (Oman, 1996; Reich, 1992).

However, the large-scale, long-term movement of capital across national boundaries also led many writers to conclude that capital had outgrown the nation-state – that the world economy was now based on 'global capital', a vaguely defined concept that emphasized capital's dissociation from any national or state location and its autonomy from state control and regulation (Luard, 1990).

By emphasizing the movement of capital and its multiple locations, these writers overlooked the structure of capital (its headquarters and its national origins and centres of decision making) which is decisive in identifying who benefits and loses, and the primary organizing centres where the fundamental strategic decisions about location, profits and sites of accumulation are located (Doremus, et al., 1998).

The claim of a new globalized capital, and, by deduction, a new process dubbed globalization, came to dominate the discussion of inter-state, inter-regional and inter-economic relations.

Along this same line of argumentation, many economists and journalists argued that this process of globalization was driven by the Third Scientific Technological Revolution (TSTR), seen both as a cause of globalization – facilitating the free flow of capital and goods (not labour) – and as an outgrowth of a global economy (Castells, 1993: 45–96). The TSTR was seen as inaugurating an emerging New Economy based on the enormous growth of investment in IT, biotechnology and optic fibres and skyrocketing stock valuations. The New Economy was credited with ending the business cycle associated with the 'old economy' (resource extraction and industrialization, producing tangible goods and services), promoting unlimited growth, high productivity and the de-concentration of wealth and power' (Kelly, 1998). However, by the beginning of the new millennium, almost all of the

arguments made on behalf of 'globalization' and the New Economy were highly
suspect and subject to a counter-thesis.

The counter-thesis argues that while private capital has indeed expanded into new
regions, conquering formerly restricted markets and economic sectors in the ex-
Communist and nationalist Third World countries, it retains a clear linkage to nation
states – particularly imperial states – in the world economy.

Second, the TSTR did not form a New Economy. To the degree to which it was
divorced from the Old Economy it was largely a speculative activity, without any
solid foundations; that is, it lacked a marketable product, and had little potential for
profit.

The *Financial Times* described the IT speculative fever as 'millennial euphoria',
and went on to note, 'The NASDAQ Composite Index, beacon of the new economy
peaked at 5,048.62 on March 10 (2000). A year later it was nearly 60 per cent lower.
The bursting of the dot.com bubble was only the start of the trouble. The rout of ...
technology, media and telecoms extended to ... established operators' (*Financial
Times*, 11 May 2001: 3). The volatility of the speculative sectors of the economy
affects all sectors of the economy as well as the economic foundations of empire.
The rise and fall of the speculative economy clearly influences the economic
strategies of empire-building.

This chapter argues that the growth and conquest of overseas markets is today a
product of giant enterprises linked to powerful Euro-American states and can best
be seen as part of an empire-building process rather than anything resembling
globalization. The claims of a TSTR are dubious. The IT economy, remains a much
reduced economic sector, in which a few giant enterprises emerge from the sharp
decline of paper companies. IT is not seen as the dynamic factor accounting for
overseas expansion, but rather as a source of instability, crises and declining
productivity. The expansion of capital is seen more as a product of speculation,
imperial conquest and illegal activity.

The Myth of the Global Corporation

A recent empirical comparative study by Doremus, Kelley, Pauly and Reich of US,
German and Japanese multinational corporations found that, on the vital issues of
investment, research and development, the great majority of decisions were taken in
the national headquarters of the multinational corporations (Doremus, et al., 1998:
Ch. 5). With regard to research and development (R&D) of US multinationals they
show that 88 per cent of the total research and development expenditures are made
in the 'home' country, and only 12 per cent by majority-owned affiliates overseas.
Technology development remains centralized in the national headquarters of the
multinational corporations. In the other key area of corporate strategy, direct
investment decisions and intra-firm trade, the authors find that the priorities of
nation headquarters predominate. The authors' findings and conclusions refute the
myth of the 'global' multinational corporations, demonstrating their ties to the
nation state and their centralized nation-centred decision-making structure. While

the multinational corporations produce in many countries and divide up operations and production across multiple sites, control and profits are centralized within nation states. Expansion and control by multinationals have not changed their enduring character as linked to nation states; nor have their international operations transformed their centralized empire-building character.

The Rulers of the World Economy

The best source, despite important shortcomings, for understanding the economic forces dominating the world economy, is the *Financial Times* listing of the 500 largest companies of the world (for example, *Financial Times*, 11 May 2001). The measure of economic power is based on market capitalization that is determined by the number of shares the company has issued multiplied by the market price of those shares on the day the survey was conducted. The *Financial Times'* May 2001 study was based on data collected 4 January 2001. There are several important shortcomings of this approach. First, given the volatility of the market, sharp changes occur in short periods of time, particularly in technology stocks, thus distorting the rankings. Second, the rankings exclude family-owned business and state-owned business without stock market listings. Third, foreign buyouts, especially by Euro-American capital of ex-Communist and Third World enterprises, continue to be listed by their national location, thus underestimating Euro-American power and exaggerating the degree of diversity.

Despite these methodological issues, the ranking by capitalization does provide us with an approximate measure of the concentration of power in the world economy. By examining the top 500 firms, we get a clear picture of which countries' enterprises control the biggest share of production, finance and distribution, since most of world production and trade is carried out by large-scale enterprises.

The most striking feature of the world economy is the dominance of Euro-American enterprises: 79 per cent of the 500 biggest multinationals are located in the US or Western Europe. If we include Japan, the figure rises to 91 per cent. In other words, over 90 per cent of the major enterprises dominating the world economy are found in the US, Europe and Japan.

Between the competing empires, the US stands as the dominant power: 48 per cent (239) of the 500 biggest firms are American compared to 31 per cent (154) for Western Europe and only 11 per cent (64) for Japan. The combined Third World continents of Asia, Africa and Latin America have only four per cent (22) of the largest corporations and most of these have been bought out by Euro-American multinationals. If we examine the biggest of the big enterprises, the concentration of financial muscle is even more one sided: the top five firms are all American; eight of the top 10 and 64 per cent (16) of the top 25 are US-based, followed by 28 percent (7) in Europe and 8 per cent (2) in Japan. In other words, at the pinnacle of global power the US–European multinational corporations have virtually no rivals. Between 1999 and 2000 the percentage of American firms among the 500 increased from 44 to 48 per cent.

This concentration of world economic power is more akin to world empire than to any notion of globalization in which private corporations are independent of the nation state. The growth and expansion of US and European capital is based on acquisitions and mergers in the North, as well as via the purchase of former public enterprises in the Third World and former Communist countries.

The distribution among the top 25 US enterprises reveals two significant patterns. On the one hand the re-emergence of the old economy – the industrial, banking, insurance, petroleum and pharmaceutical enterprises – led by General Electric and the relative decline of the New Economy, particularly the IT firms. The data collected in January 2001 underestimates the decline of the IT economy during 2001. Given the volatility of share prices and the deepening economic recession, many IT companies suffered severe decline. For example, Lucent Technologies, once the leading telecom manufacturer in the US, saw its market capitalization fall from US$52 billion to US$34 billion between January and April of 2001. Similar decline occurred with Cisco Systems. On January 4, 2001 it was worth US$294 billion while at the end of April it fell to US$124 billion. While the giant IT and communication corporations like Microsoft and Cisco are still among the top ten, most of the other IT corporations have dropped out of the top 500 and many have gone bankrupt. It is more accurate to speak of imperialism than globalization when the owners and directors of the majority of the corporations and banks controlling international flows of capital are American. Globalization in these circumstances is an ideology that obfuscates the real structure of power and domination.

The concentration and centralization of capital – the growth of mega-mergers is managed by key financial and investment institutions – is in the US. Among merger and acquisition advisors worldwide, 11 of the top 15 firms are US owned and based. One of the most revealing aspects of US dominance is found in the unprecedented concentration of profits made worldwide in the hands of US-owned multinationals, who received, for example, 36 per cent of profits in 1990 and 44 per cent in 1997.

The most striking evidence against the notion of an 'interdependent global economy' and in favour of the notion of imperialism is the nature and consequences of the financial and economic crisis that hit Asia in 1997 and that has assumed global dimensions since. While Asia, Latin America and Africa suffered severe recessions, declining living standards and catastrophic increases in unemployment, the US multinationals expanded their influence and reach. In the words of Joseph Stiglitz, former Chief Economist at the WB (from 1997 to January 2000, when he was forced to resign by Washington over policy differences) and winner of the 2001 Nobel Prize in Economics, 'something ha[d] gone horribly wrong' (Stiglitz, 2002: 4). What was a crisis in the Third World – 'the greatest economic crisis since the great depression' – was a boon to US overseas firms, benefiting some US enterprises to an unprecedented degree. While economy after economy collapsed, throwing hundreds of thousands, if not millions, out of work and impoverishing an even greater number (for example, increasing poverty by 50 per cent in Indonesia) over US$50 billion was used in South Korea alone to buy up the assets of Korean-owned enterprises.

While the US–European multinationals dominate the world economy, they do so on weak foundations. Much of their growth is based on mergers and acquisitions;

four of the top 25 are, in effect, 'merged corporations', facing debts and shrinking markets. Second, the giant oil and pharmaceutical companies are based on 'monopoly prices' rather than any great innovations or increases in productivity. Pharmaceuticals monopoly profits are based on intellectual property patents, and oil companies' profits on oligopolistic structures and practices.

Third, while the US multinationals have a dominant world position, the US national economy is increasingly vulnerable due to its soaring trade deficit. According to the US Commerce Department, the trade deficit for the year 2000 was over $435 billion – the largest annual deficit on record. Foreign savings have bridged the gap, making the US economy vulnerable to sudden shifts in foreign investors. Most economists do not think this level of deficit is sustainable (*Financial Times*, 16 March 2001: 7).

The New Economy Scam

The claims of globalization ideologues who argued that the new technological revolution was no longer subject to cyclical crises have been proven wrong on several counts. Beginning in late 2000 and continuing into 2003, a deep recession has affected the IT companies leading to widespread bankruptcies and a vertical decline in market capitalization.

Japan, which early on 'robotized' its factories and engineered and applied many of the new IT products has been stagnant (average growth of about 1 per cent since 1990) and entered a deep recession in the second quarter of 2001). The US manufacturing sector has been in negative growth since July 2000. The economy as a whole entered a recession in the first quarter of 2001 and is expected to continue for an uncertain period – estimates run from one to three years. The IT growth rate went negative in the first quarter of 2001. Prospects for an early recovery are dim as negative savings rates, huge deficits and a strong dollar inhibit domestic or export powered growth. As structural and cyclical crises coincide it is highly likely that the recession will continue for some time ahead (*Financial Times*, May 15, 2001: 17). The recession totally undermines the IT ideologues who declared that the New Economy has made the business cycle obsolete. In fact, the IT companies have been the hardest hit in the current downturn. Over 80 per cent of the dot.coms are not profitable (*Financial Times*, 10 May 2001: 12).

Second, the IT economy today is less competitive and more concentrated than ever, where a few giants have survived and many have failed. While thousands of dot.coms went under, the top five IT companies retained their position among the top five rankings worldwide (Cane, 2001: 9). The productivity revolution – growth of 2.8 per cent – was based on a short interval of four years (1996–2000) and was followed by a decline in productivity to a negative 1.2 per cent during the first quarter of 2001 (*Financial Times*, 6 June 2001: 6). Looking at the big picture, productivity was higher prior to the 'information age' than during it. Between 1953 and 1972 productivity grew an average of 2.6 per cent compared to 1.1 per cent between 1972 and 1993 (Wolf, 1999: 9). The problem of measuring productivity is further complicated by the exclusion of illegal migrant labour, amounting, according to some estimates, to five million workers who produce goods and services that are attributed to the official lower count of the labour force.

There is a widespread consensus today that the productivity arguments and claims of the New Economy ideologues have little merit. The exception is Alan Greenspan, Chairman of the US Federal Reserve Board, who, in a speech in New York in late May 2001 is quoted as saying: 'There is still in my judgement, ample evidence that we are experiencing only a pause in the investment in a broad set of innovations that has elevated the underlying growth rate in productivity.'

The multibillion dollar investment in IT drained investment from more productive uses, led to vast over-capitalization in one sector that had low returns and little spillover effects. Moreover, the biggest boost for IT came from the Y2K scam – the hype of a system breakdown, with the onset of the new millennium. Hundreds of billions were spent on IT from 1996 through 1999 to avoid a dubious project with virtually no long-term effects. No serious critical evaluation and comparative analysis was conducted between countries like Russia, China, Finland and a few others which spent a fraction of what was spent in Europe and North America on Y2K, without suffering a 'catastrophic breakdown'. Raising the question whether the IT bubble was itself an artefact of a massive promotional fraud. In any case, the data base for IT claims of a productivity revolution are extremely limited and problematical.

A study by Paul Strassman, a leading critic of IT ideologues, based on a study of 3,000 European companies demonstrates no relationship between investment in computers and profitability (*Financial Times*, 28 June 2001: 14). Thus the three basic claims of the IT revolution, that it has put to rest the business cycle, generated a sustained productivity revolution and produces high profits, are not in accordance with reality. In fact, the irrationalities of capitalism have been amplified by the IT bubble: the business cycle operates in full force, productivity tends to stagnation and there is a tendency for the rate of profit to decline.

A recent article by Robert Gordon that analyzes the increase in productivity (between 1995–1999) raises serious doubts about the claims of the TSTR (Gordon, 1999). He argues that almost 70 per cent of the improvement in productivity can be accounted for by improved measurements of inflation (lower estimates of inflation necessarily mean higher growth of real output, thus productivity) and the response of productivity to the exceptionally rapid output growth of the three-year period. Thus, only 30 per cent of the 1 per cent increase in productivity (or 0.3 per cent) during the 1995–1999 period can be attributed to computerization in the so-called 'Information Revolution'.

Even more devastating from the advocates of the TSTR, Gordon provides a convincing argument that most of the increase in productivity attributed to computerization is in the area of the manufacture of computers. The dramatic improvements in productivity claimed by the TSTR apologists is largely in the production of computers, with little effect on the rest of the economy. According to Gordon's study, productivity growth in the production of computers has increased from 18 per cent a year between 1972 and 1995 to 42 per cent a year since. According to Gordon, this accounts for all the improvements in productivity growth in durable goods. In other words, the computer has brought about a 'revolution' in the production of computers, having an insignificant effect on the rest of the economy. The basic reason is that computers have simply substituted for other forms of capital. According to a recent study, growth in computer inputs exceeded those in other inputs by a factor of 10 in the 1990–1996 period. The substitution of one form of capital for another need not raise productivity in the economy as a whole. The basic measure of a technological revolution is what authors call the 'multifactor productivity', the increase in output per unit of all outputs. The basic question posed by TSTR is not over whether computers have revolutionized the production of computers but how the so-called information 'revolution' has affected the other 99 per cent of the economy. According to Gordon's longitudinal study of technical progress covering the period between 1950 and 1996, the period of maximum technical progress as manifested in annual multi-factor productivity growth was in the period between 1950 and 1964, when it reached approximately 1.8 per cent. The period of lowest multi-factor productivity growth in this century was during 1988–1996, approximately 0.5 per cent growth – a half of one percent (Gordon, 1999).

It is clear that the innovations in the early and middle twentieth century were far more significant sources of economy-wide productivity improvement than the electronic, computerized information systems of the late twentieth century.

Computer manufacturers account for 1.2 per cent of the US economy and only 2 per cent of capital stock (1997). While corporations spend substantial amounts on computers, it is largely to replace old ones. There is no evidence to back up the claims of the advocates of TSTR. There has been no such thing as the Third Scientific Industrial Revolution – at least by any empirical measure of increased productivity in the US economy. Despite the vast increase in the use of computers, the productivity performance of the US economy remains far below the levels achieved in the pre-computer age of 1950–1972; in fact, annual multi-factor productivity growth (AMPG) between 1988 and 1996 is the lowest of the last 50 years. Even more significantly, the rate of growth between 1950 and 1996 steadily declined: between 1972 and 1979 it grew 1.1 per cent; 0.7 per cent between 1979 and 1988; and 0.6 per cent from 1988 to 1996 (Gordon, 1999).

The claim of the TSTR of a new capitalist era has no basis in any purported Third Scientific Information Revolution.

The biotechnology industry, along with IT and optical fibres were seen as the three driving forces of the TSTR driving the New Economy. The biotechnology industry is over a quarter of a century old and it has yet to deliver a consistent flow of new treatments and profits. According to Arthur Levinson, Chairman and Chief Executive of Genetech, the biggest and most successful of the biotechnology companies, 'there has been no revolution in medicine in the past 25 years' (*Financial Times*, 6 April 2001: 14). According to a CEO from another biotechnology company, Kevin Sharer of Amgen, of the billions of dollars invested in the sector, only 63 new drugs have been introduced into the market. Market analysts point out that just 25 of the 400 plus US biopharmaceutical companies will make money. Most groups founded over a decade ago have yet to achieve profitability; most biotechnology groups of the 1980s no longer exist. All the promotional publicity surrounding human genome sequences currently attracting more billions are likely to be disappointed according to Levinson. Like the IT scam, the biotechnology revolution attracted billions of dollars, deflecting investment from productive uses, while leading many down the road of bankruptcy.

In the 1990s, US President Clinton and Western European leaders, investors and academics saw a bright future for optical fibres – the third force in the TSTR. Between 1999 and 2000, over one hundred million miles of optical fibre were laid around the world as companies spent US$35 billion to build internet-inspired communication networks (*New York Times*, 28 June 2001: 1). Today, only 5 per cent of the fibre on the ground is 'on', but the astronomical costs of lighting and delivering it to the end user has led to a dramatic decline in investment in the communications industry. As in biotechnology, the collapse has had an impact on the rest of the economy: billions invested in telecommunications companies appears to be wasted. The drying up of capital investment is one reason that the economy has come to a stop. The giants in communication equipment, like Lucent Technologies and Nortel, have reported losses in the billions: Nortel announced a US$19 billion loss in the first quarter of 2001. In the first half of 2001 companies defaulted on US$13.9 billion of telecommunication bonds resulting in investor losses of US$12.8 billion (*New York Times*, 28 June 2001: 1). Once again the TSTR burst like a speculative bubble.

US and European 'global supremacy' is built on three unstable and unsustainable legs. On one leg it rests on a highly vulnerable and speculative sector prone to great volatility and entering into deep recession. The second leg is the high level of transfers of profits, interest payments and royalties from their respective colonized areas. In the case of Latin America alone over US$700 billion was transferred as payments to European and US banks and multinationals from 1990 to 1998 (Petras and Veltmeyer, 1999: 31–52). The third leg of the empire is political power (including the power to print money to cover deficits) and the security that Euro-American states provide to foreign nationals who transfer funds to the US, including billions illicitly secured from their home countries. Political power and the security of the imperial states depend on the acquiescence or consent of strategic economic sectors that are vulnerable to free-market competition by rival imperial and non-imperial countries. For example, because of the strong dollar, US steel corporations are having a hard time exporting goods or even competing in the US market.

The problem for Euro-American rulers is how to manage their empires in the face of a growing recession, a deflated IT sector and rising unemployment in economic sectors that are not competitive in the world market.

The New Imperialism: From Neo-liberalism to Neo-mercantilism

Free Market or neo-liberal imperialism was always a myth: the imperial states have never completely opened their markets, eliminated all subsidies or failed to intervene to prop up or protect strategic economic sectors, either for political or social reasons. Neo-liberal imperialism always meant selective openness to selective countries over specified time periods in selective product areas. Markets were opened by the US government to products produced by US affiliates in overseas countries. Free trade in the imperial country was not based on economic but political criteria. On the other hand, Euro-American policy makers and their employees in the IMF–WB preached market fundamentalism to the Third World: elimination of all trade barriers, subsidies and regulations for all products and services in all sectors. Imperial states' selective free market practices allowed their multinationals to capitalize on market opportunities in target countries practising market fundamentalism, while protecting domestic economic sectors which included important political constituencies. Major conflict erupted when the two imperial rivals, the US and Europe (both selective free marketers) attempted to pry open each other's markets while protecting important political constituencies.

With the advent of the triple crises of recession, speculative collapse and intensified competition, the imperial countries have resorted to greater state intervention in a multiplicity of sectors: increased agricultural and other state subsidies – US$30 billion in the US in 2001; increased resort to interfering in trade to impose quotas on imports – George W. Bush's commitment to the US steel industry (Alden and McGregor, 2001: 6) – and intensified exploitation of Third World regions to increase the flow of profits, interests and trading advantages (the US 'Free Trade of the Americas' proposal).

State-managed trade that combines protection of home markets and aggressive intervention to secure monopoly market advantages and investment profits defines the content of neo-mercantilist imperialism. Neo-liberal imperialism, with its free market rhetoric and selective opening of markets, is being replaced by a neo-mercantilism that looks toward greater monopolization of regional trading zones, greater unilateral political decisions to maximize trade advantages and protection of domestic producers and greater reliance on military strategies to deepen control over crisis-ridden neo-liberal economies run by discredited clients.

Just as the US was the leader in developing its neo-liberal empire and Europe was a follower region, so with regard to the transition to a neo-mercantilist empire the US plays a leading role.

In substance, if not in style, the transition to neo-mercantilism began during the Clinton regime and became the dominant strategy of empire-building during the Bush Administration.

During the Clinton era, the US shared the takeover of Latin American markets and enterprises with the Europeans. For example, US banks, energy and telecommunication companies competed with Spanish multinationals in the buyout of formerly public enterprises and national banks. The Clinton regime, however, sought to weaken European and Japanese competition by signing the North American Free Trade Treaty that privileged US business in Mexico. Washington's success in monopolizing the Mexican market contrasted with the relative decline of its share of newly privatized Latin American enterprises and markets.

Clinton's proposal to extend US monopoly control via Free Trade Area of the Americas (FTAA) was given greater impetus by the Bush Administration, particularly at the Quebec summit of the Americas in April of 2001. The purpose of FTAA is to privilege US companies and exporters operating in Latin America, while restricting Latin American access to US markets. While FTAA is presented as a reciprocal trade doctrine, the Bush Administration refused to concede any concessions regarding the so-called anti-dumping regulations that are habitually evoked to restrict the entry of competitive Latin products that would take market shares from US companies. Moreover 'reciprocity' is a meaningless concept when the two trading regions have such vast inequalities in productive capacity and size in many economic sectors, and when infant industries are forced to compete with established giant enterprises. In these circumstances 'reciprocity' becomes a formula for US takeovers and the bankruptcy of Latin American enterprises. As we have seen, US enterprises in banking, energy, telecommunications, mining and transport industries have a massive advantage, which they have used to displace Latin American competitors. FTAA will decisively obliterate what remains of the Latin American national economies and impose an economic decision-making structure that will be centred in the headquarters of the US multinational banks and corporations.

Of equal importance is that the US state will dictate the rules and regulations that govern trade, investment and patent laws which will reign in the Americas. This will enable the US government to be in a position to combine protectionism at home, European exclusion in Latin America and free markets in Latin America.

A clear example of the protectionist elements of the neo-mercantilist empire is the White House promise to protect US steel plants from overseas competition – including Brazil. In the first week of June 2001, the Bush Administration launched action (a Section 201 investigation into 'unfair trading practices') to protect US steel producers from overseas competition (Alden and Bowe, 2001: 6). Both Donald Evans, the US Commerce Secretary, and Robert Zoellick, the US Trade Representative, publically defended state intervention to protect uncompetitive US steel producers from 'unfair trade'. The real reason for loss of competitiveness of US manufacturing is the strong dollar and the higher operating costs in the US. As the US National Association of Manufacturers stated in a letter to the US Treasury Secretary, the current levels of the exchange value of the dollar were 'having a strong negative impact on manufacturing exports, production and employment'. The letter noted that the US dollar had risen 27 per cent since early 1997, thus 'pricing products out of markets both at home and abroad' (Alden, 2001: 8).

The strong dollar, however, is a favoured strategy of the powerful financial sector of the US economy and vital in maintaining the vast flow of overseas capital into the US to finance the ballooning merchandise trade deficit.

Laundering illicit funds by major US banks is an important source of external flows to the US. Estimates by a US senate subcommittee run from US$250 to US$500 billion a year. Like the earlier mercantilist empire that depended in part on sharing the booty of its pirate predators, the neo-mercantilist economy thrives on corrupt rulers who pillage their economies and transfer their illicit funds to Euro-American empires. The strong dollar is one of the attractions of predators and corrupt rulers. It is no surprise that the Bush Administration has significantly weakened its support for an international initiative tightening financial regulation to fight money laundering (Alden and Peel, 2001).

Mercantilist imperialism in which the imperial state combines protectionism at home, monopolies abroad and free trade within the empire is thus the chosen strategy for maintaining empire and sustaining domestic political support at a horrible cost to Latin America and to the dismay of its European competitors. In pursuit of the neo-mercantilist empire, Washington must increasingly rely on unilateral decisions and policy making. Because of its monopolistic nature, neo-mercantilism depends on excluding competitor allies and maximizing trade advantages via unilateral state decisions.

The Bush Administration's unilateral rejection of the Kyoto agreement, its unilateral decision to proceed with the new missile programs in violation of existing agreements, its increased subsidies to US agriculture and its attempt to accelerate the FTAA are examples of unilateralism at the service of neo-mercantilist empire building.

The US's openly confrontational approach toward Western Europe goes beyond its unilateral style of decision making. The Bush Administration's appointment of Richard Perle, a hardline militarist, to head the Defence Policy Board is indicative of the US swing to 'mercantilist-militarism'. His imperial posturing was evident in his arrogant rejection of European criticism of the US's escalation of the missile race. 'We are going to proceed with the missile defence and either they [the EU] can join us in that endeavour or they can sit on the sidelines and complain about it' (Spiegel, 2001: 1). Washington's anti-European strategy is linked to NATO's enlargement. As Perle describes it, 'My solution to NATO enlargement is – by all means let's bring in some new members, and if we lose some old ones, I've got a candidate'.

Mercantilism, with its heavy emphasis on monopoly profits, unilateral action and, particularly, state intervention to favour business interests against external rivals and a vast panoply of domestic classes in Latin America has historically been accompanied by armed conflicts and large military expenditures. Contemporary neo-mercantilism is no exception. Accompanying FTAA is a major increase in US military expenditures in Latin America, new military bases, the colonization of air space, shorelines, and rivers and estuaries. Plan Colombia, the Andean Initiative and related military expenditures to militarize the frontiers of Ecuador–Colombia and Panama–Colombia involves over US$1.5 billion and hundreds of US military operatives. The subcontracting of Latin American military officials, paramilitary forces and US mercenaries is an integral part of the protection and expansion of neo-mercantilist empire building. Worldwide, the US policy of provoking China with ostentatious spy plan flights off its coastal waters and escalating the arms race with Russia are part of a policy of projecting unilateral military power.

Conclusion

It is not a technological–scientific–computers driven revolution that has led to globalization but rather a political, economic and military expansion that has created a new US-dominated imperial world order.

The driving force opening the doors for US–European expansion is not the so-called TSTR, but military power and class warfare 'from above'. The contemporary world faces two major facts: the unrestrained use of military power by the US in imposing global hegemony and a full-scale Euro-American assault against all socio-political constraints on the expansion of their multinational corporations.

The US/NATO bombing of Yugoslavia, the air assaults on Iraq, the missile attacks on Somalia and Afghanistan, the expansion of NATO membership to include countries on the Russian border, the incorporation of 23 new clients as 'peace associates' of NATO and the unquestioned US hegemony over Western Europe via NATO are indicators of the increasing militarization and unilateral exercises of US world police power. The resurgent imperial power is intimately related to the tremendous growth of US economic domination in the 1990s. Information systems, computerization and the electronic media play an important and subordinate role in serving the needs of imperial power. Pentagon planners use computer-directed bombings (not always very accurate) to achieve military goals. multinational corporations use computers to relay payments on buyouts of overseas firms. The so-called 'computer revolution' is thus nothing more than a new tool in furthering historical, imperial influence. Far from breaking down national boundaries, computers increase the imperial reach of hegemonic powers and reinforce the world division between imperial and dominated countries, creditors and debtors, speculators and local producers.

The reach of US global corporations has been aided far more by class warfare against US workers than any scientific–technological breakthrough; welfare cuts, regressive taxation, corporate subsidies, corporate reduction or elimination of health benefits, pensions, disability payments, increased job insecurity, have created unprecedented profitable opportunities for US business at home and to invest overseas. The declining productivity of the US economy is highly correlated with imperialism, namely the transfer of economic surplus overseas resulting in buyouts, new investments and speculative ventures. Whatever possible positive impact computerization might have had on increasing productivity is more than offset by the flow of capital overseas, instead of reinvestment in improving productivity in the US. Insofar as computerization and the new information systems are at the service of the multinational corporations in moving capital abroad, they contribute to lowering productivity in the US.

There is little economic reason for arguing that a Scientific–Technological–Revolution has taken place. The transformation of communication systems has failed to raise productivity in the overall economy or even reverse the decline in productivity. The myth of the TSTR as the driving force of globalization has served as an ideological cover obscuring the resurgence of US imperialism and the expansion of US–European capital based on class warfare and imperial wars. The new information systems harnessed to the economic and military institutions of empire have contributed to the movements of capital and the achievement of military goals. In the final analysis, it is the economic and military interests and powers that shape the use and application of the information technologies and not vice versa.

Although the US continues to be the dominant economic power in the world today, this empire faces competition from Europe and from low-cost economic sectors in Asia, Latin America and, to a lesser extent, ex-Communist countries, particularly in light of the strong dollar.

In defence of the US empire, the Bush Administration has embarked on a highly conflictual new model – a neo-mercantilist empire based on FTAA unilateral projections of power, the militarization of Latin America and military intimidation of potential rivals. The neo-liberal empire seems to have exhausted its historical possibilities, both economically and politically. US trade deficits are ballooning, selective protectionism is insufficient, large-scale social unrest and nationalist resistance is growing, the IT speculative bubble has burst and sectors of the domestic economy are under siege. The external growth of the private US economic giants is increasingly based on weakened national foundations. The imperial state has tried to ride two horses: a strong dollar for Wall Street and increasing exports by US manufacturers. This is no longer possible. Mercantilism provides a privileged place for the US exporters, while keeping a strong dollar to siphon financial resources from the rest of the world. The transition to a neo-mercantilist empire, however, has provoked widespread opposition even among European allies/competitors. It has isolated the US in international forums. The militarization of Latin America can only temporarily hold the line – FTAA is likely to deepen the crisis and increase opposition. Massive popular movements are radicalizing in Colombia, Brazil, Argentina and Bolivia. The public relations spin given by the White House, involving presidential visits, ministerial consultations and US attendance at international conferences, will not convince many governments and provokes public opposition. Nor will or can the Bush Administration reverse its course.

Given the heightened competition from Europe, the dependence of the US on extracting an ever larger surplus from Latin America in the face of the internal crises and the close ties between the Administration and big business, particularly the extractive sectors, Washington's only solution is to militarize and tighten its control, even if it polarizes and radicalizes Latin America.

Eighteenth- and nineteenth-century mercantilism led to revolutionary wars for independence. Will history repeat itself? Will imperial monopolies lead to intensified inter-imperial conflicts? Will nationalist resistance lead to new socialist revolutions? The answers to these questions are of more than academic interest; they shape the contemporary political agenda.

Chapter 6

Neo-mercantilist Empire in Latin America: Bush, ALCA and Plan Colombia

Building an Empire is not a tea party. (Lieutenant Colonel, US Marine Corp.)

Introduction

The fundamental problem facing the Bush Administration is expanding and consolidating the US empire at a time of intensifying competition from rivals, growing economic recession in Europe and North America and crisis in Asia and Latin America, and rising socio-political opposition especially in Latin America, Russia, China and on special occasions in Western Europe and the US.

The first part of this chapter discusses the transition from Clinton to Bush: the manifest continuities in strategic goals and differences in style and tactics, as well as the sectors of capital and their political spokespeople which direct US foreign policy.

The second part of the chapter discusses Washington's historic response to crises and expansion, focusing on the provocation of 'Cold Wars' – the military build-up of ideological confrontation and aggressive intervention within Third World countries, under the guise of engaging an 'external threat' to US security. Washington's purpose in unleashing Cold Wars is to subordinate allies, impose client regimes in the Third World, and extend and deepen imperial control against emerging popular challenges. The chapter identifies three Cold Wars. The first Cold War began shortly after the end of the Second World War and was designed to defeat the revolutionary upsurge in Europe, Asia, Africa and Latin America, unleashed by the defeat of fascism and the rise of the anti-colonial movements. The second Cold War was launched by the Carter Administration shortly after the US defeat in Indo-China and was directed at isolating and defending the anti-imperialist movements in Central America (Nicaragua), the Middle East (Iran), Southern Asia (Afghanistan), the Horn of Africa (Ethiopia/Eritrea) and Southern Africa (Angola/Mozambique/South Africa). Faced with economic crises and challenges to the empire, the Bush Administration has launched the third Cold War.

The third part of the chapter discusses the crises of the empire followed by an analysis of the character and policies of the Bush Administration and specifically

69

how they affect Latin America, including a discussion of US military strategy (Plan Colombia /Andean Initiative) and its relation to the Latin American Free Trade Area (ALCA) – the twin approaches to the recolonization of Latin America.

Managing Empire in a Time of Crisis

To understand the Bush Administration's problems and perspectives in managing the US empire, it is essential to examine the Clinton legacy. This requires that we examine the vast expansion of the empire under Clinton, the domestic economic foundations of overseas expansion and the first signs of the imperial crises under Clinton. Under US president Clinton, the US empire expanded far beyond the frontiers of any President since Harry Truman. From the Baltic countries to the Balkans and then onward toward the southern tier of what was formerly the USSR, the US has established a series of client states, which are either new NATO members or 'peace associates' (clients-in-waiting). In Asia, US military has incurred in China's airspace, modernized Taiwan's military, bought into South Korea's major industries and challenged the stagnant Japanese economy for supremacy in the region. Today, the US has military bases on the frontiers of Russia, its missiles only five minutes from Moscow. Washington bombs Yugoslavia, Afghanistan and Somalia with impunity, organizes international 'show trials' in the Hague where it parades its defeated rivals, and has military bases in its new satellite states – Albania, Macedonia, Kosova and, via NATO, in the Czech Republic, Poland, Hungary, Bulgaria, and so on.

Euro-American empires have succeeded in imposing neo-liberalism on five continents, opening the door to takeovers of lucrative national enterprises (both public and private) and penetration of markets, thus extending and deepening imperial control over the economies of the Third World. The Clinton legacy, with regard to the domestic economy, revealed a two-faced reality: on the surface an expansive economy covering nine years in which US corporations were able to accrue enormous profits, but based on the paper earnings of wild speculation on the stock market, the laundering by leading US financial institutions of hundreds of billions of dirty money annually and highly indebted consumer spending and huge trade deficits. Clinton's further deregulation of the financial system and economy led to the highest level of inequalities and concentration of wealth on Wall Street of any US president since the turn of the nineteenth century. Thus overseas expansion was built on very fragile domestic economic foundations. Essentially the Empire's domestic foundations were based on speculative internal investments and costly overseas conquests. By the end of Clinton's presidency, the unviable and unsustainable economy imploded or crashed. While the crisis began in the last months of the Clinton regime, it deepened under the Bush presidency.

Economic Crisis

The signs were evident in all economic sectors. First of all, as seen in Chapter 5, the collapse of IT industries and the failure of most biotechnological enterprises were two prominent examples of the speculative propaganda that enticed millions of investors to invest billions of dollars in what amounts to a massive financial swindle. The 70 per cent decline in the value of IT sector is comparable to the fall in stocks during the Great Depression. Most of the stocks that collapsed had stock values up to 200 times their earning capacity. Most of the IT stocks never earned a profit and some had not even produced a marketable product that could generate revenue. Many simply grew because of future expectations promoted by the speculators and swindlers who entered early inflated the value, took their profits and left millions holding worthless paper. The biotechnology industry followed a similar path. Despite the market propaganda that enticed tens of billions from investors by promising 'miracle drugs' or 'miracle discoveries' only 25 per cent of the 400 leading firms made any money and only 63 new drugs were developed during the last 25 years. The crash of these investments prejudiced investors, led to large-scale unemployment and undermined confidence in the so-called New Economy. More important the New Economy siphoned off hundreds of billions of dollars from productive investments in the fundamentals of the US economy, like new power and energy sources (sun, wind, ocean, and so on). Probably the greatest loss of potential investment funds was in the Y2K swindle, where tens of billions was spent correcting computers under the dire threat of economic collapse, an event that did not take place in countries that spent under a million dollars. The IT bubble was in part stimulated by the scare from propaganda of the Y2K scam. The theoretical point is that the Clinton 'prosperity' years were based on a speculative, paper economy which was unsustainable and which was fuelled by false expectations based on market propaganda, disconnected from the real economy. Along with the predatory foreign policy that pillaged wealth overseas through corrupt privatization programmes, particularly in the ex-Communist countries, Latin America and Asia, the wealth of the empire was based more on political power and media promotion than reasoned market calculations.

The second aspect of the economic crisis carried over from the Clinton to Bush regimes is the deep and prolonged recession in the manufacturing sector. From the end of 2000, long into 2001, the manufacturing sector registered negative economic growth. During the first seven months of the recession manufacturers shed over 500,000 jobs. While some of the unemployed have been absorbed in the low paid service sector, in most cases the redeployed workers experience a 30 to 50 per cent decline in wages and health benefits.

The third aspect of the crisis is the unsustainability of the country's external accounts. The US had a US$437 billion trade deficit in 2000 that was covered only because of the flows of foreign capital, much of it from Japan but also from dirty money from the Third World. As seen in Chapter 3, US law allows major US banks to legally launder billions of dollars of overseas tax evaders and corrupt rulers. Moreover, through correspondent banks offshore US banks launder an estimated US$500 billion in illegal funds annually. The decline in US competitiveness is in large part due to the siphoning off of billions of dollars into the speculative IT and biotechnology sectors that contributed little or nothing to increasing US productivity. Soon the US will no longer be able to draw on external funds to make up its trade deficit and the repercussions will be severe on the capacity of the US to maintain its consumer-based economy and the living standards of its population.

The fourth aspect of the crisis is the increasing dependence of US corporations on earnings and profits from overseas subsidiaries. With the decline in the US economy, exports to the US will decline and severely hinder the profits and earnings of neo-liberal economies based on their export strategies. This is likely to reduce profits for US subsidiaries as their markets shrink in their host countries, as well as their markets in the US. Moreover, overseas markets are becoming increasingly competitive. European investors – particularly Spain, Germany and England – have been gaining footholds through buyouts of strategic sectors of the privatized economy in Latin America.

In summary, Clinton's economic prosperity was based on flawed foundations, leading to huge misallocations of investments based on the deregulation of the economy and the US promotion of the speculative bubble. The Bush Administration, which, of course, shares the basic 'free market' assumptions and imperial goals of its predecessor, has to confront the dual reality of an expanded empire and a deepening crisis: these are the economic parameters within which policy toward Latin America is framed.

Political Crisis

The economy is not the only crisis area in the empire confronting the Bush Administration. There is a serious problem emerging from the aggressive political and military expansion that took place throughout the 1990s. The major characteristic of Clinton's empire-building project was the indiscriminate and comprehensive intervention everywhere, without regard to region, priorities or strategy. Clinton's concept of empire was so inclusive that no region of the globe was immune to direct military assault, invasion or penetration. The Clinton Administration engaged in continuous bombing of Iraq throughout his presidency, leading to over one million children dying of disease, malnutrition, and so on. Washington declared war (via NATO) twice against Yugoslavia – once in Bosnia and later in Kosova, establishing military bases in Kosova, Albania and Macedonia. In Africa, Clinton sent troops to Somalia, which he was later forced to withdraw, and later bombed the country, which he also did in Afghanistan. Haiti was invaded in an attempt to impose a client regime. Clinton expanded NATO membership to include the new client regimes in Eastern Europe, many of which received their baptism of fire as accomplices in the bombing of Yugoslavia and in the provision of military logistical support. The Clinton Administration recruited a new tier of 'peace associates', junior members of NATO in countries from the Baltic to the Caucuses. Finally the Clinton Administration buttressed the totally incompetent and kleptocratic Yeltsin regime in Russia as a means to destroy Russia's economy and military, while the 'multinational' corporations pillaged its economy alongside the new Russian oligarchs.

But as the empire grew, so did the contradictions. Washington could pillage the economies, but it could not prevent ever-deepening economic crises nor control an increasingly restive population. Yeltsin was replaced by Putin, and some semblance of an economy and foreign policy reappeared defending Russia from the crudest forms of depredation. In Belarus and Moldavia, new regimes seeking closer ties with Russia came to power. In Eastern Europe, the Ukraine and elsewhere, the initial wave of support for incorporation into the new empire faded with the wave of corruption and plunder that accompanied the new free market rulers. By the late 1990s economic boycott of Iran, Iraq and Libya signed economic cooperation agreements with Italy and other Western European governments and corporations.

While Clinton focused on Israel and Kosova, US trade with the MERCOSUR nations, particularly Brazil, declined. The US share of the Mexican market declined. European investors, particularly Spain, bought out lucrative telecommunications, energy and transport enterprises which were privatized.

As US-backed neo-liberalism spread and extended the empire, and as exploitation and pillage via local client regimes deepened, so did the growth of opposition as nationalist regimes began to surface and regional markets expanded. The European common market expanded, MERCOSUR grew, the Chavez regime in Venezuela provided leadership to OPEC and deepened its ties to Russia, China and Cuba in defence of a multi-polar world, the UN rejected US candidates for two commissions, and even the Organization of American States (OAS) rejected the US economic policy toward Cuba.

Bush and the Third Cold War

President Bush confronts a dual crisis: a stagnant economy and an unsustainable empire. Faced with this double crisis, the Bush Administration's response in great part is shaped by the sectors of capital and the ideological forces that make up his regime. Capitalists, or their representatives, dominate both the Clinton and Bush regimes. But there are significant differences in the type of capital represented. The Clinton regime was heavily influenced by Wall Street investment bankers, financial and insurance enterprises, IT speculators, as well as overseas manufacturers. His regime depended heavily on client minority politicians (blacks, Hispanics) and trade union bureaucrats to mobilize the voters in exchange for political appointments and protection from judicial prosecution. By contrast, in the Bush regime, the influential capitalist are located in the extractive sectors – gas, oil, energy suppliers, mining, timber. They are geographically located in the south-west of the US and the Rocky Mountain states. There is strong backing from the military–industrial complex, agro-business sectors (particularly tobacco monopolies) as well as from overseas investors in the pharmaceutical industries.

The Bush regime depends on lower-middle-class religious fundamentalists, right-wing anti-Communist ideologues and the Chamber of Commerce (small business) to provide the political activists to win elections. Like Clinton, Bush provides symbolic representation to minorities (five blacks and Hispanics and several women in his cabinet) who are in agreement with his pro-imperial, foreign policy and reactionary domestic policy. Once again, classless 'diversity' serves reactionary goals.

Styles of Empire Building

While the strategic goals of the Bush regime are exactly the same as those of his predecessor, there are important differences in terms of styles of empire building partly because of the changing context and partly because of differences in the internal composition of the two regimes. Clinton was a maestro of dissimulation – a master of exercising power and pursuing the substantive goals of empire while observing the forms of consultation and 'multilateralism' whenever it was likely to coincide with US objectives. The Clinton regime's manipulation of the symbols of international cooperation was expressed via the process of formal consultation with allies and, to a lesser degree, with client states, followed by unilateral or multilateral military action. Formally 'consultative' and informally 'unilateral' – that was the style and substance of the Clinton regime. When it was possible to secure EU support for bombing Yugoslavia, Clinton proceeded via consultation; when it was not possible, as was the case in the bombing of Somalia, Afghanistan and Baghdad, the Clinton regime reacted unilaterally.

The Clinton style of empire-building combined overt economic penetration and the recruitment of new political clients with covert military and intelligence intervention to buttress influence with disintegrating regimes, or to undermine independent regimes, or out-compete EU/Japanese competitors via high-level economic espionage, the so-called Echelon Project. True to the distinction between form and substance at the ideological level, the Clinton regime, together with junior partner, UK Prime Minister Tony Blair, elaborated the idea of humanitarian intervention to justify the military invasions of Yugoslavia, the military occupation of Yugoslavia and the establishment of military bases in Eastern Europe and the Balkan States.

The domestic counterpart of this version of 'populist-imperialism' was the doctrine of the 'Third Way'. This ideology paved the way for massive shifts in budgetary priorities from social welfare to capitalist subsidies and empire-building in the name of providing an alternative to statism and the free market. Under the ideological forms of humanitarian intervention and the Third Way, Clinton aggressively pursued policies extending the US Empire via military intervention, imperial conquest and the imposition of neo-liberal doctrines.

The legacy of the Clinton extension of empire was a series of deepening structural contradictions and crises that made the Clinton policy of indiscriminate imperial expansion unviable. Clinton's policy of stimulating overseas economic investment and high profits based on low wages at home was built around cheap consumer imports from even lower wage areas to compensate for the declining real income of US workers. The result was an unsustainable trade deficit. The US Treasury and Central Bank policies were heavily dependent on large foreign inflows of capital to balance external accounts while domestic recession depended on lowering interest rates that prejudiced overseas investors. Clinton's indiscriminate empire building led to losing out in strategic economic markets while extending US politico-military influence in economically marginal regions. Clinton's drive to reassert US supremacy over Europe via NATO overlooked the decreased US economic role in European trade and markets, as well as the growing trade conflicts between the two protectionist giants.

The crisis of Clinton's empire is found in its incapacity to go beyond pillage and large-scale transfers of wealth to the US and client-building: no long-term, large-scale integration of the subordinate economies came to fruition: instead pillage led to perennial crises; indiscriminate expansion led to loss or decline in strategic markets, consultation failed to eliminate competition or to regain US ascendancy.

The Bush Administration, dominated by economic and strategic policymakers accustomed to imposing policies in their corporations and military hierarchies and to dominating markets, has reacted to this complex of crisis and expanded empire by pursuing overt unilateralist policies, justified by the defence of US imperial economic interests. In contrast to Clinton, the Bush regime makes no pretense of 'consulting' allies or clients on major strategic international policies: its calculations and decisions were directly related to the principal economic interests which are centrally located in the regime: extractive industries. The Bush regime has rejected any and all international agreements that were perceived as lowering profits and exploitation by US corporations without any pretext of masking those interests in humanitarian ideology. Bush's policy is based on unilateral, strategic involvement in confrontations with European imperialism, China, Russia and the Third World. This policy is at the same time more aggressive (unilateralist) and less directed to military intervention in marginal regions. It is more directed toward capturing strategic economic markets and less in asserting a US political presence in international forums. The Bush Administration is, in turn, divided between economic imperialists and ideological military imperialists, personified by Foreign Minister Power on the one hand and Secretary of Defense Rumsfeld and Vice-president Cheney on the other.

Counter-ruling Forces: Economic versus Ideological Imperialists

Unilateralism was the hallmark of the first year of the Bush regime. From the beginning of his Administration Bush chose to pursue policies based exclusively on what were perceived to be US corporate economic interests and to enact those policies without consulting allies or adversaries. The list of unilateral decisions continues and deepens. The first example of US unilateralism was when Bush rejected the Kyoto Agreement on control of greenhouse gases that contaminate the atmosphere, he revokes the anti-ballistic missiles (ABM) agreement with Russia and refuses to end export subsidies as demanded by the EU. Bush's trade representative threatens trade restrictions on countries that protest US import quotas and anti-dumping policies as new forms of protectionism. Unilateralism, particularly with regard to US rejection of the Kyoto Agreement, was justified by Washington in terms of raising profits for US extractive industries and manufacturers and securing competitive trade advantages over their European competitors.

The second example of US unilateralism was Washington's decision to reject negotiations with North Korea and engage in provocative military manoeuvres with the South Korean armed forces. This action was necessary in order to maintain the fiction that North Korea was a rogue or terrorist state that threatened US national security and therefore justified huge state subsidies for the new long range missile 'defence' systems (thus benefiting the military–industrial complex).

The third example of US unilateralism was the provocative violation of Chinese airspace and the subsequent public announcement that Washington would continue this practice. Once again this action was directed at creating tension to justify higher military spending, to consolidate US domination in the South China Sea, and to test the willingness of the Chinese leadership to sacrifice political sovereignty for economic goals. In this context the Bush Administration's large-scale sale of armaments to Taiwan was a further extension of US policy of encroachment and tension – to promote weapons sales and political control.

The fourth unilateral move was the decision to revoke the Missile Defence Treaty of 1992 with Russia and thus provoke a new Cold War. The purpose was, once again, to justify new multi-billion dollar government military contracts to the military–industrial complex and to force Europe to abide by US–NATO commands.

Washington's unilateral policies have had unintended and negative consequences: the revoking of the Kyoto Agreement has totally isolated the US in the international forums. The US lost two UN elections to two important committees, one on human rights and the other on the environment, in which it was clear that at least some EU countries voted against the US candidates. The US decision to break with North Korea was immediately followed by a EU visit to North Korea, the establishment of diplomatic relations and the signing of important economic agreements. In addition, the unilateral US decision alienated vast sectors of South Korea public opinion.

The US decision to abrogate the Missile Defence Treaty with Russia alienated Western Europe and hastened economic cooperation agreements between the EU and Russia. The confrontational policies toward China provoked internal debates inside the Bush regime between the 'New Cold Warriors' grouped around Cheney and Rumsfeld, who are close to the military–industrial complex, and Secretary of State Powell, who represents the viewpoint of Wall Street and the big overseas investor groups. The compromise reached between these elites led to the temporary resolution of the immediate conflict with China's liberal leaders, without sacrificing either the US strategic and military policy of encirclement or US business's lucrative access to China's markets and cheap labour. The market imperialists supporting Powell are more interested in China's multi-billion dollar trade and investment and the gradual conquest of China via economic colonization against the New Cold Warriors, who are exclusively tied to the domestic military–industrial complex and the extractive industries.

The unilateralist position of the Bush regime reflects the attempt of Washington to impose its position and push more aggressively for greater US corporate advantages, even at the expense of alienating strategic allies and the domestic public. The relative decline in US competitive position, as is evident from the huge and unsustainable trade deficit, is the driving force behind unilateralism.

Nevertheless, the political and economic realities of the contemporary world weaken the unilateralist posture. In the first place, the merger and acquisitions by

European, US and Japanese multinational corporations undermine the attempt by the New Cold Warriors to develop policies exclusively at the behest of the US military–industrial complex and extractive industries. Second, the military confrontational politics isolate US corporations, including extractive capital from lucrative market and investment sites in Iraq, Libya, Iran, North Korea, China, and Russia. The economic links between Europe and the US are as strong as their competitive differences for the time being. The problem for the Bush Administration is the growing intra-European trade (without the EU) that strengthens European autonomy from the US and limits Washington's market access.

The relative economic decline of the US in Europe and Asia means that Latin America has become one of the central areas for Washington's imperial expansion and exploitation.

Fortress America: From Neo-liberalism to the Recolonization of Latin America

Confronted by stiff competition and negative trade balances with Asia and Europe; the Bush Administration sought to consolidate and deepen its control over Latin America. Under Clinton, Washington had spread its empire over the four corners of the world, US multinational corporations had gained ascendancy, but the US national economy – that is, the exports and imports to and from the territorial US economy, had suffered a relative decline as seen in its growing trade deficit. The only region with which the US still retained a favourable balance of payments was Latin America. It was also the region where the US had historical control over the military and secret police (intelligence agencies) apparatus and a dominant influence in the economies. Yet during the 1990s, despite the establishment of client regimes and huge flows of profits, interest payments and royalties to the US and privatizations of public enterprises that benefited US multinationals, there were economic indicators showing a relative decline in US dominance: Mexico's trade with the US declined from nearly 92 per cent in 1994 to 70 per cent in 1998. MERCOSUR's trade with the US declined from 17 per cent in 1994 to 14 per cent in 1998. While MERCOSUR had an annual average trade surplus of US$66.6 billion between 1991 and 1999, service payments – debt payments, profits-remitted royalty payments – amounted to an annual average deficit of US$89.5 billion from 1991 to 1999, leading to an annual average deficit in the current accounts of US$22.9 billion. The Bush Administration strategic goal is to increase the US share of the service transfers, as well as the US share of MERCOSUR trade, and to reverse the 1990s relative decline of the US due to increased European competition. While Clinton was securing client regimes in Bosnia, Kosova and Macedonia US share of trade with MERCOSUR declined nearly 18 per cent. European multinational corporations and banks, especially Spanish ones, bought-out privatized telecommunication systems, banks and petroleum companies in Brazil, Argentina and Spain.

In addition, US dominance in Latin America was being challenged by the growing guerrilla movements in Colombia, the independent-nationalist regime in

Venezuela, and significant anti-imperialist Indian and peasant movements in Brazil, Ecuador, Bolivia and Paraguay as well as trade union and urban movements in Uruguay and Argentina. In response to these challenges, Washington has devised a two-pronged complementary strategy: the ALCA and Plan Colombia–the Andean Initiative, both of which are designed to increase US control and deepen its capacity to extract resources and wealth to the US. ALCA is a logical outgrowth of the advance of the neo-liberal doctrine imposed by US policy makers and their Latin American clients since the mid-1970s. While it purports to speak of free trade it resembles the mercantilist system of earlier imperial systems.

A discussion of ALCA should begin with a clarification of what ALCA is not. First of all it is not a free trade agreement. The US reserves the right to maintain $30 billion subsidies for its agriculture, its so-called anti-dumping legislation to protect major industries, quotas on imports in economic sectors where it is not competitive, banking legislation which permits major US banks to launder funds illicitly gained in Latin America, and a host of unilaterally decided 'health' restrictions to reduce imports of cattle and other products. Latin American countries, on the other hand, will have to eliminate all trade barriers and comply with the free trade doctrine. At the Quebec summit when President Cardoso of Brazil addressed the issue of US anti-dumping restrictions on Brazilian steel exports, President Bush told him 'that has nothing to do with ALCA; that should be taken up at the Organization of World Trade'!

Second, ALCA has no resemblance to 'economic integration'. The scenario resembles the subordination of colonies to imperial countries where the latter control strategic sectors of the economy, dominate markets and labour and dictate economic policy. Integration implies more or less equal exchange of commodities, two-way flows of capital, profits and interests, joint enterprises – in a word, more or less symmetrical relations and benefits. ALCA is totally asymmetrical, with the US multinationals accumulating Latin assets and determining the one-way flow of benefits (profits, interests, royalties) from south to north. Subordination, not integration, defines the nature of ALCA. In that sense, ALCA is very different from the EU.

Third, ALCA does not stimulate competition; it furthers monopoly. By establishing trade preferences within the trading bloc, ALCA penalizes Europe, Japan and other non-hemispheric trading partners and increases the monopoly trading positions of the dominant powers within the hemisphere, namely, the US. By increasing the advantages of the US, it lessens the Latin American countries' capacity to secure better prices, both in sales and purchases. In a word, ALCA lessens competition in the world marketplace.

Fourth, given the above restrictions in competition and trade – in other words, ALCA's favouring of a US monopoly position – it provides greater opportunity for US firms to secure privatized enterprises at 'political' rather than 'market' prices. One of the dubious arguments of neo-liberal ideologues is that 'there is no alternative to neoliberalism' (TINA). US advocates of ALCA would add, 'there is no alternative to the US market and investors'.

From the perspective of economy theory, ALCA is a denial of the basic premise of liberal (or neo-liberal) principles. ALCA is a mercantilist system, centered in the political supremacy of the US, whose economic policies are dictated by the imperial state via a set of asymmetric, monopolistic structures that facilitate the one-way flow of benefits. The transition from neo-liberalism to US–ALCA mercantilism is a result of two factors: the deepening economic crisis of the US, and the increasing competition from Europe and Asia, leading to huge and unsustainable trade deficits. In a time of internal and external crisis and sharpening competition, Washington needs to seize a greater share of the Latin American market, public enterprises and natural resources. ALCA would establish the supremacy of US multinational corporations over challengers from Europe by prioritizing US access to markets and trade. 'Free trade' within ALCA means US monopoly control over their Latin competitors, especially given the protective restrictions which Washington will impose on Latin exports.

Faced with increases in intra-regional trade, especially in MERCOSUR, ALCA will favour direct exports from the US over trade via subsidiaries in regional markets. This will increase the US trading surplus and undermine locally owned secondary suppliers of US-owned subsidiaries. ALCA is a return to asymmetric bilateral relations as opposed to regional trade in which local regimes had some negotiating leverage. Most likely regional trade as it exists in MERCOSUR will decline, as it is subordinated to ALCA. The result will be to favour US exporters, mainly agribusiness, manufacturers of services (information technologies, banking, and so on), while undercutting Argentine agribusiness and Brazilian industrialists. US multinationals in these countries will then operate according to the rules of ALCA, not their host country's regulations, particularly with regard to labour legislation, health and education.

Probably most important, ALCA will establish US-dictated rules and regulations in setting conditions for trade and investment over and against neo-liberal regional regimes. This means vast changes in education, health, labour relations, and the environment, as well as in the economy. For example, health and education would be privatized via the end of subsidies, opening the door for giant US health corporations and high tuition charges for public universities (as is the case in the US).

Basically, ALCA will allow the imposition of its mercantilist policies by establishing rules designed to favour US protectionism and Latin American openness. ALCA means the end of the last vestiges of national sovereignty – the recolonization of Latin America. It means that US multinationals do not have to transplant subsidiaries to Latin America; it can export directly from the US. ALCA is the logical extension of neo-liberal policies extended from the national and regional level to the hemispheric level: neo-liberalism within a mercantilist system run by and for the US and its local client regimes.

If neo-liberalism allowed the US to share with Latin American and European and Asian capitalists in the pillage of Latin America, particularly the privatization of public enterprises, ALCA is designed to maximize the US share of Latin American markets and resources. ALCA is designed to create 'fortress North America' against Euro-Asian competition and to maximize the extraction of surplus to finance the deepening crisis in the United States.

With so much US capital 'offshore', or in speculative or consumer activities, US banks resort to laundering dirty money, estimated by the US Senate to run to over US$250 billion a year, thus serving to compensate for the negative domestic saving rate. Criminal activity today is what 'pirate plunder' was to early capitalism: transfer of capital from the colonies to the imperial centre. As Stephan Hasam argues, the plunder strategy requires a criminal economy that can generate large sums of money to be transferred to the legal side of the economy. This means that a criminal economy must be fabricated and 'pump-primed'. Today the criminalization of drugs and the billion dollar people smuggling and white slavery trades stimulate the growth of the US banking sector. It is important that Latin American elites stay corrupt and voracious and that their activity should be criminalized so that the flow of capital northward multiplies and its possession secures imperial power.

ALCA has generated widespread opposition, from trade unions and peasant movements to sectors of the national bourgeoisie, particularly in Sao Paulo, Brazil and Porto Alegre in Rio Grande do Sul. The avariciousness of ALCA, which goes beyond neo-liberal policy to a mercantilist, imperial-centered monopoly, threatens the position of certain sectors of the bourgeoisie with displacement. While this bourgeoisie shares with the US multinationals their common support for reversing social and labour legislation, it opposes the total takeover of the economy by the imperial power. Hence Cardoso's wavering between his dependence on foreign capital and banks and his political dependence on the Brazilian big industrial groups: Cardoso's complaints about US mercantilism in the name of 'true liberalization', however, fall on deaf ears in Washington.

In order to implement ALCA, the Bush Administration has two client regimes, President Fox in Mexico and at the other end of Latin America, Economic Minister Cavallo in Argentina. Both regimes act as 'Trojan horses': Argentina by lowering tariffs in MERCOSUR for US exports at the expense of Brazil, and through deepening financial dependence on US banks (via debt restructuring); Mexico through Fox's plans to extend the maquiladora system from Puebla to Panama. These two client regimes are part of a two-stage policy of greater bilateral relations with the US (undermining Brazilian links) in the first part, to be followed by pushing ALCA in the second stage as the only 'viable alternative' to isolation from global markets, that is, the US market. The mercantilist essence of ALCA has already aroused criticism from the neo-liberal fundamentalist regime in Chile.

Chapter 7

Peasant-based Socio-political Movements in Latin America

(with Henry Veltmeyer)

Introduction

For many rural sociologists in Latin America the main object of analysis is the dynamics of social change and development in the rural sector. The social and economic conditions of these dynamics are not at issue: they have been fairly well described, at least in the Latin American context. What are at issue, however, are the social forces and processes and the change agents involved. Here rural sociologists seem to be of two minds. On the one hand, many sociologists continue to view the dynamics of change and development in structural terms – the outcome of an identifiable and comparable complex of institutionalized practices or underlying 'structures'. At this level, analysis generally takes the form of, first describing the conditions of development in objective terms and documenting the relevant experiences and, second, providing an explanation of subsequent developments on the basis of specified underlying structures and processes, with reference to a theory constructed for the purpose. This is the scientific method used by most analysts of agrarian change and rural development, both those within the Marxist tradition and those whose analysis departs from one theory or another of modernization. On the other hand, this form of analysis has come under serious question, leading a number of sociologists to rethink the issues involved and seek an alternative non-structural form of analysis and theorizing. In the context of what appeared to some as a paradigmatic crisis or theoretical impasse and to others as the emergence of a postmodernist sensibility, this rethinking has resulted in a number of scholars abandoning all forms of social scientific or structural analysis, particularly as guided by Marxist theory.

This chapter explores the ramifications of this divide in social analysis in relationship to the debate concerning the viability, nature and significance of contemporary peasant and landless workers' movements in Latin America. It presents an argument against two prevailing lines of analysis in favour of a return to a Marxist approach. To this purpose, the chapter is organized as follows. In the first part, the traditional and as yet dominant form of structural analysis is briefly reviewed. In the second part, an emerging postmodernist perspective on the dynamics of social change and development is outlined. Specific reference here is made to the writings of Florencia Mallon, a historian noted for her attempts to introduce a postmodernist sensibility among Latin American historians. The 'identical subject-object' of her analysis is the post-colonial peasantry of Mexico and Peru. In the third part of this chapter, these dynamics as they relate to the peasantry are placed within a Marxist perspective. Here both the dominant form of structural analysis and a postmodernist antistructuralist form and line of analysis exemplified by Mallon are criticized. The object of criticism in the first case is a dismissive attitude towards the peasantry as a significant social and political force. In the second case, the object of criticism is a tendency to reduce peasant-based or led struggles and movements to their cultural identities or attributes and demands. It is argued that a reconstituted class analysis, with a focus on both structural factors and forms of political struggle, still provides the most useful approach to an understanding of the dynamics of social change and development in the rural sector of Latin American society. This argument is supported by a brief discussion of four cases of peasant-based social movements.

Modernization Theory and Structuralism

The dynamics of change and development over the years have been analysed with reference to principles of a social scientific approach, namely that:

1 observable social and economic conditions of change and development are the manifestations of an underlying structure, visible only in its effects
2 these material conditions can be understood without reference to the subjective beliefs or perceptions of the individuals involved
3 these conditions can and must be understood, and explained, in structural terms and the process involved can be explained in terms of objective tendencies or 'laws', that is, conditions beyond human control and will
4 the process involved is based on modernization, the formation of a modern form of society, and has three major dimensions: *economic* (progress or prosperity – growth in the productive forces of society, with a consequent improvement in the level of income generation; *political* (increased freedom for individuals, embodied in the institution of democracy); and *social* (equality, justice or, in its most recent formulation, equity).[1]

Analysis in these structural terms has taken a number of theoretical forms, particularly in the post-Second World War context of 'international development'. In the 1960s and 1970s, economists, sociologists and political scientists advanced a theory of economic growth and modernization that dominated the study of development. In this tradition it is assumed that development requires the institutionality of a capitalist system, particularly private property, in the means of production, wage labour, the market and the state, as well as an institutional reorientation toward modern values such as universalism and individual achievement. Within this system the process of modernization is multidimensional, but essentially takes the form of capitalist development, rural outmigration and urbanization, and agrarian reform, with the restructuring of the grossly unequal and inequitable property relations in land, and access to other means of social production. The improvements and changes involved in this process are progressive in the sense of spreading benefits and gradual increases in the levels of social inclusion. In the 1970s, this form of analysis and theorizing was confronted by an alternative form of structural analysis and theorising derived from a paradigm that did not presuppose the institutionality of capitalism and that assumed the need for radical change – systemic transformation and social revolution. Analysis in this highly contested terrain of social theory also took different forms, including Marxism and Neo-Marxist Political Economy (dependency theory, and so on).

In the mid-1970s, there also emerged the search for an alternative non-structural forms of analysis. This search took diverse forms but shared a concern to establish Another Development (AD) – a form of development that is neither state- nor market-led, but small and human in scale; community-based; participatory (and empowering); generated from below and the inside rather than from the outside and above; and equitable and sustainable in both environmental and socio-economic terms.[2] One of the earliest permutations of this approach takes the form of what after Kitching (1982) could be termed 'economic populism' – a concern with small-scale enterprise and human-scale development.[3] With specific regard to the peasantry, the search for AD involved, on the left, a concern to protect the peasantry from the modernizing forces of capitalist development (urbanization, industrialization, proletarianization, and so on); and, on the right, a *culturalist* concern to protect the traditions of peasant societies from the same modernizing forces and a *populist* interest in a small-scale form of development that would correct the urban bias and the fetish of development thinkers and practitioners with capital-intensive large-scale heavy industry – industrialization. In this context, some theorists and analysts like de Janvry (1981) adopted a somewhat ambiguous position – *modernist* with regard to the belief that history was against the peasant, but *romantic* in the sense that he does not see the forces of capitalist modernisation as developing the peasants out of existence. In a postmodernist twist to this ambiguity, Gustavo Esteva and other exponents of Post-development Theory a decade later, have fought (at the level of thought) to dismantle the entire development and modernization project in so far as it concerns the peasantry and other subalterns (indigenous peoples, and so on).[4] The problem with this position, one that is rarely posed let alone tackled, is that the forces of capitalist modernization continue to resist these efforts to dissolve them in thought.

In the 1990s this search for AD proliferated, spawning a variety of experiments in development practice and shifts in thought all across the world. One recent formulation is 'sustainable rural livelihoods' (SRL), an approach advocated by the United Nations Development Programme (UNDP) that brings together sociologists and a range of scholars in other disciplines and development practitioners that share a concern for building sustainable communities (Barkin, 1999). Unlike most forms of AD in which the agency for change is located within the communities that make up civil society, the SRL approach acknowledges that localized collective actions have a structural context that must be brought into analytic focus and accommodated, if not changed. The objective, however, of SRL and other forms of AD, such as grass-roots postmodernism or post-development (Esteva and Prakash, 1998)[5] is not to bring about fundamental change or challenge the broader system – that is, social transformation – but democratization, to enlarge the space for local, community-based and people-led development.

In the 1990s, both the modernist and antimodernist approaches were reformulated and given a new form. They generally involved one form or other of modernization theory, neo-structuralism à la Economic Commission for Latin America (ECLA) or some other line of structural analysis, or the search for AD. One notable exponent of this structuralist and modernist discourse with regard to rural development is Cristobal Kay, who in a number of studies documents in some detail the economic and political processes involved in the decomposition and destruction of the peasantry as a dynamic force for change. Kay might not define himself as a modernist, at least in terms of the exclusionary capitalist form that modernization has taken in Latin America, but he is certainly a structuralist. In this context, the centre of reference for his studies into the social conditions of agrarian change and development is the long multifaceted process of change and development associated with the modernist search for economic prosperity, justice and freedom – and the inclusion of the peasantry in a project that postmodernists, among others, have given up on (Kay, 1999: 273–303). Excluded from the forces of change and modernisation, the peasantry is converted into what Kay in structuralist or class analytic terms describes as a 'permanent semiproletariat' – caught up in a stalled historical process ('the lost promise of land reform', and so on).[6]

Kay here addresses an issue of critical importance. From a conservative perspective, the peasantry is viewed as a major obstacle to change, a drag on the development and modernization process. But from Kay's more salient liberal perspective, the peasantry is viewed rather as a victim, buffeted by the structural and political forces acting on it. The peasantry is swept away by the tides of history, condemned at best to a life of marginality, at worst a decimated political force, fated to disappear. Kay himself does not come to, or spell out, this conclusion, but historians like Eric Hobsbawn, concerned with the broad sweep of changes and developments across the century, do. This conclusion is also implicit in most of the structural analysis and modernist theorising that continues to dominate the study of Latin American society, if not peasant studies.[7] Essentially, the peasantry is here viewed as a premodern social category or class that has been unable to adapt to the forces of change and that has lost the struggle for modernity – for inclusion into the development process that has brought about prosperity, justice and freedom for an increasingly greater part of the world's population. In this process, the peasantry is seen as unable to secure its own place in the modern world, the object of historical forces (urbanization, and so on) it cannot control or avert. In this context, Hobsbawn, for one, and modernists in general,[8] see the peasantry as a relatively insignificant factor in the process of change and development, a numerically reduced and politically impotent and spent social force, fated to disappear into the slums, squatter settlements and informal economies of the region's burgeoning centres.

The Postmodernist Pivot of Social Analysis

A model of science that can be traced back to the eighteenth-century Enlightenment dominated social, economic and political analysis in what Hobsbawn has termed 'the short 20th century' (Hobsbawn, 1994). Analysis in this tradition takes a scientific or structural form and is predicated on the following assumptions, elevated into epistemological and methodological principles:

1 the human mind is capable of constructing in thought and theoretically representing reality as given
2 facts have an objective reality and exist in a relation of truth to their corresponding scientific concepts.

Not all analysts have conformed to this model of social science but it has nevertheless provided an ideal, a necessary point of reference for the analysis conducted by most economists, sociologists, and political scientists – and some historians. However, in the 1960s a number of voices were raised in criticism of this mode of analysis and by the 1980s these voices reached a crescendo, provoking much talk – and writing – of a theoretical impasse, a crisis in theory and analysis that dictated a major rethinking as to the form that analysis should take (Booth, 1985; Moore and Schmidt, 1994; Munck and O'Hearn, 1999; Schuurman, 1993).

This was not the first challenge of this sort. There has been a long history of idealist attacks on a structural and materialist form of scientific analysis, including one led by exponents of the Frankfurt, or New, School for Social Research ('critical theory') in the 1930s, 1940s and 1970s. But this latest outbreak of an attack on the possibility of social science was led by proponents of a poststructuralist/Marxist/modernist analysis.[9] All of the major epistemological and methodological assumptions of a scientific approach to social analysis were challenged. As concluded by the Gulbenkian Commission (1996: 61), set up to investigate this theoretical crisis, this attack on the theory and method used in both the 'hard' (natural) and 'soft' (social) sciences shifted the focus of analysis and theory from 'the linear to the non-linear, simplification to complexity, neutral objectivity to the impossibility of removing the observer from the process of interpretation, and the superiority of qualitative modes of interpretation over the precision of quantitative analysis'. In opposition to the scientific search for objective truth, the proponents of a fundamental change in the form of analysis were sceptical or dismissive of the entire enterprise and scoffed at its scientific pretensions. Searching for the meaning rather than the cause of observed or studied phenomena, poststructuralists and postmodernists in social and development theory,[10] like phenomenologists and the ethnomethodologists in sociology, view facts as *social constructions*, mental constructs with no empirical referents and with meanings that are internal to the discourse that gave rise to them. As Norris (1997: 21) has put it, reality can be seen as 'purely a discursive phenomenon, a product of the different codes, conventions, language games or signing systems which provide the only means of interpreting experience'. Gayatri Chakravorty Spivak, another writer in this tradition and a member of the Subaltern [Historical] Studies Group, in similar terms criticises Marxists generally for reducing all phenomena to matters of class and modes of production. In reality, she notes, the concept of 'class' has no 'empirical referents'.[11] It is, she adds, 'the purest form of signifier', implying that class is but a linguistic symbol, the product of discursive practice with no concrete referent in the material world. In this poststructuralist discourse, the idea of class as a structure is just that: an idea without a basis in the immediacy of lived or experienced reality.

By the end of the 1980s this postmodernist sensibility had penetrated a range of academic disciplines from literary criticism, where it began, to sociology and social analysis of diverse issues (gender, race and ethnicity, political identity, hegemony and power), the study of economic development and social movements, and history 'from below' – from the point of view of subalterns viewed as 'conscious actors rather than simply as those acted upon' (Mallon, 1995: 10).

The effects of this penetration have been diverse and controversial. One is a reorientation of analysis from objectively given and structurally determined conditions of collective action towards an analysis of discourse, defined as 'the combination of intellectual and political practices that makes sense of events, objects and relationships' (Mallon, 1995: 5). A second effect on analysis in this poststructuralist/Marxist/modernist tradition, rooted as it is in a long history of an idealist attack on the possibility of social science,[12] is a focus on the subjectivity of experience, reality as viewed by the subjects of social action, the subalterns of popular culture and discourse. A third effect on analysis in this tradition is a culturally contextualized or localized research agenda with a consequent lack of comparative structural analysis,[13] and the corresponding absence of any directive social theory and quantitative analysis, or for that matter, empirical verification (Haber, 1997).[14] In this regard, Mallon defends herself and other analysts in this tradition from criticism by noting the essential subjectivity of experience and lived reality and the need for 'historical imagination' to uncover history from below – meanings that are embedded in the generally hidden and fragmentary popular discourse, which is generally suppressed by the dominant discourse, a medium for the exercise of hegemonic power (Mallon, 1995: 6, 19).[15] In this regard, the 'new cultural history' (and subaltern studies) that spurns the quantitative methods preferred by the earlier 'new economic history' is inspired by both a poststructuralist form of discourse analysis and the qualitative methods of hermeneutic interpretation.

In this connection, Mallon like other poststructuralists, eschews the methods of social science, opting instead for a deconstruction of hegemonic and subaltern discourses, uncovering and reconstructing hegemonic and counter-hegemonic struggles and power-relations embedded in them. Instead of relying on one form or another of structural analysis, Mallon, liked other poststructuralists, post-Marxists and microsociologists, seeks to foreground subjectivity and turns towards the social construction – and reconstruction[16] – of reality via resort to a 'decentred vision of the historical process' and use of multivocal analytic categories such as gender, ethnicity and nationalism, as well as hegemony, for capturing the fluid, ever-changing, contested and constructed nature of reality and providing 'a fine-grained consideration of the actual processes through which power and meaning are negotiated' (Mallon, 1999: 339).

Oddly enough, despite the recent spate of postmodernist theorizing, interdisciplinary conversations and research over the past decade (see, for example, the extensive notes to Mallon's writings) there has been precious little research into the actual subjective beliefs and perceptions of the co-participants in this research, the social actors at issue (the indigenous peasants of Peru and Mexico in the case of Mallon). Although Mallon spends considerable time on her 'theoretical conversations' with the 'identical subject-objects' of her analysis, and efforts to involve her subjects in the projection of her historical imagination, in these efforts we discover very little about the actual beliefs and perceptions of post-colonial indigenous peasants concerning what for them is real. Nor do we learn much about the dynamics of their day-to-day struggle to survive and their longer struggles to change the structures that bind them, structures that are not entirely the product of their own past activity notwithstanding Mallon's theoretical discourse on this point.

The New Peasantry and Social Movements: A Reconstituted Class Analysis

The peasantry, which in a number of contexts (Bolivia, Ecuador, Mexico, Peru ...) has a decidedly ethnic or indigenous character, is an important part of the rural social structure in many Latin American societies and an equally important agency for social change and development. As such, as both the object and subject of diverse social forces at work in rural society, peasants have been subject to the most diverse and conflicting interpretations, particularly as regards the dynamics of their struggles. On the one hand, they are widely viewed as a premodern social category, fighting a losing battle with the forces of change and development that have marginalized it from on-going processes and reduced its numeric relevancy. As we have noted, this is the stance of Hobsbawn, who in this regard writes of 'the death of the peasantry' as the 'most dramatic and far-reaching social change of the second half of this [the twentieth] century' (1994: 289). On the other hand, within the optics of a post- or antistructuralist analysis, the peasantry appears as a postmodern category, an advance representation of a new era of localized day-to-day struggles for ethnic and social identity; a social actor seeking to reclaim its popular culture and affirm its collective identity. In this postmodern tradition the focus of analysis is on the ethnic rather than the class character of the subaltern social movements involved or on the peasantry in terms of its collective identity. Then there are those, like the authors of this chapter, who see the peasantry in class terms, that is, with reference to both the economic and political structures that constrain them as well as the forms of their own consciousness – how they view themselves. In these terms, the peasantry are viewed as neither pre- nor postmodern but as a highly modern social class, a catalyst for antisystemic change and a dynamic force in an on-going modernization process – to create a more just and better form of society in which they are freed from oppression and in control of an economy that secures a livelihood and a decent standard of living for all members of the society within a framework of dignity and respect for their cultural values.

Paradox Confronting Structuralist Theorists

Since 1990, peasant and rural landless workers have been in the forefront of some of the most significant confrontations with national governments and international agencies. For many structuralist theorists like Roger Bartra (1976, 1993) or historians like Hobsbawn (1994), this presents a serious reality test of their ideas. Arguing from the position that structural changes based on a globalized economy have shrunk the rural sector in size and as a percentage of the gross national product, they assert that the peasantry and rural workers are no longer the significant transformative force that they once were.[17] Yet Latin American reality speaks to large-scale peasant-based guerrilla movements in Colombia, the most potent peasant-based insurgency in its history; a national rural landless workers' movement in Brazil that exceeds the peasant leagues of the 1950s and early 1960s in scope and effectiveness; and sustained peasant-Indian movements in Ecuador which seized Congress and shared power for a few hours in January 2000. And then there is the Zapatista uprising in Chiapas, which, like the 1990 *Inti Raymi* uprising of peasant and indigenous peoples in Ecuador, has challenged the existing power structure with an alternative conception of politics as well as antisystemic action.[18] These are striking cases that raise serious empirical doubts about the broad generalizations by structuralist theorists about the disappearance or bypassing of the peasantry/rural labour force. It would seem a paradox: the fewer the peasants/rural workers the more decisive a force they have become in national politics.

The facile dismissal by some structuralists of the current movements as the last gasp or a dying anachronistic class cannot be taken seriously given the systematic organizational structures of these movements, their long-term activity and their increasing effectiveness over time. The depth and scope of these movements suggest that, rather than trying to force current movements into preconceived and deductive pigeonholes based on spurious analogies with European and North American experiences, it would be better to reconceptualize the nature of these movements and introduce a new theoretical approach in the analysis of their dynamics.

Flawed Demographic Deductionism

One structuralist argument for relegating rural movements to the dustbin of history is based on a double extrapolation – one from Europe and the US, the other from Latin America. The first is that Third World countries are following the demographic pattern of Euro-America in which rural to urban migrations eventually led to the demise of rural popular movements. The second is based on a comparison of past and present demographic data showing rapid urbanization and a sharp decline of the rural population. From these demographic comparisons, structuralists argue that a shrinking minority of rural peasants and rural workers can only engage in rearguard actions, which only delay their eventual demise.[19]

However, the correlation between percentages of the labour force and political efficacy is hardly convincing, especially if we look at the role of bankers, generals and the bourgeoisie in shaping or making political agendas. By this quantitative criterion we could dismiss all social classes, including industrial workers in large plants and public employees. The only class that might be considered majoritarian is that of the low-paid service workers in the so-called informal economy and few scholars have identified this group as the spearhead of any process of change.

Deductions from aggregate demographic trends tell us very little about the crucial determinants of socio-political actions and motivations. First of all, they fail to explain the persistence of the peasantry, their refusal to leave the countryside and those urban sectors engaged in return migration to the countryside when conditions in the rural areas offer better opportunities than the city. Where successful agrarian reforms have occurred in a context of urban regression and economic crisis the demographics were reversed. Second, organized and cohesive minorities of peasants can be majorities of the best-organized sectors of society and can exercise great leverage against unpopular regimes. In other words, a strong capacity for mobilization among the peasantry and landless rural workers can provide a more effective political movement than an immobilized urban middle or working class.

Some structuralists focus on specific country cases to argue the thesis of the 'decline of the peasantry' or the 'lost promise of agrarian reform'. For example, by focusing on Chile and Peru and comparing activities in the 1960s and early 1970s to the 1990s, Kay (1981, 1982, 1999), among others, generalizes the effect of modernization in reducing the size and weight of rural labour and its political role. However, the decline of rural labour in Chile had as much to do with the harsh repression under the Pinochet regime and the retrograde rural labour legislation under the post-dictatorial regime. Second, in both countries the major peasant confederations were fragmented by left-wing sects in Peru and dependent on and manipulated by electoral parties (in Peru) and subordinated to the governing regime in Chile, thus undermining any possibility of independent political action. Third, the reversal of agrarian reforms in both countries – a kind of political counter-reform policy – seriously eroded and undermined the morale and cohesion of the peasantry and rural labour. Hence while few would argue that Chile or Peru have advanced rural movements today, it has little to do with any general concept of modernization. It has more to do with the specific political circumstances under which the economic transformation toward free markets took place as well as an endogenous dynamic originating in the actions of better-off peasants. On this point, studies on peasant dynamics by Brass (2000) in Peru, Zamosc (1986) in Columbia and de Vylder (1976) in Pinochet's Chile are instructive. The issue, identified most clearly by Brass (2000), is that the loss of dynamism in the struggle for social change in rural Latin America and the unravelling of the land reform movement is not just a question of neo-liberal capitalist development. It relates in part to efforts of the *gamonales* (landlords) and the rich peasantry, acting as or seeking to transform themselves into rural capitalists, to use land reform as a means of penetrating and dominating the production cooperatives of peasant smallholders and, in the process, to erode them from within. Needless to say, this dynamic is not entirely absent from the countryside today and needs to be factored into any analysis of rural political dynamics.

Modernization, Agrarian Reform and Peasant Movements

Structuralists, both Marxist and liberals, frequently resort to a version of the modernisation argument to argue that global changes, the New Economy and the demands of the market and international competitiveness have eroded any peasant-based agrarian reform. Some, like Kay (1999), go as far as to argue that modernization has made the whole concept of radical agrarian reform irrelevant or anachronistic.

This position poses a number of problems. First, the term 'modernization' is problematic. Unless one resorts to a tautological and ideological circular argument that identifies modernization with what passes for current free-market economies or political economic measures leading to the former, one must recognize there are many paths to modernization. If modernization means raising living standards, an increasing marketable surplus, improving productivity and combining credit, technical know-how and skilled labour to expand the reproductive capacity of investments, then historically (and today) there are a variety of market and non-market roads to modernization.

The equation of modernization with free-market or neo-liberal doctrine is a product of a particular configuration of class-based and elite-led power. In structural terms modernization under elite hegemony means the exclusion and displacement of peasants and rural workers, to benefit large-scale exporters, big landowners and multinational agribusiness. In these circumstances, modernization is equated with export surpluses, a high return to big investors, and high capital/labour ratios. Viewed from the perspective of rural workers and peasants the free-market version of modernization has resulted in a regressive de-modernization. Millions of peasants have been displaced from the market and forced into relations of subsistence to production. Many have become rural refugees swelling the low-productive, low-income sectors of the economy. Free-market modernization has undermined the access of landless workers and small peasant producers to means of production – land, technology and credit. Thus the struggle in the countryside involves not so much a conflict between modernity and tradition as a confrontation between two alternative forms of modernization: one that is elitist and exclusionary and another based on landless workers and peasants. The persistence of this conflict is not based on traditional rural sectors tenaciously holding on to their land and resisting modernity, but on a struggle over the means of production and state aid.

Discussions of the nature of rural movements and the viability of agrarian reform revolve around the notion of modernization. Neo- or social-liberal structuralists, such as Randall (1996), Seligson (1995), and the scholars associated with the Economic Commission for Latin America (ECLAC),[20] the Inter-Commission Development Bank (IDB) and the Food and Agricultural Organization (FAO), define the process essentially in techno-economic terms, with reference to technologies linked to large-scale, capital-intensive, export units. The imperatives of accumulation and investment are linked to big investors who have access to financial markets and export networks. The fundamental problem with this version of modernization is that it overlooks the class relations that define land tenure, access to credit, technical assistance and choice of markets. Notwithstanding their professed belief in the multiplicity of development paths, neo-liberal structuralists tend to assume that modernization can only be achieved by a single socio-economic configuration. They make an a priori identification between modernization and export markets and corporate farming in large-scale private units. By definition, other forms of farming and social classes are here relegated to a marginal role. Having designated modernization as a supra-historical category that transcends class and state relations, it is apparent why neo-liberal structuralists do not consider agrarian reform and peasant landless workers' struggles as an alternative route to modernization. By associating modernization with one particular configuration of power and economic strategy they overlook alternative configurations, routes, agencies and property forms within which modernization could occur.

On the record, the results of neo-liberal capitalist development and modernization are mixed. Some productivity gains measured by output per worker are counter-balanced by declining output as measured by output per acre of land.[21] First, the concentration of ownership, justified as modernization, has been as much for speculative as well as productive purposes, leaving large land tracts sparsely cultivated. Second, much of the economic progress measured in terms of increases in exports is the result of heavy government subsidies and cheap credits, not the imputed market efficiency of large-scale production. In this context, rather than describing socio-economic realities the neo-liberal structuralist conception of modernization serves as an ideological subterfuge used to justify the ascendancy of a particular power configuration as well as deny the importance of peasant struggles and the relevance of agrarian reform as a legitimate strategy for modernization. In this context, neo-liberal structuralists argue that the marginalization[22] and elimination of peasants and rural workers from the productive process is a technological outcome divorced from human will and, as such, will only be resisted by neo-luddites. They turn the struggle for resources and markets into a technological imperative rather than a form of class struggle (from above) that induces a class struggle (from below) over the content and direction of modernization. Briefly put, neo-liberal structuralists deny the importance of human agency. They impute irreversibility to the process of centralization and concentration of agricultural capitalism. They deny the possibility of reversibility based on a different political resolution of the class conflict inherent in the accumulation process. Structuralists in this regard, be they orthodox Marxists or liberals, tend to engage in a one-dimensional line of reasoning rather than a dialectical approach, which combines analysis from two converging directions: the objective process of concentration and centralization of capital, trade and government aid and on the other hand the subjective organization, internal cohesion and mobilization of peasants and rural labourers.

The intensification of rural conflicts between landowners and peasants/rural workers and their radicalization can best be understood by placing contemporary rural capitalism in the context of the larger urban-industrial economy. The assumption of neo-liberal structuralists is that the displaced rural population will be incorporated into the industrial-urban economy. And, in fact, as of at least the 1960s, the urban centres and cities of Latin America have experienced explosive pressures of large-scale rural outmigration that, in the not atypical case of Brazil, alone engaged from five to eight million migrants during the 1990s, and, it is estimated, will bring another eight million into the cities between 2000–2005. But the structuralist argument in this area is untenable. As of the early 1980s, Latin American economies have tended to stagnate, drastically reducing the absorptive capacity of the urban economies in the process. In this situation, the decision by the rural poor to take the route of urban migration is less clear-cut and the decision to stay and fight for change in the rural areas becomes more plausible. Structural constraints in the cities and increased opportunities to engage in successful social movements in the countryside have increased recruits for the rural movements. The apparent willingness of these new contingents to engage in direct action may in part account for the observed radicalization of these movements. A new type of leadership with solid roots in the peasantry can also be seen as a factor in the observed dynamism and growing radicalization of these movements.[23]

The conflict between processes of capital concentration and the counter-tendency of social mobilization may account for several new developments: the return migration of urban poor/unemployed toward the countryside, and the attempts to make claims on new agricultural land via land occupations, as well as the spread of rural resistance to hitherto quiescent regions. The demonstration effect of successful movements in winning land, building successful cooperatives, and achieving housing, schools, adequate nutrition and access to health has created a new momentum in attracting new activist households. Even where concrete achievements have been minimal, the movements have attracted new followers because they promise a vision of a better future, solidarity in resisting further evictions and strength in negotiating with established powers.[24]

Neo-liberal Structuralism: Urban-centric Perspectives

Neo-liberal structuralists tend to assume a one-way flow of influence and pressure: from the cities to the countryside – from the globalized economy inward. Their concept of power is based exclusively on an institutional or market conception of power in which the top institutional position and the flows of capital are the only source of power. Although institutions and markets are important nodules of power, they are not the only source of power. Organized masses of people are also sources of power. Power is a class relation in which the dominant class has resources like money and what it can buy and state instruments of armed force while the peasants/rural workers have large numbers, a new form of (potential) organization and grass-roots support.[25]

In several important instances, an urban-centric conception of power is not tenable: powerful rural movements have had a major impact on urban politics, converting the peasantry and indigenous peoples into an active force for social and political change.

The MST (Rural Landless Workers' Movement) in Brazil, the FARC (Revolutionary Armed Forces) in Colombia, and CONAIE (National Confederation of Indigenous Nationalities) in Ecuador have all shaped national policies and have become major challengers of state power. The MST has built coalitions with urban trade unions, urban shantytown organizations, and church and human rights groups. It has made agrarian reform a major political issue on the national agenda. The FARC is a rural-based guerrilla group with 15,000 armed supporters, overwhelmingly peasant or landless rural workers. It controls or has influence in half the municipalities of the country and is in negotiations with the government on a possible peace accord in which agrarian reform is one of the centrepieces. CONAIE, the major Indian-peasant confederation in Ecuador, has paralysed the country via general strikes and highway blockages, occupied Parliament in January 2000, and swept the highland state and local elections in May 2000.

The theoretical point here is that power is a two-way street in which rural movements can reverse urban and external flows of influence and exercise hegemony on a national basis, making agrarian reform a national issue. Implicit in most neo-liberal structuralist arguments is a virtuous view of the city. Urban economies are seen as dynamic, creative and the wave of the future. A corollary to the dynamic city is the image of a static, stagnant countryside. This is a serious misconception: city life today is actually guarded enclaves of high money turnover and seas of crime, corruption and under-employment. The dynamic view from the stock market does not correspond to the real economy of the 1990s or the new millennium: stagnant urban economies are unable to provide employment or habitation. On the other hand there are two faces in the countryside: one is the static negative image of the neo-liberal structuralists, the other is the promising dynamic growth of social movements, and the successful production cooperatives that have emerged as a consequence of do-it-yourself agrarian reforms, based on land occupations.

In their negative view neo-liberal structuralists fail to examine the class context of agricultural activity. Where rural movements have been successful in expropriating productive lands and securing credit and technical assistance they have produced virtuous outcomes, demonstrating that there are many roads to agrarian modernization.

By examining the class context of modernization we can understand the facile incorporation of elite classes and the difficult and insurmountable obstacles to popular incorporation and hence their resistance, not to modernization *per se*, but to a particular form of it. The issue of realizing modernization goals is less a problem of 'peasant embrace of traditional values' or resistance to 'structural adjustment' and 'short-term pain', but the lack of access to available alternative employment, housing and security in the urban setting. Staying in the countryside and attempting to improve rural livelihoods is a modern, rational decision based on cost–benefit analysis: the real possibility of change based on perceptions or information of other successful activity in other regions or adjoining territories. The diffusion factor is also operative: positive activities in one region have a multiplier effect, successful occupations have a demonstration effect. The demonstration effect is only successful if peasants or landless labourers already have a predisposition to want to remain in the countryside and farm if the opportunity presented itself. Illustrating what we could call 'modernization from below' is evidenced by peasant/rural worker demands for technical assistance, credit, infrastructure and marketing. These demands are associated with raising production and acquiring market shares, obviously associated with modernization, albeit in capitalist form.

Today the issue of agrarian reform is not a simple replay of traditional demands of 'land for the tiller', counterposed to capitalist modernization associated with large-scale corporate export farming. It is an alternative modernization strategy built around modern social classes. Peasants/rural workers or at least their cadres/leaders view land distribution as only the first step in an agrarian reform. Thus the conception of 'the peasant' or 'landless workers' today is vastly different from past images of atomized subsistence farmers, relying solely on traditional farming know-how and barely aware of markets, alternative cropping, non-traditional marketable crops and resistant to technological innovation.

It is precisely the emergence of a different peasantry and rural workers, with modern attitudes and with positive attitudes toward the possibility of significant, even transformative, change, that accounts for the resistance to being displaced or 'proletarianized' (more likely joining the urban reserve army of unemployed).

It is the 'new peasantry' with its new subjectivity in the current structural context that provides a challenge to Kay's notion of 'post-agrarian reform' and, in part, explains the re-emergence of dynamic peasant movements notwithstanding the prognostications of the demographic reductionists of their irrelevance and/or their anachronistic demands. However, we argue that the modernity of rural producers (peasants/rural workers) and their struggles can best be understood within an approach that emphasizes their political–economic demands (agrarian reform, credits, adequate prices, and so on) combined, in many cases, with a defence of politico-cultural rights (mistakenly described as classless 'identity politics') and, in some cases, socialist demands for a new system of production relations.

The pursuit of political and cultural rights is itself a part of the larger class struggle between elite members of exploited indigenous or black communities and militant poorer sectors. The internal class differences and the playing out of those differences in class conflicts within ethnic groups undermines attempts by postmodern writers to impose an a priori uniformity over politically heterogeneous and class-divided social groups. Specific cases of Ecuador, Bolivia, Mexico and Brazil (see below) empirically illustrate this point. If modernist and postmodernist conceptions of the peasantry and rural workers and the nature of their struggles are flawed, the same can be said of a kind of unreflective Marxism with regard to the process of proletarianization. While the *disappearing peasantry* thesis argues for the decreasing relevance of rural social movements, the *proletarianization* thesis assumes that the transformation or conversion of former peasants into wage labourers will swell the ranks of the urban-industrial labour force and provide a new infusion of troops for associated working-class struggles.[26]

There are several problems with the proletarianization thesis. First, most of the displaced rural peasants and rural workers never make it into the industrial labour force even in the best of times, let alone during extended periods of economic stagnation. Second, those that enter the labour force are usually recruited through clientelistic-family networks, most often in construction, which inhibits any expression of militancy and of steady employment. Third, most find work in the underpaid, low-productivity 'informal' sector with few of the social compensations associated with urban industrial employment. Fourth, 'proletarianization' – as well as the more dominant 'semi-proletarianization' that Kay (1999) writes of – takes place in the rural sector under very diverse social circumstances.

The formation of a rural landless working class is derived from several processes. Large families of small farmers, for example, create a surplus of sons and daughters who do not have access to land; in other cases, share croppers, renters and tenant farmers are displaced by larger farmers converting to new crops, the introduction of mechanization or new capital intensive crops. In many cases, the government's neo-liberal trade policies result in the importation of cheap food stuffs that drive small farmers bankrupt, while cutbacks in agricultural credits and loans and high interest rates have also forced a massive exodus of small family farmers, driving many to migrate to cities or to become a rural proletariat. The theoretical point is that while the segments of the rural labour force that remain in the countryside are formally 'property-less rural workers', their ties to the land are recent and relatively strong, their lineage and extended family networks are rural and their class consciousness is still tied to access to land, particularly cultivable land in regions familiar to them.

The failure of government resettlement and colonization schemes and the success of movement-based land occupations by landless labourers is closely related to this class-consciousness – that success is based on productive land, market access via roads and proximity to regional markets and transport systems. Thus proletarianization in the rural areas heightens land-class-consciousness among landless workers in a particularly market-oriented manner. The contrast between people without land and lands (under-cultivated estates or plantations) without people is one incentive to solve the landless problem in a way quite different from that espoused by neo-classical ideologues: by creating an alternative social market productive unit that combines radical collective social action with access to privately held property based on production for consumer markets.

The concept of proletarianization as the simple deflection of small holders to wage labour and the attribution of behaviour associated with the eighteenth- and nineteenth-century working-class consciousness does not apply today. Capitalist transformation and wage labour formation under current free market conditions in many parts of Latin America does not offer as attractive an option as staying in the countryside and fighting to create an alternative modern-based agrarian settlement through class struggle and agrarian reform.

Two related conceptual fallacies accompany the postmodernist and modernist views of peasant/rural workers' struggles. One relates to the exaggerated and unfounded belief that electoral politics could serve as a vehicle for social change. The second is that rural classes, and peasant and rural workers' movements, are organically or organizationally incapable of leading national struggles because their position in the national economy is strategically insignificant, they are geographically removed from the levers of power, or are firmly under the control of rural bosses and easily repressed by the military, police, local gunmen or a combination of all three. This 'organic' limitations argument revolves around the parochial and unfounded view that 'rural idiocy', in contrast to the illuminated minions of urban-industrial intellectual life, pervades the countryside. A more sympathetic view is that rural workers and peasants cannot see or understand anything beyond their turnip patch, chicken coop and their neighbours' encroaching cow. In any case, whatever the dubious validity of this view in the past, today many of the leading cadres, militants and activists in the rural workers/peasant movements are educated, have a definite understanding of national politics, and have been exposed to and engaged in national and international debates about rural alternatives.[27] They are cosmopolitan and capable of engaging in movements that articulate a broad range of positions that include credit, markets, trade and land use.

Also, the question of the relationship between rural and urban movements cannot be deduced from the supposed centrality of the urban economy. After all, everybody needs to eat. Nor do demographic changes alone account for the relative importance of classes in socio-political action. Other variables such as superior cohesion, organization, leadership and mobilizing capacity have a major role to play in measuring the relative effectiveness of socio-political movements in rural and urban areas. A deductive a priori position on this question is untenable. In fact, there are data accumulated from a variety of country studies that suggest that the major social forces confronting the neo-liberal regimes be organized from the countryside among peasants and rural workers.

Modernist Discourse and Practice

A poststructuralist discourse analysis is predicated on the notion that the meanings expressed therein do not constitute simplified theoretical representations of the real world. It is also taken that these categories of analysis are social constructions rather than representations of social facts. A structuralist discourse analysis,[28] on the other hand, assumes a relation of correspondence or truth between the categories of analysis and the real world. Concepts such as 'class' are deemed to have empirical referents and the structures to which they theoretically relate are taken as real, the basis of causally operating forces. In this theoretical context, the actual struggles and actions of the peasantry, our object of analysis, are viewed not merely as discursive but as real and therefore active responses to objectively given conditions. At the same time, the discourse of the actual subject, in our case the Latin American peasantry, is taken as a representation of the degree or form of theoretical awareness or social consciousness. As such, this discourse is viewed as a resource but not a reflection of reality. In fact, as Marx asserted in an earlier and different context, as a matter of principle one should not take a historical subject's social consciousness as a measure or accurate representation of reality, notwithstanding the fact that people will necessarily act on their subjective beliefs and seek to bring about their own reality.

In these 'structural' or social scientific terms, an analysis of peasant discourse is revealing. In all cases it makes sense of and explains the actions to which the discourse refers. The practice of the peasantry in Latin America is both informed by and consistent with their discourse. In many cases it also shows a high level of class consciousness, that is, theoretical awareness by the peasants and their intellectuals of the conditions acting on them as well as the structural sources of these conditions. In some cases, as in Mexico and Ecuador, the discourse of the peasants also reflects a high level of ethnic consciousness – a concern to assert or recover their cultural and political identity. A structuralist discourse analysis further shows that our interpretation of the dynamics of peasant-led or -based social movements in the region as modernist in character at the very least accords with the interpretation and understanding of the peasantry itself. Four very different cases of this understanding are briefly profiled in the following sections.

Examples of Peasant-based Social Movements

Brazil: The Rural Landless Workers' Movement (MST)

There are several reasons for considering the MST as a modernizing social movement. In the first instance their program is directed toward modernizing agriculture, converting fallow estates into productive units incorporating credits, technical assistance and innovative marketing strategies (Caldart, 2000). The slogan of the MST is 'occupy, resist and produce'. Over 200,000 families have been settled in cooperatives between the founding of the MST in 1984 to the present (Petras, 1999). The great majority have increased cultivation of land, increased living standards (improved health, education and housing) and produced a marketable surplus, including significant coffee exports to overseas markets. The national and regional leadership of the MST has passed through advanced training programs, many sponsored by the organization, where invited lecturers, including university professors and technical experts, teach courses on modern agricultural farming, cooperative management and contemporary political economy (Caldart, 1997).

The organization of the MST activities and its tactics and strategies have evolved into a highly sophisticated if mixed structure. Between 1 May and 7 May, 2000, over 400 land occupations were organized throughout the country, relaying information via the internet to supporters throughout Brazil. The strategy of land occupations is based on an elaborate structure of self-governance dealing with food, security, negotiations with the state, and so on.

During the 1999–2000 period, the MST engaged in direct action protests demanding greater credits and financing to stem the outflow of bankrupt small holders and impoverished landless rural workers fleeing to the cities in pursuit of low-paid, unproductive urban employment.

The MST has been a leading force in organizing urban alliances to counter-act the neo-liberal agenda of privatization and budget cuts, mobilizing trade unions, political parties, university and religious groups through a campaign called

'Consulta Popular'. In the late 1990s the MST led a march of over 100,000 urban and rural workers to Brasilia drawing urban support along the parade route across the country. The organization, leadership, productive units and activities of the MST are directed toward modernizing agriculture against unproductive landlords on the one hand and land speculators on the other, both of whom invest little in increasing productivity and producing a marketable surplus (Stedile and Frei, 1993). The MST has also counterposed its modernization strategy against large agribusiness enterprises that have expelled small holders and farm workers. In this context, the MST pursues a 'modernization from below with equity' strategy in contrast to the elite modernization strategy favoured by the Cardoso regime and its WB sponsors. One of the key differences between the two approaches is the social and ecological foundation from which the contrasting modernization strategies are organized. The elite modernization strategy is based on a small group of elite capitalist farmers, tied to chemical-intensive agriculture and almost exclusively linked to overseas foreign export firms. The modernization from below strategy of the MST is built on the inclusion of a large contingent of former landless labourers in agricultural cooperatives and pursuing a sustainable agricultural strategy that produces food for local markets and that includes a social agenda incorporating gender and racial equality. In this context the conflict is not between a 'modernizing' agribusiness elite versus a pre-modern peasantry, but a struggle between two distinct modernizing strategies, with different socioeconomic bases, strategies, markets and social values. In part, particularly in dealing with land speculators and traditional landlords, the conflict is between the modernizing strategies of the MST directed toward employment and production and the 'rentier' mentality that still pervades in many regions of the country.

Within the institutionality of the dominant capitalist system, the MST has widened its agenda from agrarian reform to include banking and credit reform foreign debt moratorium, conservation of the Amazon to protection of domestic producers. It has called for greater social spending for public health and education as part of a national project toward greater national autonomy within the international economy. It has been an active participant in many of the most important national and international conferences dealing with globalization, environmental issues, gender and minority rights (Stedile, 2000).

The effectiveness and prominence of the MST in national and Third World politics is based precisely in its 'modern' character and its capacity to build a modern program and adapt it to the primary demands of the landless rural workers and impoverished small landholder.

Colombia: The Revolutionary Armed Forces of Colombia (FARC)

The FARC was founded in 1964 as an overwhelmingly peasant movement, largely of subsistence farmers in the relatively underdeveloped region of Marquetalia (FARC-EP, 2000). The guerrilla movement was based on peasant land settlements that had developed a degree of autonomy from the national government, and therefore were perceived as a threat to its control. The Armed Forces' attempt to exterminate the peasant communities led to the formation of the FARC, which has evolved from an armed formation dedicated to defending peasantry from the depredations of the national government and landlords into a national political-military force of 15–20,000 active fighters that have influence in half the municipalities of the country. The centrepiece of the FARC program has been the issue of Agrarian Reform (*Matta Aldana*), although, as it has grown into a national political force, it has developed a political program that embraces a whole ensemble of political and economic issues that include the reform of state institutions, expansion of the welfare state and increasing national control over domestic markets, energy and communications.

FARC is a complex organization whose main constituency includes subsistence farmers, displaced peasants, landless rural workers and a sector of urban workers and employees. According to the FARC about 65 per cent of the organization is peasant and 35 per cent is 'urban' – including rural towns (private communication from FARC to author). While some of the leaders of the FARC, including its legendary leader Manuel Marulanda, are formally members of the Communist Party of Colombia, in fact, the FARC has its own leadership, program, strategy and tactics, with a decidedly distinct social base. Even in its origins the FARC developed a modern program of agrarian reform based on land distribution and government financing, credits and technical assistance. Its political program called for break-up of the political monopoly exercised by the century-old traditional two parties (Liberals and Conservatives) rooted in the urban and rural oligarchies. The introduction of a modern multiparty system was the basis of peace negotiations with the then President Betancourt in the mid-1980s. The FARC-supported Patriotic Union Party was soon decimated – over 4000 activists and sympathisers were killed as well as three presidential candidates (FARC-EP, 2000). The renewal and intensification of the civil war led to the massive displacements of millions of peasants, largely the result of the scorched-earth policies of the Armed Forces and their paramilitary progeny.

The FARC has two faces: one is the rural social base of rural small holders, displaced subsistence farmers, and landless labourers seeking to carve a niche in local markets with little technical know-how, the second is the national and regional leadership and rural cadres of the movement who have embraced modern values and organizational principles through the leadership training programs run by the FARC. Thus, though the FARC has and continues to defend under-developed rural producers tied to small-scale production, its leaders and program is directed toward introducing modern agricultural techniques and marketing strategies (FARC website, http://www.farcep.org). During the peace talks held in 1999–2000, the FARC organized a national forum on a whole series of wide-ranging national issues, including projects for alternative development, illicit crops, unemployment, privatization versus nationalization, free trade versus protection, and so on, issuing position papers that reflect a sophisticated understanding of contemporary debates (*Dialogos*; *Financial Times* 1 July 2000: 4). The forums held in the 'liberated zones' were attended by the whole gamut of social organizations, including trade unions and employer associations, Wall Street investment bankers, government officials.

The point here is that the FARC has been transformed from an almost exclusively rural movement based among small producers into a national political movement rooted in the agrarian struggle but with modernist aspirations.

The guerrilla army is closely linked with peasant and rural workers' communities throughout Colombia, drawing on support for its agrarian reform program. Its military organization is highly structured, strategically sophisticated and equipped with modern arms. It is a modern guerrilla army linked to a mass peasant base with a 'modernist' leadership which envisions the modernization of the economy and society through a mixed economy, strong state welfare and regulatory regime. What began as a rural defensive movement based on pre-capitalist rural producers has been transformed into a modern guerrilla army linked to a modernization-through-equity vision of political transformation. While the setting for much of the FARC's activities takes place in the most under-developed and impoverished regions, its organization, leadership and program is oriented toward opening Colombia's political system, eliminating extra-judicial state formation and creating a more dynamic domestic market via redistributive politics. The juxtaposition of democratic political values to vertical military organization, the elaboration of a modernist development agenda to a largely subsistence rural base, and the promotion of the home market in the context of deepening international integration are some of the formidable contradictory elements confronting the FARC in the future.

Ecuador: National Confederation of Indigenous Nationalities (CONAIE)

In 1990, a significant sector of Ecuador's indigenous peasants launched an uprising against the state and its neo-liberal policies. Over the subsequent decade the conditions that had led to this uprising generated an antisystemic social movement of significant proportions, with a series of concerted actions that included the storming in 2000 of Congress and a brief takeover of the presidency. At issue in these actions are a seriously deteriorating economic situation and a series of drastic economic reforms and policies of adjustment that include a serious proposal to adopt the US dollar as the country's currency. Other issues include concessions to transnational corporations of permits to construct oil pipelines and engage in economic development projects to the detriment of the country's indigenous peoples, their communities, the environment and their local economy. Behind these concerted actions can be found an impressive organization of indigenous communities from across the highlands that are politically represented by CONAIE. By the turn of the new millennium this peasant-based indigenous movement had clearly taken the lead both as a nation-wide social movement against the government's IMF-mandated policies and a movement of social transformation, aimed at changing not only the relationship of the country's indigenous peasants to the country's state and economy, but also at overthrowing the whole system (Macas, 2000a). In this the organization of peasant communities at the base of the indigenous and peasant movement concerted direct actions with other forces for social change, but in itself constituted the most dynamic forces for systemic social change in the country. On this point there is wide agreement among scholars and observers notwithstanding the existence of a parallel indigenous discourse on identity politics and the plurinational character of the state that bears comparison with similar developments in Bolivia and Mexico.

The beliefs and ideas used to mobilize collective action by Ecuador's peasant and indigenous peoples are clearly articulated in a series of programmatic statements by the movement's leaders and spokespeople and other forms of discourse. There is no room for misinterpretation here. Although the discourse is indigenist in nature and couched in the language of identity politics – a 'return to the good times' (*Pachakutik*), the 'reaffirmation of our historical roots', the 'plurinational character of our society and the state' – on the basis of their own accounts, the series of uprisings and the overall movement of the country's indigenous peoples and peasants are based on a clearly modernist development project. The critical dimensions of this historic project are clearly reflected in the discourse associated with both the *Inti Raymi* uprising and the creation of MUPP-NP (United Plurinational Pachakutik Movement – New Country). Both are oriented ideologically and politically towards *development* – to bring about a 'profound social transformation [in] the lives of the people'; the 'construction of *democracy*' – 'to profoundly and radically change the structures of the Ecuadorian state and existing forms of class domination'; and *social justice* – 'to determine in a manner that is ... participatory, just ... the destiny of each people' (Macas, 2000a). In terms of this modernist political project the associated discourse addresses issues of national economic development and the need for a new politics centred on community-based relations and forms of power. In other words, what is sought is AD that is constructed from below, participatory people-led and centred, inclusive, equitable and just – and empowering.

The meanings embedded in the discourse are clear enough and do not arise from within the discourse itself, as poststructuralists would have it. The discourse makes clear empirical reference to a process of capitalist modernization that needs to be combated at all levels with the combined resources and collective action of the country's indigenous peoples. To this end, CONAIE has committed itself to a process of non-capitalist modernization, an alternative form of development rooted in both the indigenous peasant economy and equitable participation in the country's resources and national development process. In this regard, CONAIE sees itself as a means of converting the country's indigenous peoples from a 'passive subject of change' into 'an active social and political subject' and, in the process, to bring about a state of development, democracy and justice.

Mexico: Zapatista Army of National Liberation (EZLN)

In Mexico it is estimated that the indigenous peoples comprise some 14 million, the vast majority of them peasants, landless workers or *jornaleros*, a subproletariat of seasonal or permanent migrants, refugees from what Marcos termed '*bolsillos de olvido*' and in official language are defined as 'marginal zones' of subsistence production, exclusion and poverty.

There is nothing 'socially constructed' about these categories – marginality, exclusion, poverty, and so on. They reflect conditions that are structural in source and objective in their effects. In terms of the directives and communiqués of the movement, the armed rebellion and uprising of indigenous peasants in Chiapas was directed against the Mexican State and the capitalist system supported by it. In the poetic language of Comandante Marcos, the official spokesperson of the movement, the cause of the uprising was the 'wild beast' (imperialism) whose 'bloody jaws' and teeth have sunk deeply into the throat of south-eastern Mexico, drawing out large pools of blood (tribute in the form of 'petroleum, electrical energy, cattle, money, coffee, banana, honey, corn') through 'many veins – oil and gas pipes, electrical lines, train-cars, bank accounts, trucks and vans, clandestine paths, gaps and forest trails'.[29] As far as Marcos and the EZLN are concerned, the enemy is imperialism and the Mexican State that sustains its globalizing neo-liberal project. This was made clear by Marcos himself as early as 1992, a year and a half before the 1994 uprising and soon after the Zapatistas' first skirmish with the government's armed forces. And the point is made not as eloquently but as clearly both at the moment of the EZLN's unexpected irruption and subsequently in the convocation of a series of national and tricontinental (intergalactic) encounters and forums that the Zapatistas have organized against neo-liberalism and for humanity.

With reference to the imperialist and class nature of the oppressive state and rapacious capitalist system, the Zapatista uprising coincided with the inception of NAFTA, viewed as 'the death knell of the peasant economy'. And in similar terms, the Zapatistas' discourse, in the form of a series of communiqués and reflections and calls for solidarity, speaks consistently of the need to combat (structural and political) relations of oppression and exploitation; and to establish new relations of power to the state and the economy based on 'independence, democracy and justice' – a modernist project if there ever was one.[30]

At the outset, the Zapatistas spoke or wrote clearly in class terms. Over time, however, this language was transmuted into terms that have given rise to misinterpretation by an international array of postmodernist intellectuals tuned into cyberspace and anxious to establish the 'first postmodernist' movement in history. In this context, historians like Florencia Mallon write of the 'postmodern condition of the post-colonial peasantry and the political (discursive) struggle for ethnic or national identity ...' and political analysts like Burbach write of the 'first postmodernist movement in history'. In this poststructuralist reading of EZLN discourse, objectively real or existent relations of cause between imperialism/capitalism/the state and Zapatista actions are reduced to a meaning derived from their discourse – relations of power and hegemony arising out of and consisting of, discursive activity. The object thus becomes not to act on and change reality, as Marx had it in the XIIIth thesis on Feuerbach, but to reinterpret it.

In the context of forming itself into a national force, the Zapatistas have been concerned to establish a new form of power and politics that is reminiscent of the theoretical discourse initiated by Foucault and reproduced by Mallon and other members of the subaltern group of historians. However, it takes a perversely poststructuralist reading of this discourse to convert the categories of this discourse into purely discursive phenomena with socially constructed meanings. As for the Zapatistas themselves there is no question about the meaning attached to their words. They reflect class-based conditions that are grounded in a modernist project – to bring about changes and improvements in the human condition of the country's indigenous peasants. Our own interviews of Zapatista activists and peasant leaders make clear that the conditions to which the discourse makes reference are taken as real and objective in their effects, requiring militant collective action. Mallon's postmodernist reconstructions on this point, based as they are on 'theoretical conversations', 'multivocal [socially constructed] categories' and 'historical imagination', do not reflect well the subjective beliefs of the country's indigenous peasants in this regard. Rather, they reflect on the poststructuralist sensibility of Mallon herself and her concern to reinterpret, but not change, reality.

Conclusions

We have reviewed and criticized various approaches to an understanding of the Latin American peasantry as a premodern and postmodern social category. In the former, the peasants emerge as a social force fated to disappear, the victim of historical forces they cannot understand or control and with little organisational and political capacity. In the latter, the peasantry appears as a discursive category rather than a social force and the dynamics of its struggle are reduced to 'discursive activity'. In this chapter, both forms of analysis, pre- and postmodern, are rejected and counterposed to an analysis pioneered by Marx.

The chapter departed from the assumption that the concept and tools of class analysis that are inspired if not directed by Marxist theory still provide the best understanding of the fundamental dynamics of rural development in Latin America. In this connection, a number of peasant-led socio-political movements have constituted themselves as the most dynamic forces for systemic social change. In the current context, peasant and landless workers' movements in Latin America are engaged in a modernist struggle to secure socio-economic improvements within a modern economy dominated by capital. In fact, it was argued that the enduring presence and increasing importance of peasant and rural workers' movements is based precisely on their modernity. Rooted in or articulated with the productive sectors of the capitalist economy they tend to resist the pressures and demands of financial and commercial capital whose free-market policies and outward (world-market) orientation threaten to undermine the livelihood of small local producers and rural workers and their communities.

The resurgence of peasant and rural movements in Latin America is built around the combination of traditional forms of cohesion based on kinship, community and, in many cases, class and ethnic identity; the adaptation of modern goals and techniques; a strategic understanding of the levers of power in the national and international system; and the quest for an alternative form of development – family smallholding or community-based collectivism in some cases, socialist or pro-socialist (cooperative) in others.

In some countries this resurgence reflects a search for ethnic or racial identity, but it would be a serious mistake to view these movements in purely cultural terms as a discursive phenomenon. As attested to by the spokespeople of these movements or relevant discourses, peasants across the region in diverse local circumstances are consciously engaged in a struggle not only for survival and development, but also for systemic change – for an alternative to the prevailing capitalist system in its worldwide operations. In some cases (most clearly the MST and FARC) the struggle for antisystemic change is directed towards socialism in some form. In other cases (CONAIE), the struggle has not acquired an explicitly socialist character but has more limited objectives. In any case, all of these and other peasant-based social movements, particularly at the level of leadership, have exhibited a consistent orientation towards egalitarian and communitarian or socialist values, as well as a capacity to transcend the traditionally narrow (almost parochial) focus of agrarian mobilisations in Latin America. The struggle for land and greater access to productive resources, and the collateral struggle over human rights – for freedom, autonomous development and social justice – are generally placed in a broader context of systemic change, that is, opposition to privatization (of the means of production), liberalization of market forces and deregulation of private capitalist enterprise, and the dominance of big capital in the marketplace. Every peasant-based socio-political movement is uncompromisingly opposed to capitalism in its current neo-liberal form, including land entitlement schemes and other mechanisms for opening up and expanding the market in land. In the name of greater heterogeneity and efficiency these schemes only benefit agrarian capitalists and capitalism.

In general, Latin American peasants tend to see themselves as combatants in a class war unleashed by the capitalist class and its state apparatus. The discourse of peasant intellectuals and the mobilization of peasant-based socio-political movements leave no doubt on this score. In their response to this situation, these movements have staked out diverse ideological and political positions, depending on the circumstances. In every case, the state is taken and confronted as 'the enemy', a depository of the most reactionary social and political forces as well as the agent of anti-peasant neo-liberal reforms. These movements continue to exhibit considerable dynamism in terms of diverse forms of struggle. In this connection, they also exhibit a disposition to enter into cross-class civic alliances, to form or participate in a broad alliance of oppositional forces while maintaining an essential autonomy *vis-à-vis* political parties and non-governmental organisations on the Left. The experience of the MST in Brazil is particularly instructive in this regard. However, the political dynamics of this class struggle are by no means settled as to their form and outcome. Despite a long history of studies on these dynamics they require a much closer look.

Notes

1   The universal values and legitimating and beliefs and ideologies associated with this
     multidimensional project or process can be traced back to the eighteenth century
     Enlightenment belief in the necessity for, and possibility of, changing the form of

society. This project was opposed from the very beginning of the nineteenth century in a conservative reaction to the fundamental ideas of the Enlightenment (human reason, freedom and equality) and the emancipatory project for liberal or radical change based on these ideas. Throughout the twentieth century the project of the Enlightenment in both its liberal and Marxist forms was attacked at the levels of social analysis, theory and epistemology. However, in the late 1950s, opposition to this project (to bring about a new and better modern form of society on the basis of scientific analysis) took a new turn. C.W. Mills in 1959 was one of the first sociologists to suggest that 'we are entering a new postmodern era in which the legitimating beliefs and explanations (of the enlightenment era) no longer serve'. Daniel Bell in the *End of Ideology* argued along similar lines, initiating a search for a new form of postmodern, postcapitalist, post-Marxist analysis. By the 1980s, the notion of a new postcapitalist, postindustrial and postmodern society was defined by a new set of conditions requiring a different (nonscientific) poststructural and postmodern mode of analysis and theorizing. As such it was widely disseminated by a new generation of French sociologists and philosophers, leading to the perception of a theoretical crisis (Booth, 1985; Schuurman, 1993).

2   On this search for Another Development see Chapter 2 of Veltmeyer and Petras (2000) and Chapter 1 of Veltmeyer and O'Malley (2001).

3   As Kitching constructs it, economic populism embraces approaches that range from the *Narodniks* in their polemic with Lenin, the ideas of economists like Schumacher and Lipton, the policies of countries like Nyere's Tanzania, and the models advanced in the 1970s by the International Labour Organization (ILO). What these approaches share is a concern for small size, cooperativism, and egalitarianism, as well as a balanced rural development.

4   Prior to his embrace of Post-Development, Esteva (1978, 1983) actively participated in the Mexican debate on the dynamics of peasant development as – to use the classification set out by Kearney (1996) – a 'peasantist', that is, a left-wing romantic. In this position, Esteva was clearly at odds with proletarianists like Roger Bartra but curiously aligned with those who adopted more of a right-wing romantic or populist position – Redfield (1956), in an earlier intellectual context, and Scott (1990) in a more recent one.

5   Admittedly, this view of grass-roots postmodernism as a form of AD can be disputed. Some scholars, including Brass (2000), link grass-roots postmodernism with economic populism on the basis of a shared concern with decentred small-scale enterprise and development. Others, including most of the proponents of grass-roots postmodernism, take a counter or post-development position, that is, rather than searching for another form of development, development as such is rejected as a misbegotten enterprise both in theory and in practice. On this see Escobar (1995); Rahnema and Bawtree (1997); and Sachs (1999).

6   Kay's (1981) conception of the semiproletariat has a greater resemblance to de Janvry's notion of 'functional dualism' than to Marx's conception. On the latter see Veltmeyer (1983).

7   A very important line of this analysis (neo-structuralism) is conducted by the economists and sociologists associated with ECLAC. As far as these scholars are concerned the dynamic forces of economic development are encapsulated in the process of capitalist industrialization. Thus in the diverse and extensive research program initiated by ECLAC, and in their publication series such as *CEPAL Review*, one can find only the most oblique references to the peasantry, namely the process of agricultural modernization and the social conditions of exclusion and marginality.

8   There is both a left- (radical) and a right-wing (liberal) stream of this modernist tradition, both rooted in the eighteenth-century Enlightenment (ideas of science, progress, and so

on). The former can be traced back to Marx; the latter is exemplified in a succession of modernization theories advanced as of the 1960s with numerous permutations: cultural diffusion and institutional reorientation (Parsons, Moore, Harrison); stages of growth (Rostow); the Green Revolution; achievement orientation (McClelland) and rational choice (Schultz, Bates); Basic Needs (Meier, Streeten, WB); and neo-liberal capitalist development – the New Economic Model (see, among others, Bulmer-Thomas, 1996; Veltmeyer and Petras, 1997). On both the left and the right of this divide, both in the past and today, there can also be found what could be termed a 'romantic reaction' to the modernization project. With regards to the peasantry Kearney (1996: 49–109) classifies these two forms of romanticism respectively as 'peasantism' (Bartra, Esteva and Post-Development Theory) and 'populism' (Redfield, Scott and Resistance Theory).

9   The postmodernist challenge to a scientific form of analysis and any associated metatheories (modernization, emancipation of the working class, and so on) was mounted in the 1980s by diverse exponents of 'post-Marxism', 'poststructuralism', 'discourse theory', or the oxymoron 'postmodern Marxism'. What the writers in this tradition share is an antipathy for any and all forms of what we term 'structuralism' – analysis predicated on the objectivity of material and social conditions. Poststructuralism in this context (discourse analysis) has some affinity with structural linguistics or what we might term linguistic structuralism. However, it should not be confused with any structural form of social or economic analysis associated with various forms of modernization theory or Marxism. On this point see, among others, Veltmeyer (2000b).

10   Major reference points for this postmodernist approach to social analysis include the writings of the French poststructuralist philosophers and sociologists such as Derrida, Foucault, Lyotard and Baudrillard. The interpretative and expository literature associated with this school of thought is voluminous. As for post-Marxism, a variant of this approach directed at the Marxist form of structural analysis, of particular relevance is a book put together by the French philosopher Mouffe and the Argentinean sociologist Ernesto Laclau (Laclau and Mouffe, 1985).

11   At a seminar at the Pembroke Center for Teaching and Research on Women, at Brown University (March 1988 (cited by Nugent, 1995: 124–5).

12   The poststructuralist/Marxist/modernist critique of universalism, structuralism, essentialism and positivism, associated with the French school of post-structuralism (Foucault, Derrida, Lyotard, Boudrillard, and so on) or the post-Marxist project of Laclau and Mouffe (1985) has a long history within sociology. It follows similar attacks made by Dilthey and the German Historical School in the late nineteenth century, the critical theorists of the Frankfurt School, phenomenologists in the tradition of Husserl and a number of 'Western Marxisms such as existentialism'. As formulated by, among others, Mallon, a supporter of the Subaltern [Historical] Group and its extension into Latin America, this form of analysis of the 'never-ending chain of human agency and structure' and the inclusion of herself within this chain (Mallon, 1995: 20) bears comparison with the diverse efforts by sociologists, such as Anthony Giddens and Pierre Bourdeau in the 1980s and 1990s to construct a social theory that incorporates or takes into account the subjectivity of experience and the subaltern point of view. What mark all of these efforts are a decided idealism and a rejection of structuralism, materialism and the objectivity of experience, principles that make social science possible.

13   As it happens, the historian Mallon, in her encounter with, and adoption of, a poststructuralist position has set up a comparative frame for her analysis (Peru, Mexico), but in this she is somewhat idiosyncratic, seeking to overcome the 'distressingly

ahistorical' nature of postmodernist writings (1995: xvi). A striking feature of the analysis of social movements in Latin America in the optics of postmodernism is the lack of any attempts at comparative analysis.

14 Haber, among others, criticizes Mallon not only for the lack of empirical verification, but also for involving herself in the object of her historical interpretation and her defence of such interpretation (discourse analysis) without the need for direct access to what peasants, women, and so on thought and did (Haber, 1997: 341, 367–8).

15 As Mallon (1995: 333) herself notes in her discourse, analysis derives not so much from a general poststructuralist emphasis on and concern with language, but from Laclau and Mouffe's post-Marxist reformulation of Gramsci's concept of 'hegemony'. Her use of this concept and other such socially constructed 'multi-vocal' categories such as gender and nation suffers from the same problem that Laclau and Mouffe's social constructions do. By her own admission these categories have no ontological existence as 'social facts' but are 'only interpretations'. On this and other problems with Laclau and Mouffe's post-Marxist discourse analysis – problems that apply equally to Mallon – see Veltmeyer (2000b).

16 It is Mallon's method for reconstructing a suppressed and non-existent popular discourse that has aroused the most criticism. True to the postmodernist principle that guides her historical investigation she herself actively participates in the process of getting the subjects of her research, the indigenous peasants of Mexico and Peru, to recover their historical memories and interpretations of reality.

17 In the 1970s this position, taken by many structuralist, Marxist and modernist thinkers at the time led to a heated and as-yet unsettled debate (especially Mexico) between peasantists (*campesinistas*) and proletarianists (*proletarianistas*). Studies by Cancian in 1987 and 1992 and a 1993 study by Roger Bartra, a key figure in this debate, suggest that the structuralist or proletarianist line of analysis represented most clearly by Bartra himself in his 1976 study, is by no means passé.

18 On the efforts of the indigenous movements in Ecuador and Mexico to redefine relations between themselves and the rest of society and the state see, among others, *Koeyu Latinoamericano* (koeyu@cantv.net) and Veltmeyer (2000a). As for the ideological orientation of these socio-political movements, there is some ambiguity or lack of clarity and direction. The actions and mobilizations launched by CONAIE and the EZLN are clearly antisystemic and oriented towards 'social transformation' rather than adjustment to a reformed neo-liberal capitalism. However, the specific form of social relations of production advocated by these movements is unclear. FARC in Columbia and the MST in Brazil are clearer in this regard. Although in practice the form of preferred economic organization ranges from the family-owned production unit to production cooperatives, the leadership shares a commitment to socialism. A survey of MST leaders conducted by the authors in May 2000, testifies to this. All but one expressed their general orientation and commitment to socialism in one form or other, most generally a Brazilian form yet to be constructed.

19 Roseberry (1989: 73), in this connection, argues that a major reason for the failure of rural guerrilla movements across Latin America was that 'the movement [was] romanticized and attempted to organize the peasantry ... when it was disappearing'.

20 The economists and sociologists associated with CEPAL or its line of analysis, including Henrique Fernando Cardoso, define themselves in terms of 'neostructuralism' (Sunkel, 1991), the theoretical basis for a policy package that might be labelled 'social liberalism', but (cf. a personal communiqué by Sunkel to this effect) they all take for granted the need for a neoliberal institutional and policy framework. This is the basis for

the theoretical convergence sought and achieved by the Cepalistas between the World Bank and its neo-liberalism and the Latin American structuralists. As far as we are concerned, they are neo-liberal structuralists.

21   This point, and those that immediately follow, relate to findings of CEPAL's Research Division of Production, Productivity and Management.

22   CEPAL economists generally do not directly address the question of the disappearance of the peasantry; they focus more on the marginality and exclusion of peasants from the on-going development process. In this connection, the Cepalistas view their model (productive transformation with equity) as an alternative to the neo-liberal model in that the latter is exclusionary – designed to benefit only those enterprises that are able to adjust to the requirements of the new world economic order (some 15 per cent) or that are deemed to have 'productive capacity' (another 35 per cent or so). The peasants, in this model, are left to twist in the winds of change. The CEPAL model in theory is designed to broaden the social base of production, to incorporate the peasant economy via the process of productive transformation. In practice, however, peasants are only thought about and tolerated to the degree that they are willing to adapt to change, to enter the modern economy, to disappear as peasants.

23   This is a conclusion drawn by the authors from a series of interviews with the leadership and activists of peasant movements in Bolivia, Brazil, Paraguay and Mexico (Petras, 1997).

24   A recent survey conducted by the authors of 32 peasant leaders and MST militants from across Brazil lends considerable support to this conclusion.

25   The indigenous movements in Ecuador and Chiapas provide important examples of this new conception of power – in the discourse of both the *Inti Raymi* and Zapatista uprisings (see *Koeyu Latinoamericano* (koeyu@cantv.net) and Cdte Marcos) – 'a construction from below, from the bases, from the roots, of power'.

26   Roman and Velasco Arregui (1997) are representative of this line of thinking, as are Bartra and Cancian (1987, 1992).

27   In a May 2000 survey of thirty-two MST leaders from across Brazil the authors found that a surprisingly large percentage (37 per cent) had at least some university education; another 31 per cent had either finished a collegiate or technical secondary education program; and only 12 per cent had not finished at least primary education.

28   On the form taken by a structuralist reading of a text or discourse see Althusser (1970).

29   See Marcos's analysis of the 'capitalist imprint' on Chiapas and the ravages of imperialism in his 'Tourist Guide to Chiapas' (1994) written a year and a half before the January insurrection to 'awaken the consciousness of various brothers who have joined our struggle'.

30   The structural-class line of analysis behind Marcos's discourse and the modernist project behind the Zapatista practice are reviewed in Veltmeyer (2000a).

Chapter 8

Brazil's Rural Landless Workers' Movement: Ten Hypotheses on Successful Leadership

(with Henry Veltmeyer)

Introduction

Sociological studies of socio-political movements in recent years have addressed a number of questions related to the social base of these movements, the issues around which collective action is mobilized, the form of struggles involved, and the context in which these struggles take place.[1] What is generally missing in these studies, however, is an analysis of the role and social dynamics of political leadership, a curious omission given the saliency of this factor in earlier studies and the non- or poststructural 'social actor' approach taken by so many social movement analysts today (Calderón, 1995; Escobar and Alvarez, 1992; Esteva and Prakash, 1998).

One possible explanation of this is the emergence of a postmodernist sensibility among sociologists and historians in this area.[2] The effect of postmodernism generally has been to turn attention away from the structural factors and to eschew a comparative and objective analysis of these movements. Indeed this lack of comparative analysis, together with a focus on contextualized and well-described but largely unexplained collective actions of a single movement, is a notable feature of sociological studies in the 1980s and 1990s (Munck, 1997).

Another feature of these studies is an orientation towards a poststructuralist form of discourse analysis and, in this new intellectual context, an abandonment of structuralisms, particularly Marxist class theory (Howarth, Alettta and Slavrakakis, 2000; Petras and Veltmeyer, 2001a; Veltmeyer, 1997). This chapter provides a counterpoint to this poststructuralist form of analysis and associated postmodernist and post-development theory. In this context it is argued, with reference to the political leadership factor, that the dynamics of socio-political movements in Latin America can best be understood in structural terms and on the basis of a reconstituted form of class analysis.

This argument is structured as follows. First, we establish the emergence of what we have termed new peasant socio-political movements (NPSMs). We then explore the dynamics of these movements in terms of a structuralist form of discourse analysis, which we contrast to the more dominant poststructuralist form. Then we

109

discuss the class and social character of the leadership of a movement that we and others[3] regard as the most dynamic social movement in Latin America today. This discussion is made with reference to ten hypotheses that we constructed for the purpose of interpreting our field research data on the leadership of the Brazilian Rural Landless Workers' Movement (MST) and for drawing a sociological portrait of these leaders.[4] With reference to these hypotheses, derived not from any general theory but from prior studies by the authors into diverse social movements, and on the basis of field research data, we argue that what is distinctively 'new' about the peasant-based movements that dominate the contemporary struggle for social change in Latin America is precisely the class character of their leadership as well as the organic ties of this leadership to the social base of the movements. We draw out various theoretical – and political – implications of this argument in the conclusion.

The Emergence of New Socio-political Peasant Movements in Latin America

In the post Second World War context of a large-scale development project initiated in the late 1940s[5] and a globalization project initiated in the 1980s under very different conditions it is possible to trace out three waves of social and political struggles against the capitalist system in Latin America.[6] In the 1950s and 1970s the social and political forces of change were mobilized in three ways:

- Via leftist political parties and the use of the electoral mechanism, a strategy exemplified in the success of Salvador Allende in bringing the working class to state power in Chile.
- Via the unionization of labour and the struggle of the organized working class against capital and the state for higher wages, improved working conditions and greater social benefits.
- In the wake of the Cuban revolution, a guerrilla form of armed struggle against the state.

Each modality of political struggle helped incorporate elements of the working class and rural producers into the political and economic development process. But none of these antisystemic struggles and strategies managed to overcome the array of forces ranged against them and the project of social revolution or societal transformation ultimately ended in defeat. In the 1980s, however, in the context of a democratization process, a region-wide debt crisis, and the implementation of a new project based on a neo-liberal program of policy measures designed to structurally adjust the economies in the region to the requirements of a new world economic order,[7] protest against the new economic model of neo-liberal capitalism and the project for social transformation was picked up by a second generation and a new form of social and political organization – a popular movement protagonized by the urban poor and a proliferation of non-governmental organizations that manifested a burgeoning 'civil society' and the emergence of a social, as opposed to the political, left. But the forces mobilized by these civil society organizations were subsequently – in the 1990s – demobilized under conditions generated by a neo-liberal program of economic and political reform measures implemented by governments in the region.[8]

In the 1990s, the region was hit by a third wave of social and political forces ranged against the system in place. The labour movement was in disarray, its forces and organizational and mobilizing capacity decimated by the forces of a 'silent revolution' wrought by the capitalist class under the agency of the state. The new social movements that had dominated the political landscape in the 1980s suffered a similar fate. With very few exceptions the forces that they had mobilized were dissipated. But in the same context there surfaced a new wave of rural activism protaganized by a number of peasant-based socio-political movements – the Zapatista Army of National Liberation (EZLN) in Mexico; an indigenous uprising and social movement led by the Confederation of Indigenous Nationalities (CONAIE) in Ecuador; the MST in Brazil; and the Revolutionary Armed Forces of Colombia (FARC). These movements, all organized in the 1980s except FARC, and all but the EZLN operating on a national scale, took centre stage in the 1990s, dominated the popular struggle for social antisystemic change.

As argued in Chapter 9, these movements constitute the most dynamic forces for social change in the region as well as opposition to the economic and political system everywhere in place. However, these movements are still not that well understood, raising more questions than answers and generating a scholarly – and political – debate as to the nature of their social base and the dynamics of struggle involved (Bernstein, 2000; Brass, 2000; Foweraker, 1995; Haber, 1996; Petras, 1997; Petras and Veltmeyer, 2001a).

The Question of Leadership – Ten Hypotheses

The debate on the nature and dynamics of the new peasant-based socio-political movements in Latin America has generally focused on the social base of the movements and the dynamics of their organization and mobilization – the general form of their struggles, the particular strategy and tactics involved, and the associated ideology. However, the character and form of leadership seems to be an equally important factor in explaining the relative success of these movements in organizing and mobilizing the forces of resistance and opposition – of social change. For example, FARC is the only peasant-based guerrilla army that not only survived the forces of counter-insurgency in the 1970s and 1980s but that has actually increased its mobilizing capacity. The one striking difference between the FARC and the other guerrilla armies of national liberation and social change formed in the first two waves of post-Cuba insurrectionary activity is the social character and form of its leadership. In terms of their social base and operating ideology these guerrilla armies were very similar if not identical (see, for example, Wickham-Crowley, 1991); the FARC, however, is the only such movement that was not only peasant-based but, like the NPSMs, peasant-led.

In the 1980s, the emergence in the region of what was conceived to be 'new social movements' whose social base could not be reduced to, or understood in, class terms led to a general abandonment of class analysis and the adoption of poststructuralist forms of discourse analysis (Calderón and Jelín, 1987; Camacho and Menjivar, 1989; Escobar and Alvarez, 1992; Mallon, 1995; Slater, 1995; Zapata, 1987). In the 1990s, class analysis virtually disappeared from the map of social movements being drawn and redrawn by political sociologists, leading the authors of this chapter to seriously reconsider the class origins and character of the leadership of the peasant-based social movements in the region today.

With the aim of sparking a return to a reconstituted form of class analysis, the authors chose to conduct a case study of the MST leadership in Brazil. To inform and direct this study we formulated a number of hypotheses, each of which is discussed below in terms of observations made and data collected on the basis of several research visits; conversations on site with, and in-depth interviews of, several MST leaders and activists; and a formal survey conducted of a cadre of 37 leaders representing every state where the MST is represented. These hypotheses were derived not from any general theory but an understanding resulting from fieldwork on a number of peasant-based social movements in the region (see, for example, Petras, 1997; Veltmeyer, 1997). Given percentages relate to a statistical analysis of the data generated by this survey.

Hypothesis 1
The MST leaders have deep and continuing roots in the countryside and among the constituency they are organizing.

One of the most striking characteristics of the MST relative to other Latin American rural movements in the past is the high proportion of leaders who have long-standing ties to the rural poor – the social base of the movement. First, close to two-thirds are sons and daughters of peasants – small producers (37.6 to 40 per cent) or landless rural workers (28.2 to 21.9 per cent). Although there are no systematic data or studies on this for comparable movements in earlier waves of peasant movements, most analysts of these movements over the years have commented on the urban middle-class origins of the leadership. In the case of the MST, however, most leaders (79 per cent) originate in families of small farmers, members of producer cooperatives or landless workers.

There is an on-going academic debate as to how to conceptualize these various categories of 'peasants' in the context of an advanced process of capitalist industrialization, social decomposition and class differentiation, but the subjects of this debate generally see and define themselves both as 'peasants' and as 'landless workers', creating problems of objective categorization if not self-definition (Bernstein, 2001; Brass, 2000; Kearney, 1996; Mallon, 1995).[9]

From our conversations with diverse MST leaders it is clear that they not only tend to have deep roots in the countryside but they maintain and cultivate their rural ties, going back to the countryside whenever possible, usually in the context of mobilizing a land occupation, and they work actively to ensure a lack of social distance from the rank and file in the field, identifying with their struggles and way of life. Furthermore, there is little to differentiate these leaders from the rank and file in terms of material conditions, including housing, eating, modes of transport and personal possessions. In this connection, it is well known that leaders who share the same material conditions as their followers are more likely to engage in struggles that relate to their common interests, as opposed to bureaucrats ensconced in hierarchies who tend to be focused on and to defend their own particular privileged position. Although there are no comparable data for other rural social movements in the past, both in South and Central America and in Mexico there are clear indications that, relative to the MST, these movements were characterized by a significant social distance between the leaders and the rank and file. On this see, among others, Wickham-Crowley (1991).

Hypothesis 2
The leaders are relatively well educated and committed to continuing education, thus securing the learning and teaching skills to diagnose social realities and develop appropriate strategies.

Successful movements of the popular classes require leaders who are well trained and capable of articulating and formulating grievances, devising appropriate strategies and diagnosing social situations. In many, if not most, situations, social movements have tended to rely on well-educated leaders from the urban middle class or rank and file leaders with little formal education. However, the MST is possessed of a large cadre of grass-roots leaders from the popular classes who are relatively well, or highly, educated. Over half of the MST leaders have some post-secondary education (either in technical schools or the university). In addition, another third (27.9 per cent) have completed or attended high school. Only 12 per cent have never attended school or failed to complete primary school. In addition, the MST invests a large part of its budget on education and has developed ties with a number of universities that provide extension courses for leaders and activists (Caldart, 1997, 2000). Women leaders, constituting 31 percent (nine out of 29) of our survey sample,[10] are particularly well educated: twice as many women as men have some university education. Thus it is clear that the MST has a cadre of popular leaders with both the formal training and class experience to develop successful national organizing drives. In this regard they differ significantly from the leaders of an earlier wave of guerrilla movements formed in the 1970s, most of whom, particularly those who were well-educated, had no organic ties to their rural constituency. With the exception of FARC's leader, Marulanda (*Tirofijo*), these leaders, like those of the Central American guerrilla movements of the 1970s and 1980s, were reliant on a much smaller leadership cadre that, with few exceptions, was drawn from the middle strata of the class structure. On this see Johnson in Dominguez (1994).

Hypothesis 3

The primary loyalties of the leaders of the MST are to that organization. They do not have any conflicting loyalties with other political groups that could lead to ideological divisions and undermine their unity of purpose.

One of the perennial and divisive scourges of popular movements in Latin America is sectarian political conflict. Since many of the leaders of these movements tend to come from a political party whose prime purpose is to use the movements to build their party, the movements are often cannibalized and immobilized in the process.[11] In contrast, the MST is a socio-political movement that has fraternal relations with other parties, particularly the Workers' Party (PT), but its leadership insists on retaining the autonomy of the movement and its capacity for independent action (Stedile, 2000). Most leaders joined the movement through participation in MST-organized land occupations and/or through attending meetings and discussions. Having been introduced to the movement through direct contact with its activities rather than 'party intermediaries', their ideological formation and practice is essentially a result of social interactions within the movement. This shows up in their political attitudes: large majorities, ranging from 65 to 100 per cent, are in agreement on the major issues of the day – the negative position of the Cardoso regime on effective agrarian reform, the negative impact of the policies designed and sponsored by the IMF and the WB. This internal consensus allows the MST to focus on building outside support and to channel available resources in the direction of organizing, and mobilizing, direct action. Again, this is not a conclusion drawn by the authors as much as a point made in as many – or few – words by Pedro Stedile himself and other leaders who we interviewed. Indeed it is clearly a matter of internal policy as well as general strategy that conflicting loyalties and other conditions that might undermine a unity of purpose be avoided if possible, and counteracted if not.

Hypothesis 4

The main source of recruitment is based on practical problem solving that attracts 'doers' rather than ideologues.

Most of the political organizations that recruit their members on the basis of ideological polemics at the level of leadership tend to create 'armchair' revolutionaries given to spinning theories and discovering ideological differences – highly ideological 'purists' divorced from the language and interests of the people at the social base of the movement (Wickham-Crowley, 1991).

As for the MST, leaders generally joined the movement through participation in land occupations and public meetings. By their own accounts, their attraction to the movement was based on its history of success in solving practical problems, including their own. In this regard, a majority of leaders (69 per cent) have participated in ten or more land occupations and over two-thirds believe that land occupations are the most effective way to bring about agrarian reform and translate theory into practice. While the MST as an organization is acutely aware of the need for both theory and practice, and to unite the two, its emphasis on continuing political education needs to be understood in the context of a concern for practical problem solving. As a result, the MST tends to recruit 'doers' rather than 'ideologues' – a perception confirmed by the leaders themselves.[12]

Hypothesis 5
The leaders have accumulated practical experience via continuing direct actions that enhance their capacity to organize and carry out successful actions that can, and do, attract new members and supporters.

MST leaders do not engage in successful action to then rest on their laurels. They are, as it were, in continuing action. Despite their relative youthfulness (88 per cent are under 40 years old and over one third in their 20s) many have been involved in multiple land occupations. These occupations frequently involve prolonged experiences in which squatters are organized to administer the settlement, negotiate with the government, and pressure for a favourable resolution. Through these multiple and varied experiences the leaders of the MST have developed the savvy to secure land appropriations in such a way as to benefit their main constituency – landless, or near landless, workers. This continuing, cumulative practical problem-solving type of leadership, and the emphasis on continuous if limited gains, appears to be a key factor in the success of the MST. At least, this is the view expressed by the leaders themselves in various discussions on this point. In this connection, over 15 years of struggle, the MST has settled over 300,000 landless families and from 1995 to 1999, at the height of the struggle for land and land reform, the MST mobilized 363,053 families of landless 'peasants' or workers for land occupations (Robles, 2000: Table 5; Petras and Veltmeyer, 2001c).[13] In the first six months of 1999 the MST organized 147 occupations involving 22,000 families, a level of mobilization maintained in subsequent years under conditions of a major counteroffensive launched by the Cardoso government. No other socio-political movement in Latin America has demonstrated anywhere close to such dynamism and relative success in making practical gains to the benefit of so many of its members.

Hypothesis 6
The leaders tend to be self-reliant and less dependent on electoral politicians, thus able and willing to engage in bringing about change via direct action.

Unlike movement leaders in other contexts (particularly the ex-guerrillas in Central America) the leaders of the MST have what could be regarded as a healthy distrust of electoral processes and politicians.[14] For one thing, they have seen many popular leaders over the years enter parliament and abandon the struggle. For another, they have seen the success to be achieved via direct action.[15] Both in terms of their own recruitment and in terms of evaluating the best strategy for bringing about the agrarian reform, over two-thirds (70 per cent) favour land occupations over the electoral process as a means of bringing about change. And the pressures to opt for what the government and the international community of development assistance organizations term 'forms of peaceful and civil struggle' (including use of the 'electoral mechanism') are considerable.[16] Although political conditions were radically different and perhaps not comparable, this finding differs markedly from findings related to socio-political movements for agrarian or land reform in Central America (see, Edelman, 2000). In addition, a significant minority (23 per cent) of MST leaders believe that a combination of direct action and electoral campaigns provides the best route to social change. Only one leader prioritized the electoral path towards social change and development, again in contrast to what analysts have found with regard to other land reform movements in the region. In this context the MST does support progressive politicians who support their program (mainly from the Worker's Party) but always from a position of the autonomy of their social movement; they do not, for example, suspend land occupations during election campaigns.

Hypothesis 7
There is a common understanding or consensus of the leaders as to who are their common enemies, the nature of state power and the impact of the World Bank, the International Monetary Fund (IMF) and other International Financial Institutions (IFIs) on their followers and the process of agrarian reform.

MST leaders manifest a high level of consensus regarding their adversaries and the nature of state power: 75 per cent perceive the Cardoso regime as completely opposed to agrarian reform; over two-thirds see the government and landlords as acting in concert against agrarian reform; over 75 per cent perceive an increase in repression over the years of the Cardoso presidency; there is unanimous agreement that the WB and IMF program of structural adjustment are designed in the interests of the rich and the well-to-do as well as the large corporations that dominate the economy. Its impact on the producing and working classes of Brazil are perceived as very negative. Specifically on this issue 90 per cent think that IMF–WB policies largely benefit foreign investors and Brazil's rich and powerful; 94 per cent believe that, with reference to the operations of transnational corporations, foreign direct investment and neo-liberal policies mandated by the IMF and the WB, the impact of the US on Brazil has been totally negative. In this connection, almost two-thirds of MST leaders are oriented to one form or another of socialism and 84 per cent are optimistic about the future. It is difficult, if not impossible, to ascertain the precise source of this ideological orientation – class background, experience or political education – but there is no question as to its saliency in defining the MST.

Hypothesis 8
The leadership has a 'realistic' view of the international and national configuration or structure of power and whose interests it serves.

Unlike the Central American ex-guerrillas (see Vilas, 1995) the leaders of the MST have no illusions about the international configuration of power.[17] For one thing, they have a clear understanding of the imperial nature of US policy and interests; and, as a result, they are generally hostile to the IFIs and have a clear understanding of the class alignments organized against them. This is evident in several survey questions in which MST leaders were asked to define their ideological orientation and to report on their views regarding the WB, the IMF and other IFIs, which are almost universally viewed by the national and regional leadership as 'agents of US imperialism'. As a result, these leaders are generally resolved to mobilize internal support rather than appeal to 'outside organizations' for support or condition their action to accommodate the interests and demands of such organizations. Both the interviews that we conducted and our survey pointed towards this conclusion.

Hypothesis 9
The movement leaders have a common vision of an alternative social system that informs their actions, thus motivating the organization and providing guidelines to action.

Many former leftist parties, especially, but not only, in Central America, have adapted to neo-liberal realities, shedding their former socialist views in the process (see, for example, Casteñeda (1993) as well as Petras (1997)). This could in part explain the divorce of so many of these movements from the mass struggle and their electoral pragmatism. In contrast the leaders of the MST and their actions continue to be guided by a socialist vision of an egalitarian, participatory society based on Brazilian realities. Unlike Central American revolutionaries (see Halebsky and Harris, 1995; Liss, 1991; Vilas, 1995; Wickham-Crowley, 1991) their socialist vision rejects the Soviet model and thus was not affected by the downfall of the USSR and the collapse of 'actually existing' socialism. Of the MST's 37 leaders 27 favour socialism as practised in Cuba; 33 per cent favour the democratic socialism advocated by Brazil's Worker's Party; and 33 per cent project a new form of Brazilian socialism. That is, 90 per cent are oriented towards socialism in one form or another but not as practised in the former USSR.[18]

At a different level, that of practice rather than ideology, the MST leadership is clearly committed to the principle of substantive or popular democracy. This is evident in the decision making related to both the formulation of political strategy and in the social organization of production. Our observations of actual practice in diverse contexts (small meetings and congresses that bring together up to 10,000 rank and file members, popular assemblies, consultations and open discussions with the rank and file in the encampments and on permanent settlements – and their constituent communities) point towards a very substantive or egalitarian form of 'participatory democracy'. Discussions are open, voting is direct but secret, and decisions, even on matters of fundamental strategy and policy, are generally reached, and made, on the basis of popular participation. For example, after a year of 'occupation', 'encampment' and 'settlement'– and successful negotiations with the government on the legal expropriation of the occupied land – peasant families are free to choose whether or not to form a production cooperative and collective, the strategy preferred and promoted by the national leadership, or to work the land on an individual household basis.

Hypothesis 10
The leaders have the élan and mystique required in bringing about change in the future, thus providing the motivation to sustain action in times of repression and opposition by formidable adversaries.

Unlike the leaders of so many left-wing parties and movements, who tend to be sceptical about large-scale change and pessimistic about socialism, the leaders of the MST manifest a high degree of optimism (84 per cent) based on their own practices and successes as well as faith in the righteousness of their cause. It is difficult to operationalize the concepts of 'élan' and mystique as critical factors in the mobilizing capacity of a social movement. But with regard to the former ('élan') we took cognizance of the degree of enthusiasm and positive spirit exhibited by the leaders in their response to questions about what the movement means to them and their sense of its future prospects. The degree of enthusiasm and optimism about the future was striking, much greater than that exhibited by leaders of various urban-centred social movements who we have interviewed over the course of research visits undertaken over the last four years. To some extent this enthusiasm and what we have termed *élan* is generated and maintained via the movement's anthem, flag carrying and other rituals that precede and accompany each official act or daily training sessions at the MST's leadership training school in Santa Catarina. As for *mystique* it defines the particular relationship that most peasants have to the land and is exhibited in the quasi-religious spirit of solidarity generated by ritualized events such as the annual gatherings of the leaders and activists at regional and national congresses and national meetings of regional leaders such as the one in Sao Paulo where we conducted our interviews. The mystique of the movement is also reflected in the many symbolic representations of the movement's historic struggle against the forces of reaction such as banners, insignias, and the songs of struggle and conquests written to lift the spirits of the movement's members and to mobilize them to collective action. The use of such symbols is a characteristic feature of events staged by the MST, including meetings and daily openings of sessions of lectures and classes at the Leadership Cadre School in Santa Catarina.

Class as a Dynamic Factor in Political Organization and Leadership

Despite the propensity of recent sociological analysts armed with a postmodernist theory to downplay, if not ignore, the class factor in social movements, namely the objectivity and subjectivity of class conditions, there is little question about the centrality of class in regard to the social base of the most significant and dynamic socio-political movements in Latin America, including the MST (Veltmeyer, 2000; Petras and Veltmeyer, 2001a). But when it comes to leadership the issues that surround the concept of class are more clouded. A number of peasant- or worker-based socio-political movements in the region draw much of their leadership from the urban-centred middle class, particularly its intellectual stratum. In the case of the MST, however, the movement is peasant led as well as peasant based; class is a salient feature of leadership as well as the social base of the movement.

As to the role of class as a factor of analysis, our research suggests that the principles of class analysis established by Marx, and generally used by Marxists, continue to be useful as a guide to analysis and practice: that is, the dynamics of social movements such as the MST are based on a dialectical interplay between the objective and subjective – between the *objectivity* of the structural conditions shared by the MST leadership with their members and the corresponding *subjectivity* of shared awareness as to these conditions. This is not to say that the radicalism and orientation toward direct action exhibited by the MST is directly attributable to the class origins of the leadership and the rank and file. The political landscape in Latin America and elsewhere is littered with counter-examples. However, the leadership of the MST exhibits a high degree of class-consciousness of the socially shared conditions generated by the economic structure of Brazilian society. The mobilizations and direct actions taken by the movement clearly reflect this class-consciousness as well as the class origins of the leadership. This consciousness is also reflected in the political education programming at the MST's leadership training school. Also, the responses of the MST leaders who we surveyed and interviewed clearly establish the centrality of class as a dynamic factor in both the social organizations of the movement and the struggles involved, as well as the subjective consciousness of the leaders and activists. Class, defined as both a relationship to the means of social production and to the instruments of political power, is clearly a central factor in the thinking, and actions, of these activists.

Conclusion

Our case study of a successful leadership group is based on a leadership whose social origins are proximate to their organizing constituency, that is, who have organic ties to the social base of the movement that have achieved a higher education than the norm; are directly involved in practical struggles that engage supporters; and are independent of other political organizations. These leaders have a unified political vision of the future, a positive view of the efficacy of their action and are highly motivated regarding future success.

The antithesis of this positive profile of successful leadership would be a leadership drawn from social classes that are distant from their constituency (part of the rural elite or urban professionals) or who are from the same class but poorly educated, drawn to the organization for purely ideological rather than pragmatic reasons, remote from the actions taken (leaders ensconced in central headquarters) and relying on the electoral process for solutions. Leaders who have illusions about concessions and reforms from established regimes or international donors are likely to lack both vision and initiative and to misdirect the organization with false expectations that tend to lead to internal divisions, ideological conflicts and political demoralization – a sense that there are no alternatives.

The bane of many popular movements is the 'prodigal son' phenomenon: leaders who are renegades from their class, usually in the middle strata of the class structure,[19] who identify with the lower classes but who, upon achieving institutional positions, return to a middle class 'centrism' and shift their politics accordingly, thus undermining or derailing collective actions in the direction of fundamental and sustained social change. Drawn, to a large extent, from a class of landless or near-landless workers in the rural sector, the MST leadership has shown no propensity toward accommodation to the *status quo* as a means of feathering their own nests. While the organization has grown and to some degree has become institutionalized, and it has its national headquarters in a two-story building in Sao Paulo as well as a network of professional accountants and agronomists, it still depends heavily on the voluntary actions of lawyers, clerics and, above all, its own members to carry out daily operations. Institutionalization without bureaucratization seems to work well in providing regularities and order while supporting a decentralized and innovative style of leadership that is very responsive and accountable to the membership. Arguably, the small material differences that separate top leaders from rank and file members are a critical factor in the MST's successful mobilizations. At least we put this forward as a tentative suggestion that warrants further comparative study. The idea is that a relative equality of material conditions, a similarity in social origins and shared social perspectives make for long-term commitments and sustained struggles.

Land occupations are a key element in the MST's strategy for effecting agrarian reform. The success of this strategy is based on democratic participation by the mass of beneficiaries in the planning, organization and execution of the occupations and in resisting repression by local gunmen and the military police. The importance of the land occupation strategy in the thinking and actions of the MST leadership is closely linked to the participatory style of social change practiced by the movement.

The centrality of the MST in the lives, beliefs and practices of the leaders is a critical factor in the creation of the high degree of cohesion that sustains their activity. The movement is the social, political and economic organization for realizing activity. There is no separation between 'party', 'trade union' and 'enterprise' with parallel and competing loyalties as is the case in most Latin American countries. A unified and combined socio-political movement provides both social practice and ideological direction, thus avoiding the typical problems of social movements dependent on political parties and subject to their separate agendas. Over the years, we have come across innumerable complaints by activists of being used or manipulated by their political or guerrilla leaders, the practical and essential goals of the organization sacrificed for supposedly higher ends. However, the self-reliance of the MST leaders has guaranteed that the fundamental issue of interest to their constituency – land reform – has remained in the forefront of their programme, struggles and negotiations with political authorities.

In conclusion – and this is the theoretical point of our analysis – successful leadership seems to coincide with material equality within the organization, social solidarity as an outreach strategy and participatory democracy in the realization of organizational goals. The fact that there is no gap between the goals of the movement and everyday practice means that cynicism and pessimism do not take root; the coincidence of everyday realities and idealism fuel optimism, faith and a belief that people can change the world.

Notes

1   For examples of these studies see Burgwal (1990); Calderón (1995); Calderón and Jelín (1997); Camacho and Menjivar (1989); Eckstein (1989); Latin American Perspectives (1994); Zapata (1987).

2   On this point see Brass (1991, 2000); Haber (1996); Mallon (1995); Slater (1985); and Veltmeyer (1997).

3   See, for example, Robles (2000).

4   The data for this study were derived from three sources: (i) systematic observation, over a ten-year period (1992, 1995–1996, 1998–2001), of behaviour at an annual School for Leadership Cadres in Santa Catarina, periodic Conferences, workshops and meetings, and various encampments and settlements (11) and cooperatives (eight) in Santa Catarina, Rio Grande de Sul, Parana, Ceara, and Sao Paulo State; (ii) a survey conducted of this movement's leadership cadre: 32 regional and national leaders representing every state where the MST operates (conducted at a seminar on 12–14 May 2000, in Sao Paulo); (iii) a series of in-depth interviews with Pedro Stedile, the Leader of the MST, several regional leaders and activists, and a caucus of women leaders.

5   On this project see McMichael (1996). In the optics of post-development (Escobar, 1995; Esteva, 1992; Rahnema and Bawtree, 1997; Sachs, 1992) this project is viewed as an imposition of an idea (development), which is 'at the centre of an incredibly powerful semantic constellation' ('modern mentality'), able to exert a most powerful force in 'guiding thought and behaviour' (Esteva, 1992).

6   On the theoretical and practical postulates of these two intellectual and political 'projects' and the processes to which they gave rise, see Veltmeyer (2001a). A periodization and analysis of these waves of struggle to bring about change and implement an emancipatory project in Latin America can be found in Petras (1997).

7   On this new project – globalization — see Bulmer-Thomas (1996); Green (1995); and Petras and Veltmeyer (2001b).

8   On the diverse strategies implemented by governments against antisystemic movements see Veltmeyer (2001a).

9   In the context of a process of industrial capitalist modernization a part of the 'peasantry' is converted into a class of rural capitalists who most often invest their accumulated capital in the purchase of land, new technology, export production and transportation; another part is converted into a class of independent medium-sized proprietors and producers and a large part, at least 50 per cent, is converted into a rural proletariat and a semiproletariat of *jornaleros*, landless or near landless workers, many of whom migrate to, and are absorbed into, the burgeoning slums and the informal sectors of Brazil's cities. On the basis of census data the rural exodus from 1986 to 1996 is estimated to have reached a level of 5.5 million, leaving an estimated 4.5 million landless workers or peasants in the countryside, many of whom are expected to migrate to the cities in the next few years (INCRA, 1999; Petras and Veltmeyer, 2001c).

10 In its second to last Congress (in 2000) the MST adopted a resolution to increase the current representation of women in the regional delegations of leaders from the current level of around 40 per cent to parity with men.

11 This relationship of social movements to political parties is well-known and is one of the key issues on the agenda for debate and discussion at the annual *Foro de Sao Paulo* where representatives of leftist or Marxist political parties and associated social movements meet each year and have done so for the past eleven years.

12 Notwithstanding this perception, as pointed out by a reviewer of this chapter the key to success in building a social movement is an ability to theorize political practice and to convert theory into practice – to combine theory and practice. On this point, one of the very few truisms of sociological thought on social movements, all of the MST leaders are in agreement.

13 Not all 'occupations' have led to permanent settlements; the conversion of land occupations into settlements requires a process of negotiation with the government that has its own land reform agenda. Nevertheless, from 1990 to 1999 the MST managed to create 2194 permanent settlements involving 368,325 families of peasants/landless workers (Robles, 2000: Table 6). To appreciate the scope of the problem – and success of the MST – it is estimated that there are in Brazil upwards of 1.5 million landless workers or peasants.

14 On the penchant of Central American ex-guerrillas for electoral politics, and their accommodation and absorption into the 'political class' see, among others, Zanora (1995) on El Salvador, as well as Jorge Castañeda (1993), who explains (or constructs his theory of) the widespread abandonment by the Latin American left of what he regards as its utopian quest for transformative or revolutionary change largely in terms of the shift in political orientation and behaviour of these and other such ex-guerrillas.

15 Apart from their own experience this is also the lesson that the MST leadership (Stedile, 2000) has drawn from the history of other movements in the region such as the EZLN, CONAIE and FARC, as well as peasant social movements in Bolivia, Paraguay and Central America. On this point see Petras (1997).

16 In this connection the MST has for over a year and at the time of writing (June 2001) been subject to a major offensive by the government based on a multi-pronged strategy that included outright repression, a major public relations media campaign and concerted efforts to channel grievances and land claims into the WB sponsored Land Bank program. On the political dynamics of this process see Veltmeyer (2001a). As part of the intellectual weaponry marshalled by the WB the Brazilian government has also turned toward the sustainable livelihoods approach (SLA) to tackling the problem of entrenched rural poverty. Based on the agency of civil society organizations (CSOs) in partnership with the government, the SLA is predicated on empowerment of the poor, increasing their access to society's productive resources, and encouraging the use of the 'market mechanism' (land titling, land banks) and the 'electoral mechanism' (Amalric, 1998; Chambers and Conway, 1998; Liamzon, et al., 1996; UNRISD, 2000).

17 A question might be raised as to what might constitute 'political realism'. We define it as do proponents of the Realist School of political science, namely in terms of the centrality of power relations in politics and the tendency for power holders to pursue their own class interests. However, it is not unusual for those without political power who seek to advance their own interests to harbour all sorts of illusions about the motives of power holders.

18 This supports similar findings about the ideology of other peasant-based and -led social movements in the region such as FARC, CONAIE and the EZLN. On this see FARC-EP

(2000) with regards to FARC; Macas (2000a, 20001b) with regards to CONAIE; and Harvey (1994) and Veltmeyer (2000a).

19   On the role of the middle strata or class in Latin American social movements see Johnson in Dominguez (1994). A characteristic feature of the new peasant socio-political movements that have swept across Latin America's political landscape in the 1990s is that they are peasant-led as well as peasant-based (Petras, 1997). Although this factor needs to be examined more closely it might very well explain the fact that FARC is the only peasant-based guerrilla movement of the many formed in the wake of the Cuban revolution that not only survived the counter-insurgency movements of the 1970s and 1980s, but that has actually continued to build social and political forces of resistance to the point that it now controls up to 40 per cent of the countryside in Colombia (FARC-EP, 2000).

Chapter 9

The Unemployed Workers' Movement in Argentina

Introduction

Latin America has witnessed three waves of overlapping and interrelated social movements over the last 25 years.

The first wave roughly coincided with the late 1970s to the mid-1980s and was largely composed of what was dubbed 'the new social movements'. They included human rights, ecology, feminist and ethnic movements and in large part NGOs. Their leadership was largely lower-middle-class professionals and their policies and strategies revolved around challenging the military and civilian authoritarian regimes of the time.

The second wave of social movements developed into a powerful political force from the mid-1980s to the present. The second wave was largely composed of mass peasant and rural workers organizations engaged in direct action to promote and defend the economic interests of their supporters. The composition, tactics and demands varied among these rural movements, but they were all united in their opposition to neo-liberalism and imperialism (dubbed 'globalization'). The most prominent of these movements included the Zapatistas of Mexico (EZLN), the Rural Landless Workers of Brazil (MST), the Cocaleros and peasants of Bolivia, the National Peasant Federation in Paraguay, the Revolutionary Armed Forces of Colombia (FARC) and the peasant-Indian CONAIE in Ecuador.

These movements were led by peasants or rural workers and struggled for agrarian reforms (redistribution of land), national autonomy for Indian communities, and against US intervention, including coca eradication programs, colonization of territory via military bases, penetration of national police/military institutions and militarization of social conflicts, such as Plan Colombia and the Andean Initiative. The centrepiece of their struggles was the neo-liberal economic regime and the growing concentration of wealth in the hands of local and foreign elites.

The third wave of social movements is centred in the urban areas. The dynamic growth of barrio-based mass movements of unemployed workers in Argentina, the unemployed and poor in the Dominican Republic and the shantytown dwellers who have flocked to the populist banners of Venezuelan President Hugh Chaves.

In addition to the urban movements, new multisectoral movements, engaged in mass struggles that integrate farm workers, small and medium sized farmers, have emerged in Colombia, Mexico, Brazil and Paraguay. The nature, mode of operation and style of political action of these movements challenge many of the stereotypes and assumptions of conventional liberal social science thinking and post-Marxist orthodoxies. For example the new social movement writers declared the end of 'class politics' and the advent of cultural and 'citizen based' civic movements concerned with democracy, gender equality and identity politics. The subsequent explosion of peasant and urban class movements throughout Latin America in pursuit of land and political power shattered that assumption. The notion that the advent of economic and political liberalism would lead to the end of mass ideological struggles evaporated before the emergence of the Zapatistas in Chiapas (Mexico), the FARC in Colombia, and CONAIE in Ecuador. Each in its own way was expanding territorial influence as well as deepening political participation. The elite and authoritarian civilian electoral systems, dubbed democracies by liberal ideologues, were challenged by popular assemblies from below, which defined a new substantive form of direct democracy.

After decades of abusive, corrupt and reactionary rule by elite selected executives and congress people, the urban poor, rural working class and peasants turned toward direct action to realize their legislative goals of jobs, land, credit, housing and public services. The centrality of direct action struck at the centre of the organized systems of exploitation, pillage, wealth and state power, frequently paralysing the production and circulation of commodities essential to the reproduction of the neo-liberal regime. While some discursive theorists like Eric Hobsbawm have used specious 'demographic' arguments to dismiss the centrality of peasants movements in contemporary political struggles, others have argued that the mass of urban poor, engaged in fragmented and marginal employments or divorced from the means of production are incapable of challenging established political power.

The Hobsbawm thesis was refuted by the splendid display of political power embodied in the Indian takeover of the Ecuadorian Parliament in the year 2000, the FARC's formidable influence in almost half the municipalities of Colombia and the MST's show of force in 23 of Brazil's 24 states.

The development of a mass urban unemployed workers movement in Argentina challenges the assumptions of the atomized impotent urban poor, a case worth exploring for its innovative features and its explosive possibilities for the rest of urban Latin America.

Theoretical Issues: The Unemployed

One of the major arguments of orthodox Marxists for asserting that the industrial working class was central to any social transformation was its strategic location in the productive process. Despite the enormous growth of under-employed, unemployed and informal or 'marginal' urban masses it was argued that their fragmented job structure atomized them, and their relative isolation from the main sectors of the economy undercut their capacity to undermine the accumulation process. It was further argued that this urban mass was a benefit to capitalism in so far as it kept wages down and served to lower the demands of employed workers via job replacement.

More recently mainstream social scientists and NGOs have emphasized the micro-activities, subsistence economies and reciprocal exchanges among the urban poor as a solution and not a problem. The absence of stable employment, declining living standards, growing social discontent, increasing violent outbursts and the enormous growth of illicit economic activities emanating from the barrios has called into question the idyllic picture painted by mainstream ideologues of 'self-help'.

In August of 2001 a nationwide mobilization of highly organized unemployed groups, numbering over 100,000 people, shut down over 300 highways in Argentina paralysing the economy. In the previous months and weeks, five *piqueteros* (picketers) were killed and over 3000 were arrested by the federal police in violent clashes throughout the country. At the same time, the organized unemployed were able to pressure and secure thousands of minimum wage temporary jobs from the state, food allowances and other concessions, while retaining their independent organization. By September 2001 the unemployed were able to organize massive highway blockages (*cortas de ruta*) throughout the capital of Buenos Aires and a successful general strike in association with sectors of the trade unions, blocking government activity and the entrances to all the major private industries.

There were several key factors accounting for the success of the unemployed workers organization and activities:

1   Organization took place at the point of habitation, in the suburban barrios, where there was a high concentration of unemployed industrial workers and never employed young people and female heads of households.
2   The strategy of cutting highways, which was the functional equivalent of workers downing the tools of production, paralysed the circulation of goods – inputs for production and outputs destined for domestic or overseas markets.
3   The massive assembly style of direct representation and decision-making and allocation of benefits, prevented personalistic and opportunistic leaders being bought off during individual negotiations.
4   There were unemployed industrial workers in the barrios with organizational experience and awareness of the advantages of collective, assembly style democracy in carrying out a consequential struggle.
5   The prolonged nature of the crises, the chronic impoverishment and its devastating effect on households led to a disproportionate number of women among the most militant *piqueteros*.

The absence of any prior work experience and the bleak future prospects of employment activated a large number of adolescents, especially young women, to become activated and engaged in direct action politics and a willingness to confront the federal police. Previous but half-hearted attempts by trade unions to organize the unemployed workers had failed, even in the case of 'militant unions'. Despite programmatic demands to organize the unemployed, all unions concentrated their efforts on their members and their sectoral struggles. Where the unemployed were organized, they frequently served as 'auxiliary' partners in one-day demonstrations and had very little impact on the economy and securing reforms. Likewise political parties whether rightist, populist or leftist 'organized' the unemployed in a clientelistic manner providing one-off pay-offs for their votes or, at best, a few jobs for the privileged few vote hustlers.

The success of the unemployed movement in Argentina today is due to the fact that it learned from experience to avoid the pitfalls of the past by organizing independently from within the barrios, autonomously from the electoral parties, trade union bureaucracy and state apparatus.

These organizations overcame the occupational diversity of the informal workers, the insecurity of the precariously (part-time, occasional) employed and temporary workers and the unemployed, by organizing at the point of concentration in the barrios and engaging in action on proximate highways. They organized prolonged mass road blockages, rather than forming the tail of symbolic trade union marches in the downtown plazas.

Argentina: The Unemployed Workers Movement

Several factors facilitated the organization of the unemployed in Argentina:

1   The high concentration and density of the unemployed in quasi-segregated, relatively homogeneous barrios, distant from the centres of lower-middle-class influence.
2   The massive firing of factory workers with some trade union experience and downward mobility.
3   The privatization of mineral and energy centres, accompanied by the massive closure of certain installations and the discharge of workers creating virtual ghost-towns in which all socio-economic sectors were adversely affected.
4   The relative proximity of major highways supplying and transporting goods and commuters to and from the major cities and across national frontiers.

The road blockages of the unemployed workers draw on a long history of working class picketing intended to prevent employers from using scabs to undermine strikes. The *piquetero* is thus a respected figure within popular culture and even among sectors of the Argentine middle class.

The unemployed workers' application of the road-blockage tactics and mass picketing began in two towns of the interior Cutral Co. and Plaza Huincul, on the 20 and 26 June 1996 and again in April of 1997. These demonstrations mobilized thousands in protest against job cuts and plant shutdowns resulting from the privatization process. By the late 1990s massive route blockages occurred in the working-class suburbs of Buenos Aires protesting high electrical rates of the privatized light and power companies and the disconnection of unemployed consumers unable to pay their exorbitant bills. By the year 2000, mass demonstrations took place in cities of Neuquen and General Mosconi, which had previously been relatively prosperous oil producing centres. Privatization led to the closure of work sites and massive expulsion of the labour force, while the state and federal government failed to comply with its promises to finance alternative employment, largely because of budget cuts to meet IMF fiscal requirements.

The governments (municipal, state and federal) refused or were unwilling to heed the petitions and demands of the unemployed, and ignored their peaceful demonstrations. The irate workers and unemployed turned on the state and municipal office buildings, occupying and occasionally torching them. The federal government responded with force.

The unemployed demonstrations drew support from a wide swath of citizens and social classes: local merchants threatened with bankruptcy as consumer power declined precipitously; thousands of provincial and municipal employees who had not been paid for months, or were paid in 'funny' money; unemployed public employees and professionals fired as part of the budget reduction and fiscal austerity programs; pensioners suffering a reduction in payments, public health workers and school teachers suffering pay cuts and worsening work conditions. In the ghost towns, the 'industrial cemeteries', the privatization policies had a devastating effect.

The speculative economy financed by foreign borrowing, the sell-off of lucrative public enterprises, and the movement by the Argentine bourgeoisie of over US$130 billion overseas (equivalent to Argentina's public debt) led to a chronic recession that began in 1997 and deepened into a full blown depression by 2001. Unemployed and under-employed workers varied from 30 to 80 per cent depending on the location. In Greater Buenos Aires, official unemployment figures of 16 to 18 per cent were multiplied by two, as most employed workers in the urban suburbs held temporary or precarious employment. In the big working-class suburbs, unemployment extended from 30 to 50 per cent and under-employment from 40 to 50 per cent as the great majority of households fell below the poverty line.

These economic and social conditions converged with favourable organizational opportunities to produce mass organization.

Political Conditions

In the post-dictatorial period the mass of the working class, employed and under-employed, had been denied their most elementary social economic demands. The three presidents, Alfonsin, Menem and De la Rua each in his turn aggressively pursued a political economic agenda that totally reversed existing social legislation, exonerated the military officials responsible for 30,000 deaths and disappearances and handed over the economy's 'family jewels' to Argentine and foreign capitalists at prices far below their market value.

To pacify the growing discontent among the burgeoning army of impoverished and unemployed workers, the two major parties, the Radicals and the Peronists, organized clientelistic electoral machines that distributed occasional food baskets and employment to their loyal followers. With the deepening crisis, the clientelistic relations were totally inadequate to contain the rising discontent. The barrios immersed in 'passive poverty', crime, disorganization and clientelistic manipulation began to organize.

Fundamental to the new organization of the unemployed is their rejection of patronage–clientelistic politics directed by the electoral party bosses and trade union bureaucrats. The Unemployed Workers' Movement (MTD) began and continues as a grass-roots movement organized and led by members of the barrio and the municipality. The MTD has a very decentralized structure: each municipality has its own organization based on the barrios within its frontiers; within each barrio, each few blocks have their informal leaders and activists; each municipality is organized by its general assembly where all active members participate. Policy is decided in assembly; the demands and organization of the road blockages are decided collectively in assembly. Once a highway or principle artery is designated, the assembly organizes support within the barrios. Hundreds and even thousands of women, men and children participate in the blockage, setting up tents and soup kitchens at the side of the road. If the police threaten, hundreds more pour in from the adjoining shantytowns. If the government decides to negotiate, the movement demands that negotiations take place with all the *piqueteros* at the blockage. Decisions are taken at the site of the action by the collective assembly.

From experience, the *piqueteros* distrust sending delegates – even militant local people – to individually negotiate in government offices because, as one piquetero leader stated, 'they buy them off with a job'. Once the demands are secured – mostly a quota of state funded temporary jobs – the distribution of jobs takes place by collective decision according to prior criteria of family needs and active participation in the blockages. Job allocation is on a rotating basis in cases where there are fewer jobs than unemployed.

Once again, the *piqueteros* have learned by experience that when individual leaders negotiate and distribute jobs, they tend to favour family members, friends and others, turning themselves into 'caudillos' (personal leaders) with a patronage machine that corrupts the movement.

The organization and activities of the MTD has had an electrifying effect on the unemployed. From passive sufferers of poverty and social disorganization and clientelistic manipulation they have become active in a powerful solidarity movement, engaged in autonomous grass-roots social organization and independent politics.

The early success of the MTDs in Salta, Juijuy and Matanzas led to the rapid extension of new MTDs throughout the poverty-stricken suburban belt surrounding Buenos Aires, Cordoba and Rosario as well as in the 'ghost towns' of the interior. The multiplier effect was also evident in late 2001, when two major national congresses with over 2000 delegates met in Matanzas and La Plata to discuss a common platform of national struggle.

The success of the movement in mobilizing tens of thousands of unemployed workers, energizing thousands of trade union activists and actually securing (limited) concessions from the regime is the principle reason for its expansion at the local, regional and national level. The strength of the movement, however, continues mostly at the local level based on neighbourhood ties, mutual trust and concrete demands.

The success of the *piqueteros* has spread into the central cities, drawing support from the public employees facing major wage cuts and massive firings. Human rights groups, principally the *Madres de Plaza de Mayo*, school teachers, health workers and university and secondary students have joined in blocking major intersections in downtown Buenos Aires.

In the first major nationally coordinated action over 300 major highways and city thoroughfares were blocked by over 100,000 *piqueteros*. All the major cities, the former petroleum towns, were affected causing the bourgeoisie endless delays and monstrous traffic hold-ups, effectively paralysing economic activity in many sectors and including the hitherto invulnerable financial sector.

On the picket lines and in mass assemblies there is a disproportionate number of women – estimated at 60 per cent of the participants – and young people, including numerous adolescents with no job prospects.

The attraction of the MTD is that they catalyze action – direct action – in a society exhausted by the endless structural adjustment policies (SAP), budget cuts, multiple low paid jobs and the corruption and impotence of Congress and the authoritarian elitist nature of the Execute branch. The trade unions, particularly the General Workers Confederation (CGT) in both variants has been run by a venal group of high-paid repressive bosses closely aligned with the Menem regime and unwilling to confront the De la Rua regime or its regressive policies. The occasional denunciation, and even general strike, is understood by everyone – the regime and the workers – as a meaningless symbolic ritual to 'blow off steam' and submit. Given the coincidence of the two parties in perpetuating the neo-liberal regime, in sharing the spoils of office and keeping the working majority on a downward spiral and given that the mass of employed industrial workers are subject to the control of millionaire trade union bosses, the unemployed workers are the only pole for opposition. The MTD has the only effective tactics: direct action – the prolonged blocking of highways until minimum demands are met.

The immediate demands of the unemployed movement centre on state-funded jobs to be administrated by the local unemployed workers' associations. Second, they demand distribution of food parcels, the freeing of hundreds of jailed unemployed militants, as well as a host of public investments in water, paved roads, health facilities, and so on. The demands for employment go beyond subsistence temporary work and include stable employment with a living wage. In the town of General Mosconi, the leaders of the movement have formulated over 300 projects, some of which are successfully operating, to provide food and employment, including a bakery, organic gardens, water purifying plants, first-aid clinics in the barrios and many other projects. The town is de facto ruled by the local unemployed committee, as the local municipal officials are marginalized.

The leaders, General Mosconi, Pepino, Hippie and Piquete, are local workers who have most forcefully articulated the demands of the community. These grass-roots leaders are the ones who are the least fearful of speaking out and making demands. The general populace is supportive but fearful of speaking out and losing their slot in the work plans. However, they become massively involved in supporting the road blockages and preventing the gendarmes from arresting their leaders.

The power of the unemployed in some working-class suburbs has led to quasi-liberated zones, where the power of mobilization neutralizes or is superior to that of local officials and is capable of challenging the state and federal regimes on the particular issues that are being raised. The emergence of a 'parallel economy', on a limited scale, in General Mosconi sustains popular support between struggles and offers a 'vision' of the capabilities of the unemployed to take command of their lives, neighbourhoods and livelihoods.

Beyond the local and immediate demands, the national meetings of unemployed in August and September of 2001 demanded an end to debt payments and austerity programs, the reversal of the neo-liberal model and the re-emergence of state-regulated and state-financed economic developments.

The most promising national organizational development is the convoking in August 2001 of two national meetings of unemployed groups from around the country (in Matanza and La Plata) on 5 September 2001. The meetings drew over 2000 delegates from dozens of unemployed, trade union, student, cultural and NGO groups. The purpose was to coordinate activities, share ideas and forge a national program and plan of struggle. The assembly of delegates in La Plata agreed to six immediate demands:

1   Derogation of the structural adjustment, the zero deficit policies and the judicial process against arrested and other activists.
2   The withdrawal of the austerity budget.
3   The extension and defence of the public employment schemes and food allocations to each unemployed worker over 16 years of age, the establishment of a massive register of unemployed under the control of the unemployed organizations meeting in the assembly.
4   One hundred pesos (peso=US$1.00) per hectare for small and medium-size farmers in order to seed their fields.
5   Prohibition of firings.
6   The immediate withdrawal of the gendarmes from the town of General Mosconi.

The Assembly convoked two nationwide road blockages in September to back up their demands. In addition to their immediate demands, the Assembly embraced five strategic goals:

1   Non-payment of the illegitimate and fraudulent foreign debt.
2   Public control of the pension funds.
3   Renationalization of the banks and strategic enterprises.
4   Forgiveness of the debts of small farmers and sustainable prices for their products.
5   Ousting of the hunger-provoking regimes and any reshuffle of politicians. The Assembly ended by calling for an active thirty-six hour general strike and a national committee to coordinate activities with the dissident trade union confederation – the CTA.

Social Alliances: Uneasy Allies

As the unemployed movement grew in numbers and capability for action, it attracted allies from university students, dissident trade unions, human rights groups and small leftist parties. The most numerous and significant tactical alliances were forged with the public employees unions (ATE) and with local teachers' unions. The *Madres de la Plaza de Mayo* gave moral support and mobilized its supporters, as did a number of leftist university student organizations.

Throughout the joint activities, especially with the trade unions, the unemployed movements jealously guarded their hard-won autonomy and freedom of action. The movements rejected the demagogic interventions by conventional politicos who sought to capitalize on the unemployed movement's growing power.

State Repression: General Mosconi and Salta

Early on, the De la Rua regime turned to violent repression to destroy the movement: five *piqueteros* were killed, dozens wounded by gunfire and thousands were arrested. The town of General Mosconi, where three piqueteros were killed, was taken over by hundreds of national gendarmes in the best style of the military dictatorship.

In order to impose the harsh austerity policies, including massive firings and a 12 per cent cut in salaries of public employees, measures, proposed by the IMF and supported by US and European private bankers, the regime criminalized collective action by the unemployed. The failure of the regime to stem the slide into economic depression, at the time of writing (2001) in its fourth year, and its pending debt default, only hardened its resolve to impose new austerity measures in the hope of attracting speculative funding from Wall Street and a new bail-out from the IMF.

The increasing militancy of the unemployed movements, evidenced in the expansion and frequency of mass road blockages, was the desperate response in the face of the regime's policy of replacing nutrition with coercion. As malnutrition spread, the workers' anger deepened as they watched trainloads of grain and beef shipped to export markets overseas.

Contradictions: New Challenges for the Unemployed Workers' Movement

The dynamic and unprecedented growth of the unemployed movement and its success using road blockages to paralyse the movement of commodities was accompanied by robust discussions and debates on how to proceed. Several basic issues arose within the movement debates.

Localism

The initial and continuing strength of the movements is based on their close ties to their communities, barrios and neighbours. Yet as the repression and cutbacks proceed it is evident to many movement activists that only collective action at the national level will provide the leverage to weaken state violence and secure concessions from the regime. Nevertheless, some of the leaders who have been most successful in consolidating popular participation resist and are distrustful of national meetings and organizations. The movement in General Mosconi is a case in point: they refused to formally participate in the two national meetings in September 2001.

Competing Groups

The decentralized origins of the movement have been a necessary and important element in promoting local initiatives and leadership and guarding the autonomy of the various movements. But in several cases political and personal differences have emerged which could undermine future unity of action. While most unemployed movements reject electoral politics, a few leaders have been offered a place on the lists of left parties, particularly the new formation called 'the Social Pole'. Other differences relate to the relationship with the established dissident trade unions. While few unemployed leaders would object to tactical cooperation, many are fearful that the CTA and ATE will eventually dominate the action and manipulate the movement to fit the moderate agenda of the progressive trade union officials. For example in one of the national days of action in August, under the influence of ATE, the *piqueteros* allowed alternative roads to be clear while they blocked main arteries. The purpose of this concession was to 'win over' middle-class commuters and as a good will gesture to the Minister of Labour. Many unemployed activists rejected the 'alternative routes' strategy as effectively undermining the purpose of road blockages and opening the door to the demoralization of the unemployed and the demise of the movement in favour of traditional trade union wheeling and dealing to secure the approval of electoral politicians.

Penetration by Politicians

The powerful thrust of the movement comes from its autonomy of action, its rejection of patronage–clientelistic politics. As its successful mobilization accelerated, conventional opportunistic politicos from the nominally 'opposition' parties (Peronist and other) attempted to take up some of the demands, offering to 'mediate' between the *piqueteros*, offering to secure jobs, gain a section of the movement, divide the movement and rebuild their depleted ranks. While the movement retains its power of convocation and capacity to mobilize against repression, it has successfully resisted the blandishments of these opportunistic demagogues. However, if the repression becomes more severe and its basic needs are not met, the stark choice will be either a further political radicalization, or the temptation to accept 'mediation' by the old political bosses.

Students: Allies and Dangers

The unemployed workers convoked the 7–8 September national encounter. In addition to the unemployed movements, a large number of student, cultural and even self-help groups turned up, diluting the social composition of the conference. The long and many times tedious presentations of the student orators did not add a great deal of clarity to the movement's future. While the delegates of the unemployed movements did maintain control and welcomed student and other participation, there was concern that they would introduce the usual ideological riffs that paralyse action. The genuine search among some student groups to 'articulate' with the unemployed movements was matched by a student harangue explaining to the Assembly why 'globalization inevitably condemned the movements to failure in this period'. The unemployed delegates unanimously rejected this type of intervention, and proceeded to outline a series of practical immediate and strategic demands. The Unemployed Movement of Lanus called attention to the pressures of unholy alliances following mass demonstrations and for the retention of leadership by autonomous unemployed workers' movements.

These contradictions of growth point to the new challenges that face the movement. The important point is not that there are problems, but that these are open assemblies at the local, regional and national level where the unemployed can debate and resolve these issues.

Conclusion

One of the debates about the declining power of the labour movement focuses on the issue of the proliferation of precarious work, the growth of the informal sector and the increase in the number of unemployed. When questioned, trade union leaders constantly cite the 'difficulty' of organizing the unemployed, their lack of leverage over the economic system, and their lack of interest in collective action. The massive growth of the organization of the unemployed in Argentina calls into question many of these assumptions and raises new questions. The experience in Argentina demonstrates that unemployed workers can be organized, will engage in collective action, possess leverage to paralyse the economic system, and are capable of negotiating and securing concessions in a manner that the organized labour unions have not been able to accomplish in recent years.

This suggests that the decline of labour has less to do with the nature of the unemployed and informal labour and more to do with the structure, approach and leadership of the trade unions. The unemployed movement organizes from the bottom up, in face-to-face recruitment in the barrios. The trade union bureaucrats ignore non-dues-paying workers, and send 'professionals' in to organize – and usually fail to gain the confidence of the unemployed. Second, the unemployed movement has a horizontal structure in which leaders and supporters come from the same class and discuss and debate as equals in open assemblies. The trade unions are vertical structures built around personal loyalties to the top bureaucrats many of whom draw salaries comparable to CEOs. The unemployed movements engage in sustained direct action and collectively negotiate demands in open assemblies. The trade union elites engage in symbolic protests and then negotiate with the State or the employers behind closed doors, reaching agreements that ignore workers' key concerns, and then 'sell' or impose the agreements onto the membership.

As a result, the unemployed leaders have the confidence and support of their constituents while the trade union bosses are seen with distrust if not as active collaborators with the austerity-minded state and the employers.

The problem then is the subjective and organizational nature of the trade unions, not the condition of the labour market.

The labour market, the large pool of unemployed, presents a challenge to the conventional way of top-down organizing, automatic dues check-off and formal organization. No trade union boss is willing to trudge through the muddy unpaved roads of shanty towns organizing, attending meetings in icy or sweltering improvised meeting places among crying children and women militants demanding food now, or unemployed young men bored by long-winded lectures on globalization and unemployment.

Few trade union leaders stand behind the barricades of burning tyres with slingshots blocking highways, and facing live ammunition. They prefer to secure a half-hour appointment in the offices of the Minister of Labour in order to form a tripartite committee to discuss how to cushion the austerity program and secure governability.

The fact is that almost all trade unions as they are organized today are only concerned with their electoral ties to the official parties and are totally irrelevant, if not a major obstacle, to organizing the unemployed.

Through the initiative and social inventiveness of the unemployed, via trial and error, they have found a way to secure leverage over the economic system by cutting the highways that link markets and production sites. The early success of the road blockages by unemployed petroleum workers in the ghost towns of Neuquen in 1996 has spread throughout the country.

Road blockages have become the generalized tactic of exploited and marginalized groups throughout Latin America. In Bolivia, tens of thousands of peasants and Indian communities have blocked highways demanding credit, infrastructure, freedom to grow coca and increased spending on health and education. Likewise in Ecuador massive street blockages protest the dollarization of the economy and the absence of public investments in the highlands. In Colombia, Brazil and Paraguay road blockages, marches and land occupations have been combined in pursuit of immediate demands as well as redistributive policies and an end to neo-liberalism and debt payments.

What all these groups have in common is that they are non-strategic groups in the economy acting on strategic areas of the economy. The export sectors, the banks, minerals and petroleum and certain manufacturing sectors are the principal foreign exchange earners (to pay the debt) and revenue and profit producers for the elite. Food is imported, as are manufactured intermediary and capital goods. From the perspective of the elite accumulation process, the activities of the peasants, unemployed, Indians, farmers and local commercial and small manufacturers are superfluous, expendable and irrelevant to the main activity – exports, financial transactions and imports of luxury goods. But these flows of goods and capital require free passage across roads to reach their markets. This is where the 'marginal groups' become strategic actors whose direct actions interfere with the elite circuits and disrupt the accumulation process. Road blockages of the unemployed are the functional equivalent of the industrial workers stopping the machines and production line: the former blocks the realization of profit, the latter, the creation of value. Mass organization outside the factory system demonstrates the viability of this strategy when it takes place outside of the electoral party – the bureaucratic trade union structure. Autonomous organization is the key in Argentina and the rest of Latin America. Experience demonstrates that the new mass movements – unemployed workers, peasants, Indians – can sustain struggles, resist violent repression and secure temporary and immediate concessions.

Alliances between workers who have occupied factories and put them to work, and the unemployed workers' movement is a promising development since 2002. The formation of a national coordinating committee of unemployed organizations in Argentina and similar national organizations among the peasants and small farmers throughout Latin America demonstrates that local movements can become national and potentially can confront the State.

Many questions remain unanswered. Is it possible for these new movements to unify into a national political force and transform state power? Can alliances be forged with employed urban-industrial workers and employees and downwardly mobile middle class to create a power block to transform the economy? Can local assemblies become the basis for a new assembly-based socialism?

In Argentina, the success of the unemployed workers' movement has opened a new perspective for advancing the struggle in the face of a prolonged and deepening depression. With the advance of similar direct action movements growing throughout Latin America it is not difficult to imagine the convergence of these 'marginal' classes into a formidable challenge to the US empire and its local collaborators.

Chapter 10

Non-governmental Organizations in a Conjuncture of Conflict and War Psychosis

Introduction

The 11 September 2001 attack on the World Trade Centre in New York and the Pentagon in Washington and the ramifications define a new conjuncture for social movements and non-government organizations (NGOs). The global context preceding September 11 is important in understanding Washington's reaction afterwards and the effects that both have on the perspectives and the role NGOs can play in global politics.

Prior to September 11, Washington's international position showed clear signs of weakening. The anti-globalization mass movements from Seattle to Genoa were creating greater obstacles to the 'free market agenda'. Washington's rejection of the Kyoto protocol on global warming, its unilateral renunciation of the ABM (missile treaty) and its failure to sign the Biological and Toxic Weapons Convention isolated it from the rest of the international community. In the Middle East, Iraq was breaking out of the US-imposed boycott, becoming an active member of OPEC, and increasing ties with Arab neighbours. Iran has economic relations with Japan, Russia, the EU and most of the rest of the countries in the world contrary to the US boycott. In Latin America, formidable social movements in Colombia, Brazil, Argentina and Ecuador challenged the neo-liberal model. The deepening recession in the US and Europe profoundly affected the 'export model' in Mexico, Central America and the rest of Latin America and Asia. Moreover, the recession within the US was leading to massive job losses and bankruptcies, provoking a greater volatility in the stock market, already shaken by the collapse of the information technology speculative bubble.

In short, US global hegemony was deteriorating, the internal foundations were weakening and discontent was rising – before September 11.

Post September 11

The immediate aftermath of the trauma of September 11 was, at the governmental level, a concerted effort at world mobilization based on a discourse of war. The key phrase came from President Bush: 'Countries have to choose, you are with us or with the terrorists.' The effect of this discourse was to mobilize predictable NATO followers like Prime Minister Blair of the UK, Berlusconi of Italy and President Aznar of Spain. Other NATO countries entered the 'alliance' with some hesitation. While most of the rest of the world condemned the terrorist attack and expressed sympathy with the victims, very few countries were eager to join an open-ended worldwide military campaign against loosely defined terrorists and nations which provide havens for terrorists. Only by tactically specifying the enemy to a narrow set of targets (Osama bin Laden and the Taliban) was Washington able to secure minimum cooperation within the Middle East and Central Asia. But Washington has a wider agenda: war against Europe and Japan's principal oil suppliers in the Middle-East – namely Iraq and Iran.

The key to President Bush's worldwide anti-terrorism campaign is to reverse the decline of US global hegemony. The aim is to force Europe to submit to US leadership, to secure the total obedience of the Arab rulers in the Middle-East and to encourage client rulers in Asia and Latin America to increase their repressive capacities against political opposition to the neo-liberal model and US hegemony.

George Bush junior seeks to recreate a new world order that his father, George Bush senior, tried to project after the Gulf War and which deteriorated shortly thereafter. After the Gulf War emergency, the competitive interests of Europe and Japan came into conflict with US hegemony, as did the emergence of social movements, North and South. It is likely that, once the initial war psychosis dies off, divisions and rivalries will reappear with even greater virulence than in the early 1990s. The extension of the war beyond Afghanistan, worldwide recession and Washington's attempt to gain economic advantage from its leadership of the wartime coalition could easily provoke divisions.

Nevertheless, in the short run, the war mobilization involves a worldwide socio-political offensive to reverse the advances of the late 1990s. This offensive has several common characteristics:

- increasing repressive legislation, curtailing democratic freedoms and widening police power
- attempts to reverse the recession via 'military Keysianism' with higher military spending and billion dollar subsidies to the 'adversely affected' (airlines, tourism, and so on)
- restoration of US hegemony via military dominance – 'leadership' – and strengthening client regimes
- silencing anti-globalization movements by refocusing world attention from the evils of multinational corporations to international terrorism
- reversing US isolation because of its unilateral rejection of international agreements on peace and the environment – the Kyoto Agreement on greenhouse gases; the antiballistic missile agreement; the protocol banning biological warfare; the UN resolution on an International Human Rights tribunal; the UN protocol against the use of land mines.

The anti-terrorist alliance strengthens US global leadership since power of decision is vested exclusively in Washington. The 'alliance' is an association of followers with no influence on tactics or strategy. Even NATO is excluded from any operational influence. In effect, the anti-terrorist alliance is another manifestation of unilateral state action. The imperial use of anti-terrorism extends far beyond Afghanistan; the term as applied by Washington is so loosely interpreted as to apply to any country in which resistance fighters are located, any movement engaged in social transformation, any supporters of movements, including NGOs.

The Coordinator for Terrorism for the US State Department, Francis Taylor, stated: 'My office is working with different agencies of the government in order to design an anti-terrorist strategy for Colombia and other Andean countries. This strategy is designed to complement Plan Colombia ... and the Andean Regional Initiative.' Taylor went on to state: 'Today, the most dangerous international terrorist group in this hemisphere is the FARC.' The State Department centred the second part of its anti-terrorist strategy (after the Middle East) as 'an offensive against terrorism in the Americas'. The US Congress approved the appropriation of an additional US$730 million 'for war against terrorism ... in the region'.

Imperialism today is firmly anchored in the state – the imperial state, which intervenes in the world and domestic economy to subsidize, promote and protect its multinational corporations as well as to organize continuing military attacks to destroy challenges to its domination. Today more than ever, the imperial state is the centrepiece of empire and the driving force for multinational capital expansion.

Acting in concert, the imperial state and multinational corporations have polarized the world along class, racial, gender, national and regional lines. Imperial ideology attempts to obscure this division by polarizing the world between democracy (empire) and terrorism in order to consolidate imperial power. This polarization has also entered into the world of NGOs.

The Polarization of Non-government Organizations

NGOs have multiplied by the tens of thousands over the past decade, reflecting a variety of political and social perspectives, sources of funding and political allegiances. The majority of the NGOs and the 'richest' in funding are open collaborators with the Euro-American states and local neo-liberal regimes, actively working against public/social ownership. Nevertheless, in recent years a growing number of NGOs have played an active role in the anti-globalization, anti-racist and anti-war movements that have taken place from Seattle to South Africa.

The most significant fact in the world of NGOs is their polarization or tripolar nature. To simplify, NGOs can be divided into three groups that tend to coincide with their levels of funding.

1   NGOs that are active promoters of neo-liberalism, working with large sums from the World Bank, USAID, and other international and state funding agencies on a 'subcontracted' basis to undermine national comprehensive welfare institutions.

2 Reformist NGOs that receive middle-range funding from private social democratic foundations and progressive local or regional governments to fund ameliorative projects and to correct the excesses of the free market. The reformists try to 'reform' the WTO, IMF and World Bank and regulate capital.
3 Radical NGOs are basically involved in the anti-globalization, anti-racist, anti-sexist and solidarity movements. Among the radical NGOs there are differences in tactics (civil disobedience, direct action) goals (anti-capitalist, anti-corporate, anti-speculative capital) and alternatives (communitarian, deep ecology, socialist, self-management).

The polarization of NGOs can first and foremost be seen in the responses to major events like the Durban Conference. The radical NGOs denounced Israel as a racist country, while the reformists tried to oppose racism without naming Israel and the neo-liberal NGOs supported Washington or were silent.

A second area of differentiation can be seen in the major demonstrations, from Seattle to Genoa, where the radical NGOs call for the abolition of the IMF, the World Bank and the World Trade Organization, while the reformists only pursue greater regulation of speculative capital (the Tobin tax), debt forgiveness, more responsiveness to poverty needs and internal reform to make the IFIs more 'responsive' to popular welfare and the environment.

A third area of differentiation is between those NGOs (neo-liberal and reformists) who seek to collaborate with imperial (global) institutions and those that collaborate with popular mass movements. The 'institutionalists' conceive of 'divisions' within the institutions, and then take it upon themselves to reason with bankers and officials to demonstrate how big business interests and environmental/welfare reforms are compatible with profits and stability. The movement-oriented radical NGOs believe that basic structural changes from below – redistributing power, property, and income – are necessary to achieve sustainable development and social justice.

Up to now, the lessons are clear: the neo-liberal NGOs have only succeeded in coopting local leaders, while the neo-liberal economic model has collapsed in crisis, increasing the number of poor and destitute. The reformist and radical NGOs have grown and their actions have multiplied; the size of the anti-globalization movement has grown – while the tensions within the movements have increased. In the face of deepening polarization and economic crisis in the world, the reformist NGOs are losing ground as interlocutors, as the imperial powers of Brussels and Washington turn toward war against the Third World and attack living standards in the North.

Non-government Organizations: Rethinking Policies and Structures

In the face of this deepening polarization between empire and the popular movements, both North and South, the NGOs must rethink their internal organization, their relations to mass movements and their funding policies. Most reformist and radical NGOs are basically cadre organizations made up of professional staff and volunteers who 'mobilize people'. While many of the causes are just, the structures are elitist. Today the most promising and dynamic movements – the unemployed workers' movement in Argentina, the MST in Brazil, the cocaleros of Bolivia, the Zapatistas in Mexico – are based on popular assemblies and consultation, direct democracy. There is a contradiction in style and substance between the movements and the NGOs in terms of their conceptions of struggle and organization. To resolve this contradiction, which has important tactical and strategic consequences, the NGOs must democratize their structures, and convert to forms of organization compatible with their movement partners.

The first area that NGOs need to consider is funding. In large part, the structures and orientation of the NGOs are shaped by their funding sources. The more dependent they are on institutional financial support, rather than voluntary funding, the more they retain a hierarchical structure. The greater the degree to which a NGO approximates a movement, the more likely it is that it will depend on popular/voluntary contributions. Institutional funding involves limits on the political agenda, social demands and tactical activity. Dependence on voluntary contributions means greater engagement with the people in struggle and responsiveness to their demands along with greater political education.

The second area in which the polarization on a global scale requires NGOs to rethink their activity is in terms of strategies. In the past, progressive (radical and reformist) NGOs focused on micro-projects (in Central America and elsewhere) and more recently on anti-globalization mobilizations. While the micro-projects improved some communities, it did not reverse the neo-liberal assaults on living standards and the takeover, via privatization, by foreign and domestic capital of the national wealth. The shift toward anti-globalization activity was a step forward, in so far as the progressive NGOs recognized some of the major political-economic forces attacking the poor. However, several new problems emerged. First, the anti-globalization ideology has obscured the centrality of the imperial states and their drive for world domination – exaggerating the autonomy of the IFIs and the MNCs. Second, the anti-globalization activities focus largely on occasional dramatic events (Genoa, Davos, Melbourne, Prague) while doing less in terms of day-to-day organization and supporting struggles. The question is not one of eliminating the international confrontations, but combining them with mass regional and national struggles against firings, unemployment, intensification of exploitation, and so on.

The third area for rethinking involves sponsorship and collaboration with private enterprises, international institutions and governments. The NGOs have been involved in a lengthy debate on these issues. The debates have focused on a cost-benefit assessment of accepting financial aid and sponsorship from this or that institution. For example, many NGOs discuss whether the compromises on programs and activities are worth the financial contributions and 'legitimate' sponsorship. Some NGO leaders have become experts in the double discourse of presenting a moderate image and securing substantial financing for militant solidarity work. Be that as it may, the larger historic record demonstrates that long-term, large-scale association with the 'power structure' leads to the corruption of NGO leaders, and the conversion of the NGOs into an adjunct of the neo-liberal project.

A cost–benefit analysis is too narrow a framework in which to evaluate NGO funding and alliances, because it fails to take account of the structure of power and the historical trajectory. Tactical compromises become strategic subordination where principles are sacrificed to maintain a burgeoning and expensive bureaucracy and infrastructure. What is to be done? The fundamental point of departure is a class commitment, a program deeply rooted in principles, a clear ideology and a transition from a cadre organization to a social movement that engages in solidarity struggles overseas and mass struggles at home.

Today both President Bush and Osama bin Laden have tried to polarize the world, the former between war and terrorism, the latter between empire and religion (Islam). The role of NGOs is to reject this polarization and develop alternatives to empire and fundamentalism that affirm the self-determination of people and secular states with comprehensive social welfare programs.

Before 7 October 2001, when Washington launched its air war against Afghanistan, the progressive NGOs (both reformist and radical) confronted the socio-economic and political polarization between the Euro-American empire and the Third World. Today that polarization includes the empire's war against the Third World: the first phase, according to the Bush regime was the war against Afghanistan. Phase two was the war against Iraq, to be followed by other wars. The war against Afghanistan is part of a long-term, large-scale offensive to regain US global hegemony: the empire is engaged in salami tactics slicing off each independent regime that does not subordinate itself to the Euro-American alliance.

One of the most resounding victories of the empire was its ideological victory over sectors of the left and progressive NGOs, when the latter supported the NATO bombing and invasion of Yugoslavia, the Kosovo Liberation Army (KLA) terrorists in Kosova, the fundamentalists in Bosnia and the KLA-directed invasion of Macedonia. In each instance the empire manipulated democratic symbols ('minority rights') and humanitarian rhetoric to expand its sphere of influence. Many NGOs became the tools of empire, receiving millions of dollars in exchange for their pro-imperial, humanitarian services. The imperial war logic from Iraq to Yugoslavia to Afghanistan to Iraq, from the Middle East to the Balkans to Southern Asia to the Middle East, has led to the new colonization. NATO military bases are present in occupied Kosova, Bosnia and Macedonia. A puppet regime is in place in Afghanistan and a US military government in Iraq. New wars are planned for the Middle East and beyond, under an open-ended definition of the war against terrorism. Military threats are directed against countries that refuse to subordinate themselves to the empire's military logic (refuse to 'join the alliance'). The US Marines replace the functionaries of the IMF as the emissaries of conquest. In times of economic crisis, the ruling classes deflect popular discontent and anger to external enemies; the popular movements and progressive NGOs must oppose imperial wars and turn attention to the internal oppressors. NGOs must link the anti-globalization struggle to the anti-war struggle and the anti-recession movements.

The Movement Runs on Five Legs

The challenge for the NGOs today is to build movements that elaborate alternatives to five interrelated problems:

1 war and terrorism
2 militarization and repression
3 deepening economic recession and global crises of markets
4 collapse of export strategies and vulnerability of neo-liberal regimes
5 mass unemployment and spread of poverty north and south.

Imperial wars today are 'total wars', in which all civilians and the most elemental conditions for survival (water, electricity, food, and so on) are objects of military destruction. Total war contains the seeds of genocide: whole people, as in Afghanistan, flee mass destruction and face imminent starvation; war-induced deaths in Afghanistan exceed those in New York and Washington in geometrical proportion. Police-state, anti-democratic legislation is rushed through Congress and parliaments without debate, abrogating basic democratic rights in the name of security, but in reality strengthening the repressive powers of the state to limit democratic popular opposition.

War and repression displace social-economic reform as responses to the deepening economic crisis. Employers and multinationals take advantage of the war psychosis to fire millions of workers, increase temporary workers, intensify exploitation and lay exorbitant financial claims on the state for subsidies.

Crisis in the North is catastrophic in the South. The infamous neo-liberal 'export strategies' in the Third World collapse with the decline of Euro-American markets. Further structural adjustments provoke major confrontations. Basic imports are unaffordable, debts cannot be paid, the export sectors face bankruptcy, the neo-liberal state has no resources: vulnerability is everywhere, capitalist solutions are nowhere to be found. Meanwhile, war spending, subsidies for bankrupt multinationals and declining markets lead to increasing unemployment in the US and Europe.

This is a time of deepening problems, but also great challenges and opportunities to pose basic questions and radical alternatives.

Perspectives and Strategies: Short and Medium Term

In the short term we face a right-wing offensive headed by the US-Euro War Alliance backed by powerful multinationals and police military forces. This offensive, through the mass media that have openly accepted to be a mouthpiece of the War Alliance, has secured the temporary supporter passivity of the majority of the population in North America and Europe, but not in the Middle East or many other areas of the Third World.

Today, particularly in the US and the EU, there is a war psychosis manipulated by the state and amplified and transmitted by the mass media. In the short run, this has led to the ascendancy of an irrational unanimity in which sectors of public opinion have been led to believe that dissent or criticism of the war is a form of 'collaboration' with terrorism. In the US the directors of the mass media have been told by the state not to publish or announce bin Laden's speeches or to relate Taliban speeches without identifying them as terrorist propaganda. There was probably no need for direct state intervention as the self-censorship of the media and its wholehearted support of the war made state control unnecessary.

In this context popular social movements and progressive NGOs have a vital educational role to play in countering state propaganda and its intellectual exponents in the mass media. It is through systematic critiques of the war propaganda and its distortions that an informed public opinion, particularly in the popular classes, can be mobilized to oppose the war and the accompanying injustices and insecurities.

Political education can follow four lines of counter-attack. The first is to emphasize the blatant inconsistencies and contradictions of the war message. For example, the idea that this is a humanitarian war when millions of Afghan people are displaced by the carpet bombing and are experiencing mass hunger, thirst and destruction of basic necessities (electricity, water, food, transport, and so on); the idea that state violence will uproot terrorism instead of engendering a multiplying and deepening hatred and violent retaliation. War will create a spiral of violence and the logic of prolonged and extended wars will multiply the attacks on US and EU civilians. Only through changes in policy toward the political sources of discontent in the Middle East and Gulf States (Palestine, Iraq, for example) can the conflict be minimized and the levels of violence reduced.

The second line of political education requires an exposé of the way in which socially reactionary forces in the state and in the class structure are taking advantage of the self-created 'war crisis' to further their interests at the expense of the majority of working people. This is a war, like many previous wars, where the many sacrifice and the few benefit. Already social spending in the US is being reduced and military expenditure is soaring. Multinational corporations are firing millions of workers and receiving huge subsidies for so-called 'war damage', while unemployment benefits are being denied. The state calls for 'national unity' are being manipulated to obscure the class divisions and injustices – who is benefiting and who is losing from the 'war on terrorism'. A familiar sight in the US is one of fired workers driving home with a flag flying from their antennas while their corporate bosses sit down with state officials to negotiate new subsidies. The key point is that the economic crisis preceded the conflict, and the war gave the corporations a 'legitimate' pretext to massively 'restructure' their enterprises in order to lower costs and increase profits. By linking socio-economic losses to the war it is possible to reach millions of working people with a peace and social justice program.

The third line of political education can focus on the major divisions between Western Europe and the US. One particularly explosive conflict is over Washington's project to widen the war to include Iraq, Iran and Syria. The EU's principal source of petroleum is the Middle East, and new wars will lead to a catastrophic reduction of oil supply and a geometric increase in the price of oil, that could lead to a major depression. Likewise, US clients, particularly in Saudi Arabia, Egypt, Pakistan and elsewhere, are under enormous pressure from below and any further push from the US to support the current war in Iraq or an extended war in neighbouring countries could lead to national uprisings. The war against Iraq has already narrowed support for the US, in comparison to the broad international sympathy with the victims in New York and Washington. Today (February 2003) the great majority of the people in Europe, Asia and Latin America oppose Washington's war against Iraq. Even in the US a majority of public opinion was against a war lacking European support.

Fourth, many people around the world reject Bush's (and bin Laden's) dichotomous view of the world ('either you are for us – and the war – or you are against us'). A majority of moderates opposed the US bypassing the United Nations and launching its bombers against Iraq. Many people think that the US and EU should take up the UN weapons inspectors demand for more time. Most people do not believe the US has provided evidence of Iraqui possession of weapons of mass destruction.

Activism: Engaging the Public

There are three possible axes of political action in this conjuncture. The first involves taking an 'indirect approach' and mobilizing communities, trade unionists and neighbourhoods against the socio-economic consequences of the deepening economic recession (firings/unemployment) and the elite benefits from the 'war crisis' at the national/international level. The decisions by multinational executives to fire workers because of 'world market conditions' are a powerful argument against the export growth strategies and globalization. Linking local social adversity to globalization and war is important in developing movement activity in this conjuncture.

The second axis involves focusing on the weakest link in the so-called War Alliance: Israeli violence and dispossession of the Palestinians. Outside of the US most commentators recognize that the Israeli war against the Palestinians is the detonator of the current crisis. The genocidal policies of the ultra-rightist Sharon regime have united the whole Arab world, most of European opinion and, outside of the Jewish pro-Israeli lobby in the US, sectors of public opinion. Even President Bush and US Secretary of State Powell have paid lip service to the idea of a Palestinian state. The political point is that focusing on Israeli intransigence can favourably polarize public opinion against the war and become the starting point to reactivate the anti-globalization movement.

The third area for activities is around the humanitarian disasters caused by wars in Afghanistan, Iraq and Colombia. According to the UN, seven million Iraquis face death due to war and hunger because of the war, a figure comparable to the Holocaust. This issue has moved millions to pressure for an end to the war.

The 'war on terrorism' has already turned into an escalation in the war against popular insurgent forces in Latin America. The head of the US Drug Enforcement

Agency (DEA) in Mexico declared that the Zapatesta Army of National Liberation (EZLN) is a 'terrorist' organization. A spokesman for the State Department has declared a massive increase of US$700 million for 2001–2002 and additional military personnel to fight 'FARC terrorism'. The human casualties of these new wars are grotesque: between 1 and 15 October the Colombian military backed paramilitary killed 150 peasants and workers, ending the year with 3000 killings. The issue of *state* terrorism is graphically illustrated as the real content of our definition as the war against terrorism.

An international tribunal on the humanitarian catastrophe in Afghanistan, led by international notables, could focus world attention and educate public opinion on the real meaning of the war. In summary, progressive NGOs should link their anti-globalization strategies to the deepening internal economic crisis and develop programmatic alternatives based on socializing production, redistributing income and deepening internal markets based on increased social expenditures. NGOs should link their support for humanitarian relief with the anti-war movement and the catastrophic economic consequences for Europe resulting from an extension of the war to other Middle Eastern and Gulf countries. International alliances based on international crises require the building of rank and file organizations in each barrio, municipality and region. The NGOs should learn the lessons from direct action movements like the MST in Brazil and the unemployed workers' movement in Argentina, who apply non-violent road pickets and strategic pressures in production and distribution.

Conclusion

It is clear that a right-wing offensive is underway on a world scale: so-called 'security measures' are strengthening the arbitrary powers of the state at the expense of individual freedoms and collective social rights. It is also clear that a growing movement of resistance is emerging, particularly in the Muslim countries and to a considerable degree in Europe (Italy, England, France). The very extremism of President Bush's total war strategy is having a boomerang effect: the prolongation of the war and the mounting casualties is increasing the number of voices from the humanitarian, human rights groups and citizens in Muslim countries. The right-wing offensive can be turned against itself. As fears and insecurities multiply, as the war erodes the economy and as the number of people adversely affected multiplies, these 'mass casualties' in the domestic economies of the EU and even the US can become potential recruits for social movements. The international war alliance is likely to lead to a counter-alliance for peace and opposition to militarism. Repressive legislation can heighten democratic sensibilities; authoritarianism breeds pro-democracy movements.

Polarities and forced choices (war or terrorism) can bounce back, isolating their proponents before their extreme formulations. The movements must redefine polarities: globalization and war, or democracy, self-determination, humane assistance to the victims of war and jobs for the unemployed. The vast majority of people refuse to choose between imperial wars and fundamentalist terror. Most will choose the alternative of secular, peaceful nations in which people are free to choose the social system which most fulfils their lives. Today the greatest threat to humanity is unilateralism – the decision of Washington to go to war, to bomb a country into the 'stone age', to reject Kyoto, missile controls, the abolition of land mines, international courts of justice and UN decisions which demand that Israel withdraw from the occupied territories. Unilateralism today means militarism. In the face of the world economic crisis and heightened competition, unilateralism means intensified struggle to expand control over vital resources and markets, via non-economic methods.

Unilateralism undermines any pretence of building durable alliances. Militarism alienates those who pay the cost of war: the majority of humankind. Unilateralism forces allies into opposition; economic crisis forces a re-evaluation of priorities, models, and markets – challenging neo-liberal orthodoxy. Tactically it is imperative to seek the broadest possible strategic alliance against unilateralism, militarism and neo-liberalism.

From the First and Second World Wars, and the Algerian and Vietnam Wars, history teaches us that deprivation, unequal sacrifice and the political and social cost of war undermine the initial unanimity and heighten resistance. As opposition grows from below, vertical and horizontal cleavages deepen and the imperial arrogance of a 'new world order' crumbles, while opportunities open for transforming the world and the eternal hopes for peace and justice become the programmatic bases for new socio-political movements. To be part of the solution and not part of the problem, progressive NGOs must draw a clear line of distinction between themselves and the millionaire NGOs, like Foster Parent Plan which collects US$300 million a year, MISEREOR US$214 million a year, World Vision US$500 million, and CARE with US$50 million budgets. These millionaire agencies collaborate with Euro-American imperialism and are funded to undermine social movements via class collaborationist 'community' and 'family development'. Today the foundations of multinational corporations, the World Bank and the Euro-American empires invest over US$7 billion for NGOs to undermine comprehensive public development and antisystemic movements. Progressive NGOs can only engage in popular struggles to oppose war and resist globalization by rejecting funding from these sources that limit their commitments. All funding from the power structure carries 'strings' – limits in struggles, programs, tactics and strategy. To think otherwise is self-delusive. To truly become an independent force, progressive NGOs must go to their roots, and win the allegiance of their people in order to become self-financing and live and work on voluntary donations from the people they purport to service.

This is not an easy time for NGOs or for the popular movements – but times change, reaction oversteps boundaries; people struggle out of necessity. I believe that there is a powerful resistance movement that reaches from the countryside and urban slums of Latin America, Asia and Africa to the streets, cities and anti-globalization movements of Europe and America. We must seize our opportunities and advance and reject the siren calls of defeat, death, destruction and demoralization.

Chapter 11

On Revolutionary Politics

Introduction

To understand the present and future of revolutionary politics requires an historical analysis of the previous half-century. An historical survey of the political left is a complex project, recognizing the uneven development of struggles in different continents, the contradictory tendencies, the achievements and limitations, the short- and long-term legacies, the relationship between economics and politics (the impact of growth or crisis on revolution), in a word, a nuanced analysis that defies intellectual fiats which pretend to define 'world processes' via economistic and ethnocentric views.

Intellectuals, including academics, are sharply divided across generations between those who have in many ways embraced, however critically, neo-liberalism or have prostrated themselves before 'the most successful ideology in world history' and its 'coherent and systematic vision', and those who have been actively writing, struggling and building alternatives, both socialist and others.[1] The role of intellectuals in the process of social transformation is complex and significant, but never decisive. They have more often reflected shifts in power between classes than defined 'independent' and 'realistic' positions as they sometimes, in a self-delusionary fashion, claim. Historically, the great mass of intellectuals have, at best, sided with democratic and nationalist movements, against colonial, dictatorial or fascist regimes. Their support for social revolutionary movements and events has been transitory, contradictory and limited. The bulk of the Russian intelligentsia was opposed to the Russian October Revolution, as was the Chinese, Vietnamese and Cuban, as these revolutions turned toward egalitarian policies and confronted US imperialist blockades.

During periods of counter-revolutionary ascendancy, following temporary or historic defeats, many of the former radical intellectuals revert to their 'class origins', pursuing private advance, discovering the virtues of right-wing ideologies (spiritualism as in Russia between 1906 and 1910) and converting their sense of private despair and isolation into a doctrine of the invincibility and irreversibility of the dominant right. Concomitant with their prostration before the power, realism and eloquence of the right is their denigration of the left, its defeats, mistakes, failures, delusions and self-deceptions (Anderson, 2000: 9, 12, 15, 19, 24). From this 'repentant' posture emerges what C. Wright Mills called 'crack-pot realism', a kind of theorizing that reifies a particular one-dimensional configuration of contemporary power as the reality (Mills, 1956) and the historical defeat of the left as the starting point for new political thinking.

This kind of pseudo-theorizing of past, present and future developments of the left lacks any historical depth. Through the lens of lost youthful enthusiasm and middle-age intellectual impotence, emerges a contemporary view of a barren left-wing horizon devoid of any redeeming features, except the brave light emanating from the intellectual cronies of historical defeatism. This chapter argues that the view of the leftist past is much more complex and contradictory than the picture of 1950s' conformity, the revolutionary upsurge of the 1960s–1970s and the 1980–2000 defeat and dissolution (Anderson, 2000: 6–11).[2] I argue that the cultural and ideological forces in play in these periods had counterpoints and reflected contradictory political realities, which, in turn, played a role in defining the future direction of the left. A critical revaluation of the past and its relation to the left today sets the stage for a systematic understanding of the ascendancy and contradictions of Euro-American imperialism, its limitations and the radical and revolutionary challenges confronting it, both externally and internally.

An analysis of the contemporary context requires a principled analysis of the objective and subjective realities, one which resists the temptation to magnify the current configuration of power and minimize the left in a kind of self-flagellation to expiate the excessive exuberance of the past (a kind of *mea culpa*). This is important in pre-empting any pretence for moving further right or toward a kind of apolitical or arcane self-indulgent intellectualism.[3]

Historical Survey: The 1950s and 1960s

The uneven development of left politics between North and South was never sharper than in the 1950s: in Africa, Asia and Latin America major leftist eruptions took place. World-historical struggles took place in Algeria, Indo-China, Cuba, Korea (among other countries) involving millions of revolutionary fighters, confronting Euro-American imperialism and their neo-colonial clients. In the US and the UK this was a period of relative 'quiescence', but it is a monstrous distortion to refer to the 1950s as a period of 'conformity' (Anderson, 2000: 7). Even in Europe, in Italy, France, Greece (despite the defeat in the Civil War) and Yugoslavia, powerful mass Communist parties engaged in class politics (except in regard to the anti-colonial struggle). Even in Eastern Europe, contradictory workers' revolts occurred in East Germany, Poland and Hungary and a critical underground cinema burst on the scene. Only blind Eurocentrism would understate the importance of the 1950s struggle to highlight the 1960s resurgence of the left in the US and the UK. The interconnectedness of these struggles (the extra-parliamentary action against the Algerian War in the early 1960s) created the atmosphere for the uprisings in the late 1960s as the early victories of the Vietnamese in the 1950s set the stage for the emergence of the anti-Vietnam War movement in the US.

Historical materialism describes the interconnection of political processes across time and place; it has nothing to do with anecdotal accounts that pick and choose 'facts' to fit a conservative mood. The theoretical point is that the uneven development of left politics across space and time defies political fiats reflecting particular conjunctures in specific regions. Methodologically, the development of mass struggles without theoreticians (at least without Anglo-American name recognition) does not lessen their significance as history-defining movements, as Sartre (1961) and Sweezy and Huberman (1960) later recognized during their visits to Cuba in the early 1960s.

From the Marxist perspective, the fact that revolutionary struggles emerged in countries where the general level of the 'forces of production' was low, but the level of exploitative social relations was high strengthened theoretical perspectives which looked at human agency as central, discrediting the mechanistic 'forces of production' argument used by the European Social Democrats and Communists to justify their active or passive pro-colonialist policies (later theorized by Bill Warren in NLR/Verso (1990) and, much later, not surprisingly reaffirmed by Anderson (2000).[4] If the 1950s was not a period of worldwide conformity, neither was the 1960s, in all of its manifestations, an age of uniform revolutionary upheaval.

Although there was clearly an upsurge of mass struggles in North America, Europe and regions of the Third World, during the 1960s important reversals took place in important countries and there were severe contradictions and conflicting tendencies within the mass movements. Theoretically, the results were a positive revaluation and creative development of Marxist thought and its extension into new areas of intellectual work and new problem areas.

The robust activity of rural workers and peasant-based guerrilla and social movements in Indo-China, Cuba and other countries led a few Marxists to revaluate the role of the peasantry and rural struggle in their theories of revolution (Wolfe, 1969). Likewise, the bloody Euro-American imperial interventions in Cuba, Indo-China, the Congo and elsewhere forced some Western Marxists to put imperialism back into their analysis. New non-Western theorists–activists like Fanon, Cabral and Guevara were read and influenced Euro-American militants and not an insignificant group of Western intellectuals. The negative side of this 'intellectual exchange' was the influence that some Western Marxists had on the struggles North and South. Regis Debray's book *Revolution in the Revolution*, with its ill-informed, distorted theorization of the Cuban Revolution and his militarist–elitist prescriptions took a heavy toll on the revolutionary left in Latin America (Debray, 1967). His later deluded and aborted attempt to join Che Guevara's guerrilla movement led to his capture and interrogation which, in turn, led to his informing on the location of the guerrillas and their subsequent decimation. Debray was then freed and returned to later become an advisor to the neo-liberal Mitterrand regime, an apologist for France's nuclear bomb, and a self-proclaimed French chauvinist. This did not prevent him from remaining a highly respected intellectual in some sectors of the Anglo-American left, on the basis of some banal rumination on the mass media and rather arrogant interview with Subcommandante Marcos of the Zapatistas (Anderson, 2000: 18).[5] If Debray was emblematic of the negative influences of the European left's influence on the Third World, Althussar and his followers elaborated a theoretical artifice devoid of any operational meaning: a set of abstract propositions of elegant deductive logic and irrelevant to any practical struggles or empirical reality (Althusser, 1970). E.P. Thompson,

Poulantzas and Miliband engaged in theoretical debates which contributed to broadening the understanding of the 'political' and 'cultural' spheres, while ignoring the problem of imperialism, particularly the imperial state. Thompson, in a fit of ethnocentric amnesia, denigrated the significance of the imperial-Third World struggles as the greatest source of threats of nuclear war. For Thompson, the threat of nuclear war resided in the Cold War between NATO and the USSR (Thompson, 1983). He maintained his Eurocentric views despite published accounts that revealed that the greatest threats of nuclear war occurred during the US blockade of Cuba in 1962, during the early stages of the Korean War and in Indo-China in 1954 and during the late 1960s. When I published an essay for Spokesman (edited by Ken Coates) critiquing Thompson's thesis, he chose not to reply (Petras and Morley, 1983–84: 105–107). Reading the Miliband–Poulantzas debates on the capitalist state, one would never know that the major ideological/economic resources and institutions of the US 'capitalist state' were engaged in a major imperialist war. The 1960s witnessed a great deal of intellectual creativity, with significant political and intellectual limitations.

The massive anti-war movements and urban black insurrections and civil rights movements in the US, and, more significantly, the student–worker uprising in France and Italy, raised fundamental political questions, and, in the latter countries, the issues of state power. The resurgence of the left put closure to the 'end of ideology' ideologues like Daniel Bell, the pessimistic assessments of radical 'power elite' theorists like C. Wright Mills and the proponents of 'The American Century' like *Time*'s Henry Luce. Likewise, the resurgent left marginalized and discredited social democratic ideologues who had thrown in their lot with Western imperialism in the name of 'democratic values'.[6] Curiously enough, many of these discredited ideas, like the unprecedented and total dominance of the US, the absence of opposition and the demise of leftist ideology were recently recycled in Perry Anderson's ironically titled article, 'Renewals' (2000).

A new generation of Marxist and new left writers and activists emerged who linked up with the best of the older generation of intellectual-activists: Lelio Basso, Ernest Mandel, Jean-Paul Sartre, Herbert Marcuse, Bettleheim, Hal Draper, Paul Sweezy, E.P. Thompson, to name a few. The 1960s' left was multifaceted, even as publicists and later historians saw, and described a single dimension: what was dubbed the 'new left', the ephemeral rock celebrities and the drugged-up snorting apolitical mystics and poets.[7] In reality, the political and cultural sphere of 1960s' left was a rich mosaic of contradictory and conflicting movements. In the US, for example, a major anti-war mobilization committee was strongly influenced by Trotskyists, particularly in New York City; the anti-racist campaigns in the San Francisco Bay area were influenced by the Communist youth group, the W.E.B. DuBois Club. The subsequent attempt to equate the 1960s' left with the 'new left' and the latter with the Students for a Democratic Society (SDS) was largely a self-serving exercise by former members of the SDS-turned-academic-historians claiming insider knowledge over a movement which deliberately marginalized itself from the major anti-war movements, was rejected as an equal ally by the most militant sectors of the Black Power movement, and was an insignificant factor in the

Berkeley student movement (Gitlin, 1987). Within the intellectual left, several distinct intellectual styles were present. One tendency was actively engaged in linking the big issues of the property regime to the struggles in which they were themselves directly involved. Another tendency included the high priests of abstract theory (structuralists) who set the stage for the poststructuralists who spun theories and spawned endless and inconsequential debates on how many modes of production could be 'articulated' in a social formation. A third tendency involved anti-intellectual 'populist' intellectuals, who embraced and theorized the apolitical protesters and their rock entrepreneurs as the most significant 'new medium for politics'. Finally, there was the marginalized, professional, anti-Communist Social Democrats, who published screeds in the pro-imperial media bemoaning the student left's illusions about Stalinism, namely, the left's support for the liberation struggles of the Vietnamese National Liberation Front.

The programmatic left, which combined its intellectual work with practical activity, engaged in a difficult two-front struggle: on the one hand against the anti-intellectual celebrants of 'revolutionary rock music' and on the other with the abstruse and disengaged intellectual apparatus of the armchair structuralist theorists. The so-called counter-culture movement was in a very deliberate way a backward and inverted individualism, which later easily lent itself (and many of its practitioners) to being coopted by the ideologues of 'market populism': drugged-up snorting stock brokers, long-haired IT hucksters and hip-hop slogan writers for public relations firms.

In the US, the *de facto laissez-faire* drug policy of the Federal Government led to a massive inflow and consumption of drugs in the ghettos and among the activist left, driving many out of politics. Opium became the opium of the left. Burroughs and Ginsberg and their acolytes promoted a philosophy closer to the mystical reactionary ideas of Ann Rand than Karl Marx. What passed for a 'radical critique' of capitalism was a passing reflection on a lifestyle that embraced ego-centred individualism and led directly into the self-styled 'entrepreneurial right' of the 1990s (Frank, 2000). The rock, sex and drugs left made deep inroads into the political movement, its raucous sounds and evangelical fervour drawing huge crowds. But the nature of crowds is easy come and early go. Most counter-cultural academic writing was nothing more than populist pandering to adolescent hormones and middle-aged retarded adolescents. What is significant is how quickly and decisively the rockers joined the capitalist class in outlook, income, stock holding and lifestyle. Mick Jagger Incorporated, with his US$250 million assets, still struts his stuff before the crowds singing 'Street-fighting Man', while hob-nobbing with investment brokers in the suites. Jerry Garcia, the hip lead of the Grateful Dead, was a police informer for many years, turning on and turning in his friends and followers. The Beatles, the more sedate, Liverpool proles, receiving annuities and dividends in casual clothes, providing a role model for the new hip IT millionaires. Rock music, the musicians and the counter-culturalists did not 'create' the political movement; they lived off of it and later abandoned the occasional benefit concerts for the left when the struggle ebbed, retaining their 'populist' costumes and rhetoric while touring for top dollar. The crucial analytical point is that the 'evangelical' style of the rock culture profoundly depoliticized an emerging left-youth constituency, undermined programmatic politics in the name of radical lifestyles and physically and mentally destroyed many young people with its drug excesses and a pseudo anti-work ethos. While the rockers had the money to 'bum around', enter a detox clinic and hire expensive lawyers to keep them out of jail, most of their followers wandered aimlessly, slept in the streets, drifted into 'lumpen' day work or ended up doing long stretches in jail or in asylums.

The theoretical point is that there are links between some variants of intellectual and cultural life in the 1960s and 1970s and the right turn in the 1990s: the substantive differences in political activity in the two periods, particularly in the Anglo-Saxon world, are bridged by the pseudo-radical individualist cultural practices and values in both periods.

In the UK, the 1990s' inheritance from the rock culture of the 1960s was a millionaire knighted 'street fighter'. In the US it was Jerry Rubin, the promoter of drugs and left politics in the 1960s, who led the mass conversion of yippies to yuppies. The counter-cultural 'rebellion' of the 1960s carried the seeds of the mass-commercial youth-consumer marketeering of the 1990s.

The significant political–cultural breakthroughs in the 1960s and early 1970s were found in the politicization of the military conscripts and the spread of anti-militarist ideology in the Armed Forces and in the general public, leading to the virtual paralysis of the Army, which contributed to the ending of the Indo-China war. This political and cultural transformation led to the end of conscription in the US and the biggest reduction of military budgets in the Cold War period. Equally, it contributed to the long-term weakening of the use of US ground troops in overseas combat. In the sphere of music, anti-war folk singers like Joan Baez and Phil Ochs were important influences. Malcolm X, Che Guevara and hundreds of activist–intellectuals made major contributions in shaping the anti-militarist culture.

Powerful social movements emerged among women, racial minorities, and environmentalists that broadened and deepened radical thought and practice. Within these movements important divisions emerged between liberals pressuring for a limited accommodation to capitalist power and those who challenged the property regime. These divisions continued throughout the latter half of the twentieth century, with one wing adopting a pseudo-radical post-modernist position emphasizing 'identity' politics, while others hewed closer to a class-analysis perspective. Two points need to be emphasized in this regard. First, the 'new social movements' even in the 1960s were politically divided between radicals and liberals. Second, the 1990s' accommodation to power of some leaders merely reflected their historical origin and did not reflect the totality of the movements, nor were they a particular novelty of the 1990s capitalist ascendancy, as Anderson claims.

In cinema the academic–apolitical political intellectuals looked toward the elite *Cahiers du Cinema* and the *Nouvelle Vague* to inform their avant-garde posturing, while the activist intellectuals looked to Cuban film and documentaries, Gillio Portocarrero, Costa Garvis, Litten and films like *The Battle of Algiers, Burn, Z, Missing, The Battle of Chile*. These films and film-makers reached out to connect with tens of thousands of activists, catalyzing a new aesthetic breakthrough linking art to politics.

Deep divisions appeared between Western Marxists and anti-imperialist writers. The former denied the significance of the massive revolutionary struggles in Indo-China, Latin America and Southern Africa. 'Third Worldism' became a common deprecatory label among the Western Marxists who focused exclusively on developments in the 'advanced capitalist countries' and, more particularly, on their own nuclear campaigns, library research and polemical tiffs in their literary–political journals. The anti-imperialists contributed to theorizing, analyzing and debating the contradictions between imperialism and the Third World, the internal class structures and revolutionary perspectives. Some writers wrote from an abstract 'globalist' perspective,[8] others from a 'class analysis' approach. The former virtually wrote off class and political struggles in the imperial countries, mirror images of their Western Marxist adversaries. The latter optimistically envisioned an eventual class linkage across the imperial divide, based on the French revolt of 1968 and that in Italy of 1969.

What is important to note is that the intellectuals entered *en masse* late on the political scene, after the mass movements gained energy and national dimensions, and departed from active engagement early. For them, the major breakthrough was the university administrators' forced acceptance of left intellectuals as academics. On the other hand, many left-intellectuals-turned-academics 'institutionalized' leftist thought into part of their professional life: they ceased to write from a political perspective. Academic Marxism, with its journals, conferences and debates, helped fill curriculum vitae, facilitated promotions and led to state-financed research centres and even distinguished chairs for the most entrepreneurial. The movements and struggles became 'objects' to write about, not to be engaged in. The institutional intellectuals in the West, particularly subsequent to the military coups in Latin America, introduced their exiled Third World counterparts to the world of foundation-funded academic leftism, a world in which the 'material existence' of accommodation, and the norms of success would ensure an evolution toward, and assimilation into, apolitical literary–political Leftism.

The 1960s was a complex period of intellectual political engagement. The opening of academic institutions became 'terrain for struggle' and vehicles for social mobility and access to the prestigious journals of the dominant culture.

Counter-revolution within the Revolution

Even at the height of the 1960s' upsurge, ominous developments were occurring: US-supported coups in Indonesia and Brazil, two of the biggest and most promising countries in the Third World, decimated millions of activists in the former and undermined the left in the latter. China's Cultural Revolution, which began as an egalitarian challenge to bureaucratic power, was turned into a plaything of elite factional wars, alienating activists, emptying revolutionary slogans of their content and setting the stage for the ascendancy of capitalist restorationist forces in the late

1970s. Khrushchev's post-Stalin revelations loosened the Stalinist repressive apparatus, while also encouraging the emergence of a new generation of avaricious pro-Western professionals, functionaries and clandestine marketeers.

While 'Soviet Marxism' became a state ideology manipulated by a relatively privileged elite, living standards of the Soviet population rose significantly, with universal employment, free and accessible medical care, low-cost housing, free education and month-long vacations in workers' resorts. Significant socio-economic and political improvements in the Soviet Union, however, went unnoticed by important sectors of the new left, who continued to rely on the outmoded 'anti-Stalinist' rhetoric in place of a more nuanced analysis of the contradictory and complex Soviet reality. As one editor of *New Left Review* told me during the Trotskyist romance with the Vatican–CIA funded Solidarity movement in Poland, 'anything is better than Stalinism'.[9] Thus, the ideological seeds for the Russian catastrophe of the 1990s were sown in the Stalinophobia of the 1960s and 1970s.

There were outstanding intellectuals who spoke and acted against the imperialist pressures and enticements: Jean-Paul Sartre's rejection of the Nobel Prize and his collaboration with Bertrand Russell and Lelio Basso in the organization of the Russell Tribunals on Indo-China (and later on Latin America), provided a European platform for the victims and fighters against US genocide.

Any worthwhile attempt to survey and compare the present period with the previous four decades is obligated to go beyond superficial dichotomous simplifications, which overlook the contradictions and counter-currents, the potentialities as well as the limitations in any upsurge or downturn in popular struggles. This is particularly true in looking at cultural and intellectual movements, where one must be careful to separate personal preferences for certain types of film or music, for example, with its real political impact and influence. What is intellectually dishonest is to overlook the counter-tendencies of the past, (particularly in the 1960s and 1970s) and in the present period in order to paint a black-and-white picture. This methodology defines struggles and movements by intellectual fiat dictating that the political environment of the 1960s was revolutionary and the 1990s was a period in which the left, Marxism, and significant social struggles have no importance and in which US hegemony reigns supreme and uncontested.[10] This is not only a thinly disguised reactionary politics, it is shoddy social and political analysis devoid of any historical–theoretical underpinnings. One-dimension theorizing distorted by a pessimistic mood and an ill-informed infatuation with science leads to an anecdotal method more akin to a lawyer's brief, in which selective facts replace careful analysis of the complex and changing realities of the 1990s and the new millennium.

Restoration, Imperialism and Revolution in the 1990s

The 1990s cannot be understood simply by issuing a 'political manifesto' that proclaims that US hegemony rules supreme, revolutionary struggles no longer exist,[11] the ideology of the right is coherent and systematic,[12] Leftist ideas have been coopted, are fragmentary and irrelevant.[13] Nor can we speak of the decade as a coherent 'whole' without taking account of the crises that opened the decade, the speculative bubble that burst at the end of the decade and the unstable volatility in between. Nor can we overlook the sharp and deep opposition to US imperial intervention that preceded the Gulf War and the rising tide of resistance to Euro-American economic domination at the end of the decade. It is the height of wilful myopia to ignore the imperial defeats and the emergence of significant anti-imperialist movements in the Third World and the mass struggles that call into question the whole repertoire of imperial 'neo-liberal' policies, their international financial sponsors and their domestic political underpinnings.

No doubt there have been significant imperial victories, and severe reversals on the left that need to be taken into account. But certainly only an ahistorical and hasty judgement can claim that the decade was a period of unprecedented historical defeats, which surpasses anything in prior history.[14] From the early 1930s to the early 1940s the left was totally destroyed in most of Europe (Germany, Italy, Russia, Spain, Hungary, Japan, Poland) or reduced to a shell of its past influence (France, Norway) or isolated from the main centres of power (China, Indo-China, for example) or coopted into imperialist regimes (UK, US). Tens of millions of workers, peasants and others were killed; hundreds of millions were ruled by bloody tyrants who allowed not even elemental class organizations. There were theorists then, both on the right and left, who saw the new rising fascist or 'bureaucratic' power (Burnham, 1941) as 'the wave of the future' (Lindbergh), impregnable and all-powerful. Some intellectuals turned toward philosophic and literary exercises in the occupied areas (Sartre, Camus). Fascism and imperialism surged from the capitalist economic crisis of the East and West and the passivity of the left. Social Democrats in Germany and Austria offered to share power with the Nazis until they were physically driven from office; some were jailed, others fled to exile, a few remained in Germany unmolested.

Nothing similar has occurred during the 1990s, despite the bloody repression and imperial bombings in Iraq (one million dead), Yugoslavia (thousands dead) and elsewhere. If anything, US violent reaction was more severe in the 1960s, 1970s and 1980s. During the 1965–1976 decade four million were killed in Indo-China, 50,000 in the Southern Cone (Chile, Argentina, for example). During the 1979–1989 decade, the US, with its death squads and client terrorist regimes, killed close to 300,000 workers, peasants and others in Central America alone, not to speak of the millions killed in its proxy wars in Angola, Mozambique, Afghanistan and Cambodia. Any serious discussion of US 'hegemony' in the 1990s cannot avoid the bloody class and imperial wars that preceded the decade, nor can it evade examining the highly exploitative class relations and servile regimes that emerged to serve the imperial power.[15]

US 'hegemony', a rather vacuous concept that inflates the role of 'political persuasion', is totally inappropriate when one considers the scope and depth of violence in the recent past and its continuous use on a selective but demonstrable basis in the present.[16] The theoretical point is that imperial power has been cyclical, based on political and social relations and state violence and never 'totally dominant' (even with so-called 'totalitarian' regimes) and was certainly more destructive and dominant in other decades of this century. From this historical perspective we can dismiss some of the declamatory remarks emanating from Western Marxists, prostrate before the US Empire.[17]

But it is not only historical arguments that militate against the prostrators, there is a growing body of evidence that sharply challenges the thesis of unchallenged US imperial power – in the socio-political, diplomatic and economic spheres.

Throughout the 1990s, and in most regions of the world, significant anti-imperialist, socialist and populist leftist movements have challenged the rule of imperial clients, the international financial institutions of imperial power and, more specifically, the neo-liberal policy agenda. Mass demonstrations of trade unionists, community organizations, environmentalists, peasant and farmer organizations, students, feminists and many others against the imperial ruling classes were evident in Seattle, Washington, Melbourne, Prague, Nice and many other Western cities. Hundreds of thousands of farmers in India organized to defeat the intrusion of US and European based biotechnology, chemical and agribusiness, multinational corporations attempting to appropriate local varieties and impose monopoly seed control (hardly 'archaic movements' as some Western Marxists would have it). In every continent farmers and peasants, consumer groups and trade unionists (despite their leadership) have battled multinationals, blocked highways, taken over parliaments and provided a deeper understanding of the role of the IMF-World Bank than ever before in history. The scope, depth and consistency of these movements vary by region and historical moment. Some expressions are sustained and large-scale, others are massive and made up of diverse coalitions, but all share a common opposition to imperial domination. In some regions significant advances, political and economic victories have occurred leading to the accumulation of forces and a radicalization of the struggle. In others, waves of massive social action are followed by an ebbing and regrouping of forces.

These revolutionary and radical movements are different from the earlier period and have to be examined in the new context. Some of the 1990s movements draw from the earlier Marxist programs, others have introduced a more extensive and profound integration of a multiplicity of struggles into the vortex of anti-capitalist or at least anti-big-business movements. In addition to the growing consumer movements (the opposition to genetically modified food, Mad Cow disease and other corporate-induced 'innovations') a new wave of environmentalist–social justice advocates and feminists have emerged who question the property regime. Anderson's attempt to amalgamate the 'Greens' with the German Green party bosses and the feminists with pro-Clintonite feminists is engaged in shoddy scholarship and unethical political polemics.[18] New international networks and organized international struggles surpass efforts of a similar kind in the 1960s.

Methodologically it is a false move to enumerate the demise of the 1960s' left institutions and type of activities and equate that with the absence of a left in the 1990s. It is like counting oranges and forgetting the apples. Only someone completely divorced from the realities of the 1990s or in a 1960s time warp could perform such an act of unblinking incomprehension.

While the 'Soviet bloc' disappeared, it was not even then part of a 'Marxist culture' in its practice – internally or externally. Its theories had ceased to exercise much influence, not only in Western Europe and North America but also throughout the Third World. The importance of the Soviet bloc was as a counter-balance to US imperial power, an alternative market, source of trade, investment, loans and arms – strategically important in sustaining non-aligned countries, and some revolutionary regimes, even as it imposed blinders and, in some cases, destructive policies on those parties which followed it. In the 1990s, there is no claim to a revolutionary centre or false oracles of revolutionary verities.

There are, however, powerful revolutionary guerrilla armies in the National Liberation Army (ELN) and the Revolutionary Armed Forces of Colombia (FARC) challenging for state power, recognized by Washington as a major challenger of US imperial power, even as some leftist intellectuals, more papist than the Pope, preach undisputed US hegemony. Together the two guerrilla armies number 20,000 and have many times that number of peasant supporters and urban militia units. In comparison to the 1960s, guerrilla challenges to US Empire, the Colombian guerrillas in the 1990s are far more formidable than anything earlier, both in territorial influence, military political strategic capacity, leadership and most important sustainability.[19] In size, population, geopolitical location and economic resources, the US–Colombian confrontation is much more significant than the Cuban or Nicaraguan revolutions.

The same can be said for the mass revolutionary struggle of the Rural Landless Workers' Movement (MST) in Brazil. With over half a million members and sympathizers, tens of thousands of politically conscious activists – twelve thousand delegates attended their national Congress in July 2000 – the MST's banners of agrarian reform, national liberation and socialism have served as a pole of organization for a great part of the urban movements, dissident left trade unionists, radical Catholics and Marxist intellectuals. No rural movement in the 1960s had the capacity for successful action that the MST demonstrated during the 1990s: occupying thousands of Latifundios, settling over two hundred thousand families (one million people) and growing despite hundreds of killings of rural activists. No 1960s' extra-parliamentary movements were capable of building such broad, strategic and durable alliances with church, university, parliamentary, trade union, and human rights groups as the MST has constructed. Few, if any, mass based movements in the 1960s invested as much time and effort in political education for its activists, cadres, regional and national leaders as the MST.

The argument is not that the MST is in a position to challenge for state power today or in the near future; rather, the theoretical point is that, in a large swathe of the biggest country in the Western hemisphere, there is an avowed heterodox Marxist mass social movement successfully challenging US imperial domination and its client Cardoso regime. The peculiarity of the Brazilian situation in the 1990s is the perverse position taken by one of Western Europe's leading Marxist theoreticians[20] who early on declared that 'Cardoso could be Brazil's best President of this century', a judgement made by ignoring Cardoso's alliance with the most retrograde landlord forces in Brazil, and the staunch opposition of the MST and a whole continuum of the left. Needless to say, Cardoso's craven sell-off of the most lucrative resources to foreign capital at a 'political price', makes him the unprecedented *entreguista* (sell out) of the century. It is not surprising that those European and US Marxists, or ex-Marxists, who put their faith in the Cardosos of the Third World, who failed to live up to their expectations are the same believers in the 'unchallenged power of US hegemony'.

If Brazil and Colombia are two of the most powerful examples of challenges to US imperial power, there are numerous other significant socio-political movements that are at least worthy of note. Ecuador, Bolivia, and Paraguay have witnessed massive peasant Indian–trade union coalitions organize massive general strikes that have toppled pro-US regimes, paralysed IMF dictated neo-liberal measures and politically polarized the country.[21]

Now, to be sure, the prostrators will argue that these struggles are 'episodic' (despite their repetitions), not 'party based' (extra-parliamentary movements do not count), and lack revolutionary 'theory' (they do have detailed programmatic agendas, obviously distinct from the scholastic exercises on cultural exotica found in the politically irrelevant literary–political circles of certain Euro-American intellectuals). In the final analysis, the prostrators argue that the demands of these mass movements can be 'assimilated' to capitalism, and their leaders 'coopted' (according to their 'idealized' version of US 'hegemony').[22] These Western intellectuals babbling about 'hegemony' forget the continual mass murders and assassinations of popular leaders, massive repressive apparatus and death squads organized by US imperialism, who trust more in the traditional violence of imperial power than in the persuasion associated with US 'hegemony'. Some Western intellectuals might concede that some sort of challenge to US hegemony occurs in the Third World (though they cringe to use that term any more) but certainly not in the 'advanced capitalist countries', they would argue, where all the major decisions affecting world power are made. As Debray once told some friends from Bolivia when he was a French functionary: 'The Third World is like a drum: loud noises, inconsequential politics.'

Once again, the prostrators overlook the significant growth of burgeoning social movements in the imperial countries, whose scope and depth of opposition to corporate power exceeds comparable movements in the 1960s in terms of impact and partial victories. The obvious events emblematic of this new turn include the mass demonstrations against international capital in Seattle, Melbourne, Prague, Washington, London and elsewhere. With all of their contradictory elements (protectionists versus internationalists), these demonstrations cut deeper into the core elements of capitalism than the vague 'out of Vietnam' slogans of the 1960s. Unlike the 1960s, there are significant working relations between trade unionists, farmers, students and intellectuals. Naturally there are sideline intellectuals who do not see the radical potential (and reality) of these struggles because they don't match their preconceived ideals of what a revolutionary movement should be, illustrating once again the total absence of realism and the prostrators' inability to situate themselves in the changing political realities of the 1960s.

This is clearly illustrated by the powerful worldwide opposition to genetically modified food by the imperial chemical companies. From India to France and beyond, consumers, farmers, peasants, students, and workers have fought genetically modified foods and the states and regimes which promote them, with a virulent and informed passion that has successfully forced a major retreat by Monsanto and other multinational corporations. The populace versus big-business polarization, the anti-imperial content and anti-corporate ideology and the sustaining power of these movements, as they move from one issue area to another gives these struggles more than a symbolic, transitory and cooptable character. It is very odd indeed in this regard when a leading Western Marxist deprecates this movement and the empirical research informing it and embraces the pro-genetic press handouts put out by the most reactionary chemical corporations as the real revolutionary force, borrowing the market populist propaganda of the ideologists of the new economy.[23]

The new radical movements engaged in extra-parliamentary struggles, have seen their ranks expanded with the re-emergence of trade union activists and workers in challenging the existing consensus between the new right, (ex-Social Democratic and Democratic parties) and the old right. These struggles in France, Germany, Norway, and Denmark put a question mark over the neo-liberal agenda of free markets and the hollowing out of the welfare state. These movements are not revolutionary in theory, but are certainly starting points for the reconstruction of class-based politics.

Most Marxists understand that reforms are the starting point for all revolutions in the twentieth century; the question is how reforms are attained and how they are linked to broader struggles. To the intellectual prostrators, reforms are simply adaptations to capital, which, they argue, has the unlimited power and the will to concede reforms, although no significant reforms have been accepted in the last quarter of a century.[24]

Even in the US the degree of popular hostility to free market capitalism is evident in every survey over the last decade. A majority favours a national health plan, company paid pensions, social security, full employment policy, and state regulation of utilities. Substantial majorities oppose free trade, sending US troops abroad to fight, existing levels of inequalities, corporate dominance of electoral campaigns and government policy. Significant social movements exist on many of these issues. These anti-neo-liberal attitudes call into question the notion of a US ruling class 'hegemony' (the ideas of the ruling class are not the ideas of the popular majority). The real question is not 'hegemony' but the absence of representative democracy: the gap between popularly expressed interests (values) and the political class's policies defending ruling class interests.

Apart from the collective actions and majoritarian attitudes calling into question US free market 'hegemony', US imperial dominance has suffered several blows in the diplomatic arena. In a region of the highest strategic significance (the Middle East) and among the oil producing states the US State Department has suffered several setbacks. Iran and Iraq have effectively broken the US-sponsored boycott and have jointly participated in international conferences with Saudi Arabia, the major US oil supplier. In addition, Libya has broken out of the US-orchestrated boycott and has intensified its links with Europe, particularly Italy. Venezuela, under

Chavez has revitalized OPEC and has developed commercial and political links with Washington's *bête noir* – Cuba. The latter has totally isolated the US at the UN, the Ibero-American Summit and even at the OAS on the US economic boycott, Helms-Burton and other regional issues.

In the meantime, sharp and escalating commercial rivalries between the EU and the US are emerging, even as deepening inter-penetration of each other's multinationals occurs. Likewise, while NATO still remains dominant the EU countries are making efforts to create their own rapid deployment military forces to protect their imperial interests. The point is that while these European initiatives have nothing progressive about them, contrary to the eloquent lugubrigations of French literary nationalist Regis Debray, they do reflect challenges to the notion of unassailable US hegemony.

The regions most susceptible to misunderstanding by impressionist Western intellectual prostrators are the former Communist countries, particularly China, Indo-China and even Russia and Eastern Europe. While on the surface, China seems to be creeping under Western hegemony (dubious in itself as most investment comes from the overseas Chinese plutocrats and Japan) and certainly entrance into the WTO will greatly accelerate Euro-American takeovers of market shares, firms and local savings, the other side of the picture is the rising tide of mass protests by unemployed, unpaid and exploited factory workers, peasants and day workers. The growing inequalities, vast network of party-state-private corruption and the conspicuous Asian opulence in the face of increasing immiseration, grates against a population still imbued with, and cognizant of, Communist values of equality, rectitude and the iron pot – the full employment, free public health and educational policies of the Communist era. The blatant surrender of China's sovereignty, markets and strategic industries, the humiliations accompanying gross acts of deliberate military aggression like the bombing of the Chinese Embassy and the heightened missile encirclement of China (which Washington has predictably dubbed the missile shield) have aroused nationalist, popular sentiments even among the intellectuals and students, among the most notorious pro-Western, pro-capitalist groupings. The structural underpinnings for a new round of civil warfare are all present. Opposition to the neo-liberal agenda is widespread, dispersed, localized and, despite being constantly heavily repressed, growing. Even Western gurus of China's market opening foresee serious social resistance and the possibility of reversion if (as is expected) massive unemployment occurs.

To simply count China as another counter in adding up the sum of countries under US hegemony is too facile. It means ignoring the deep structural contradictions, the egalitarian thrust in the Cultural Revolution and, even further back in history, the cyclical swings between nationalism/socialism and liberalism since the middle of the nineteenth century. Moreover it ignores the fact that below the leadership level and the wealthy, private elites, there are hundreds of millions of Chinese who reject the restoration of Western dominance and the return of what Marx called 'all the old crap': humiliation, unemployment, chronic diseases, opiates, regional fiefdoms, and so on. Even within the Communist party apparatus there is a sector of vacillating neo-statists and nationalists, who could opportunistically seize the chance if the current crop of neo-liberals falter.

In Eastern Europe and Russia, the most blatant servants of Euro-American hegemony have been frequently rejected at the ballot box. Lech Walesa's party did not break double digits in the last Polish presidential election. In Rumania, Poland, the Czech Republic, Belarus and elsewhere the most fanatical neo-liberals were toppled by ex-Communist demagogues who promised socialist measures (full employment, end of Western impositions, particularly IMF austerity measures) and then implemented liberal policies. While at one level the alternation between liberals and pseudo-nationalists/ex-Communists have confirmed Euro-American hegemony, at the level of mass behaviour the politics of rejection of imperialist dominance and free market economics is palpable. Ending the welfare state and full employment, and the unprecedented catastrophic decline of living standards, production and health in Russia and the rest of the USSR, has certainly undermined popular belief in the beneficence of US hegemony among the mass of the people.

Any discussion of US hegemony cannot rely on breezy tourist accounts of developments in Cuba (Blackburn, 2000).

To read into the general public, the behaviour and outlook of the client elites is an unwarranted assumption – both on methodological and empirical grounds. To assume that electoral processes aggregate the interests of the electorate and in some way reflect and represent majoritarian interests is to overlook the gross concentration of institutional power, especially in the mass media, the flagrant manipulation of campaign financing and the use of force, corruption and poverty to pervert and manipulate voting outcomes and elected officials' behaviour.

US World Hegemony and Domestic Decay

The key to understanding the relative strength of US hegemony is to examine its structural foundations as well as the external constraints discussed above. To engage in general projections based on a misreading of structural fundamentals can lead to the kind of monumental nonsense that predicts an Asian century shortly before the Asian crash (Arrighi, 1994).[25] Underlying the claims of unprecedented and absolute US global hegemony are the arguments of the New Economists' ideologues who describe an unprecedented period of US economic expansion and its economic superiority based on its advanced IT, and greater productivity (read: competitiveness). The convergence of views between the prostrate left intellectuals and the huckster ideologues of market populism is a result of the same method, grandiose generalizations and celebrations of US global power based on the slender reed of a limited conjuncture and highly selective anecdotal data. In fact, the prostrators show an unmerited respect for the spin masters of globaloney and their rhetoric about the Third Scientific Technological Revolution. As one Western Marxist admirer describes it 'commanding the field of direct political constructions of the time, the Right has provided one fluent vision of where the world is going, or has stopped, after another' (Anderson, 2000: 19). These right-wing ideologues, we are told, 'unite a single powerful thesis with a fluent popular style'. Written a few weeks before the crash in the NASDAQ bubble, the year 2000 provided a vivid demonstration of the emptiness of the 'powerful thesis' of US economic supremacy, the 'fluent popular style' notwithstanding.

Every assertion which the old right or the new right (New Economy hipsters) affirmed about the US economy (and taken up by the prostrate left) was, at best, dubious and, at worst, simply hot air devoid of any relation to the real economy (simply a huge Ponzi put-on comparable to the Albanian pyramid schemes of the mid-1990s).

First, the claims of an IT revolution simply fail to explain the below average growth in productivity between 1975 and 1994 in comparison to the previous 20 years before the so-called 'Information Revolution'. Second, the increase in productivity between 1995 and 1999 was comparable to the earlier period (1955–1974) and was mainly concentrated in the computer field itself with little industry-wide effect. In other words, computer makers became more efficient in making computers. Third, studies showed that the claims of the gains from interactive exchange of information were mainly bogus: over 60 per cent of the information received or exchanged within firms had little to do with the projects at hand (Wolf, 1999: 10; Gordon, 1999).

More decisive is the fact that the majority of IT companies never generated a product or a profit and some never produced any revenue. The rates of bankruptcy skyrocketed throughout the year 2000 as the speculative bubble burst. The NASDAQ fell 40 per cent and the value of the most important and biggest companies declined precipitously into 2001. The most singular development: US global superiority in the IT field, cited by rightist ideologues, in their fluent populist style, as the mainspring of sustained growth in the 1990s collapsed. Millions of small investors attracted by the market populist ideologues lost their entire savings, pensions and even their ability to pay health insurance.

But the profound structural weakness of the US was not confined to the speculative IT economy. US overseas expansion and exports back to the US exacerbated an unsustainable trade and current accounts deficit. The US economy runs on consumption, accounting for 75 per cent of the GNP. The growing trade deficit was covered by the inflow of US$400 billion annually. With the economy in recession and the dollar weakening, foreign investors are more reticent in sustaining the US dollar. Despite record low unemployment at the end of the year 2000, it was also the period of the greatest growth of low-paid workers, living off charity, without any medical coverage (close to 50 million) with soaring educational costs and unsustainable household debts. The obscene growth of social inequalities under the Clinton regime (CEO to worker ratio increased 470 to one) were largely the result of the close ties with millionaire labour officials, who were more concerned with having a tolerant Attorney General to avoid prosecution than a Labour Secretary supportive of workers' demands. The possibility of reviving the economy through 'pump priming' or demand-side stimulation has and still is outside the current political parameters.

The economic crisis has already hit several sectors (automotive, IT, telecommunications) of the economy and is spreading rapidly to the rest of the economy. Unemployment is growing. The 'negative savings' and the lost paper economy offer no unused resources that can be mobilized to stimulate consumer spending. In trade, investment, finance and technology the US economy is moving toward a 'converging crisis' that threatens the fragile neo-liberal edifice built around (and for) the US throughout the world. All the Third World countries that bought into the export-led strategies, will suffer severely from a deep US recession. The overproduction of consumer and transport (mainly automotive) is leading to massive lay-offs by Ford, General Motors and Chrysler–Daimler, which will have a multiplier effect on the suppliers and service sectors.

The military economy could be revved up, but it falls short given the channelling of the budget surplus into massive tax reductions for big business. The surplus itself is likely to disappear with the recession and a sharp decline in revenue.

What is striking about the weaknesses of the economic fundamentals of US imperial power is the lack of any perceptive or coherent understanding by the right. Neither Huntington, Brzezinski, Fukuyama, even less Yergin, Luttwick or Friedman had a clue about the impending speculative collapse, busy as they were propagating their delusional belief in the sustainability of the US empire.[26] Huntington was off in his own self-concocted world of 'clashing civilizations' (Muslim versus Christian), at a time when Washington's staunchest allies were Muslim Turkey and Egypt in the Eastern Mediterranean, Morocco in North Africa, Saudi Arabia in the Middle East, Pakistan in South Asia, and so on. Faced with the bankruptcy of his notion of the 'end of history', Fukuyama backtracked on his celebration of liberal democracy and free markets, without developing any new theoretical gloss to embellish the power of empire in the new period. Parenthetically, it is ironic that Fukuyama has begun to question the solidity of US hegemony when some of his supposedly apposite counterparts on the left (the prostrators) attempt to revive it.

Brzezinski without the Soviet Union spins strategic visions of new challenges and threats without substance, ignoring the internal economic rot a few blocks from his old stomping grounds at Columbia University. It is true that he can still provide an historical–theoretical rationale for covert operations in Chechnia, and in other ex-Soviet republics, to sustain Washington's mafia clients in power. For the rest, Yergin and Friedman (the journalist) have little to say in the face of the collapse of their vision of a high-technology US retaining world power. The visions of Main Street millionaires, of adolescent day traders and Wall Streeters sharing the growing wealth has gone down the tubes. As growing millions of US pensioners lose their Health Management Organization (HMO) private medical plans, and other millions of former welfare recipients can't make a go of it on minimum wage jobs, and as the paper incomes of tens of millions of Americans becomes a bitter memory, the arrogance of Yergen's and Friedman's claims of US superiority over backward Europe (particularly France) for sustaining the social welfare, becomes a self-delusional bad joke.

Left-wing advances and challenges to US world dominance and the collapse of delusions of sustainable US economic supremacy based on the IT 'revolution' call for an end to the prostrate politics on the left.

Today there are numerous activists and critical intellectuals from the 1960s to the 1990s who have been providing direct political critiques and constructions of where the world has been, where it is, as well as elaborating alternatives in a fluent popular style. In the US, and Canada, these are activist intellectuals like James O'Connor on the ecological-capitalist crisis, Bob Fitch's brilliant demystification of globalization as 'globaloney', Maurice Zeitlin on the US class structure, Chomsky and Petras on US foreign policy, Magdoff on US imperialism, Meiksin on class analysis, Howard Zinn, Leo Panitch and Mike Parenti on history, politics and the media. Outside of North America there is the world-class photographer of work, Sebastian Salgado, novelist José Saramago, literary-political critic Michel Lowy, and scores of other political intellectuals who provide comprehensive critiques and elaborate alternatives to US imperial domination, while being deeply engaged in the popular struggles. The left in the 1990s possessed some of the outstanding political strategists of the half century, including the brilliant military-political leader of FARC Mañuel Marulanda, probably the best military strategist since the Vietnamese Commander Giap; the brilliant tactician of the militant French farmers movement Bove; the brilliant theorist of the Brazilian Landless Workers' Movement, Joao Pedro Stedile, the principled American populist and anti-imperialist Ralph Nader (capable of garnering three million votes against all the odds).

Power is a relationship, not a static position in an organizational hierarchy. The US empire is based on an unstable and changing relationship with a vast array of heterogeneous forces. The power of ideas, including the ideas of the imperial ruling class, is embedded in this class relationship. While it is true that the (contested) ascendancy of imperial power includes control over the mass media to project their ideas, (and seducing sectors of the ex-left intelligentsia with the persuasion of power) the neo-liberal dogma has been under constant attack from all sides. This is so to such a degree that the ruling classes have sought to disguise their rule through the cooptation of the language of the left – what some pundits describe as 'market populism' (Frank, 2000: Chapter 2).

Perspectives for the Future

Over the next decade, the left has to continue developing a systematic and specific focus, and avoid the romantic pessimism that engages in sweeping and diffuse generalizations devoid of substance. The left intelligentsia must identify the class agents of the victories and defeats of neo-liberalism, the class relations and state violence behind the veil of persuasion that sustains Euro-US imperialism. Above all, they must analyse the new intensifying contradictions and emerging crises in the US as well as the on-going crises in Asia, Latin America and the former Communist countries and the impact these will have on the EU.

The left must reject the flaunting of novelty as an excuse for adapting to neo-liberal ascendancy. The Third Way doctrine has its roots in more reformist and failed versions from early in the twentieth century. Neither Bernstein nor, later, Kautsky understood the relationship between capitalism and imperialism and imperialist wars, nor the immanent tendency towards crisis, class polarization and fascist power. The current version of Third Way reformism has none of the apparent reformist platitudes of the earlier version and all of their reactionary vices: extending the neo-liberal agenda while undermining living standards and deepening inequalities. Few illusions exist today about the reactionary nature of Anthony Giddens' (Blair and Clinton's) Third Way; it is hardly mentioned as the stock markets dive and budget surpluses shrink. Likewise the right-wing course of European Social Democracy is readily understandable to any critical intellectuals except those suffering from chronic amnesia or those who seek to bolster their thesis that there are no alternatives.[27] One needn't go back to the overtures that the leading German Social Democrats (Schneiderman, Noske, and so on) made to the Kaiser's General Staff in 1918. Closer in time was the role of the British, French and Belgian Social Democrats in violently defending their colonial empires in Algeria, Kenya, Cyprus, Indo-China, the Congo and elsewhere. Their servile collaboration with the US in building NATO, their unswerving Atlanticist postures, provoked strong criticism even from the traditional right. To argue that the adoption by the Social Democrats of the US model is a 'world historic' novelty is to overlook the historical legacy of Social Democracy, its pronounced and advanced toadyism, particularly among UK Labour. The whole edifice of the welfare state had less to do with programmatic Social Democracy and more to do with the challenges from the Communist bloc, the trade union militancy following the end of the Second World War and the presence of Communist parties and the extra-parliamentary movements pressuring from the left. With the disappearance of the Soviet bloc, the diminution of the extra-parliamentary left and the transformation of the trade union leaders into state clients, European Social Democratic leaders, with a few notable exceptions, are able to compete with the right for the allegiance of the financial and industrial moguls. Jospin of France is a partial exception that proves the rule. Elected in the aftermath of a general strike by public employees, pressured by strong extraparliamentary movements and the parliamentary Communist Party, he conceded the 35 hour work week in principle, combining it with aggressive privatization, liberalization and 'flexible' labour legislation.

If the most significant fact of the 1980s was the disintegration of the Soviet bloc and the Communist regimes, the most salient fact of the 1990s was the catastrophic socio-economic conditions, the unprecedented levels of pillage and corruption and the repressive institutions that resulted from the transition to capitalism in Russia and the former countries of the Soviet Union. Russia alone is 'missing' ten million people who would otherwise inhabit the country according to demographic projections of 1987. Millions have died prematurely because of disease, stress, suicide and alcoholism resulting from job loss, poverty and the demise of the public health system. While tactically the pro-capitalist Putin regime remains firmly in control, the total failure of the capitalist transition under US 'hegemony' has certainly brought the positive features of the prior planned, collectivist economy into sharp contrast.

Western pillage of the economies of the ex-Communist countries, the massive trade in white sex slavery and immigrants, the reign of a billionaire parasitic oligarchy that washes its illicit riches in Europe, the US and Israel, has certainly given substance to the notions of Western imperialism and capitalist rapaciousness. More convincing than a ton of Communist era tracts, the experience of the people of the ex-USSR with real existing Euro-US imperialism has undone years of disbelief in the rhetoric of Soviet bureaucrats, and credulous trust in Western propaganda. This world-historic shift in popular beliefs, has important strategic importance in the rebuilding of a socialist perspective in the East. Even in Eastern Europe, bastion of pro-Western client states, the incorporation and subordination to NATO and the EU has provoked opposition, demonstrations and, in some cases, the revival of Communist influence. In the Czech Republic, Grovel Havel is more a favourite of the London/New York literati than he is in Prague, where the Communist Party is fast becoming the major opposition party. The widespread rejection of liberalism and US imperialism and the growth of programmatic socialism *sans* Stalinism is a world-historic event. The theoretical point is not to identify with certainty a time and place for a new revolutionary upsurge, but to locate the direction of history and to reject the facile belief that every left defeat is an irreversible world-historic defeat.

We have no intention of engaging in a 'tit for tat' intellectual game of naming left advances against the prostrate intellectuals' laundry list of defeats. Given the superficiality of the latter it would prove to be an easy and not very significant contribution to clarifying the present in order to advance the struggle in the future. Least of all should we resort to the prostrators' cheap psychobabble to justify their inaction and non-commitment to the ongoing struggles. In facing the future we must recognize that there are numerous intellectual dead-ends. We must recognize the barbarities committed today in the name of Western victories, hegemony, democracy and free markets: the premature death of ten million Russians, 20 million African AIDS victims denied medicine by Western pharmaceutical corporations backed by their governments; the killing of one million Iraqi children due to the Anglo-American War and blockade; the 300 million Latin Americans living in poverty, the tens of thousands of Colombians killed thanks to US military training and aid. One could add to the list but the point is clear: in the East and South, barbarism is an integral aspect of the US empire.

In discussing what is to be done in the face of imperial barbarism it is useful to recall the last days of the Roman Empire – a time like ours of tyrants, plunder, corruption, and the brazen flaunting of wealth in the face of misery. The similarities with contemporary barbarism are obvious and so are many of the responses by those who find the empire or aspects of it equally repugnant. There are many and varied intellectual responses to imperial barbarism, depending on the social conditions and political predispositions of each. The stoics among us are repulsed by the irrationality of the empire, its military brutality and the pervasive immorality. However, they feel politically impotent and declare that any political response is futile. They turn to small circles of friends or like-minded individuals to guard the flame of rationality. They retain their personal loyalties in the interstices of the system, with a modicum of comfort, distant from the imperial powers and distant from the degraded masses. Their debates about cultural studies and the relation of postmodernism and Marxism are tolerated and ignored by the elite and are incomprehensible and remote from the masses. In a word, they live by and for themselves.

Cynics do not deny the bloody barbarism, the cultural vulgarity and predatory pillage of the empire; they amalgamate victims and executions. They condemn both the victims of empire and the imperial predators as equally avaricious (afflicted with 'consumerism'). For the cynics, the social solidarity of the exploited is an ideological subterfuge of the weak in order to seek advantage and thus to reverse roles. For the cynics the difference between exploited and exploiters is only a question of opportunity and circumstances. The cynics point to the failed revolutions, the circulation of elites, the exploited who become exploiters, the victims of genocide who practise genocide to justify getting their sensitive snout in the trough of empire. More often than not, the cynics are repentant leftists: their occupational specialization is providing testimonials on the perversions of liberation movements. This is a specialization that provides lucrative honorariums and not infrequently a scholarly chair in a prestigious Euro-American university.

Another familiar intellectual posture is that of the leftist (or ex-leftist) who bathes in historical defeats and finds in them a pretext for what they dub a new realist or pragmatic accommodation with the *status quo*. While over-dramatizing political losses, as profound and irreversible historical defeats, they fail to recognize the new revolutionary struggles emerging in the Third World and in the West, the new social movements opposed to the WTO, the militant farmers and transport workers movements, the massive producers and consumer movements rejecting the corporate sponsors of genetically modified foods, seeds, and so on. Pessimistic pathos becomes an alibi for inaction and disengagement or a one-way ticket to liberal politics, since it is perceived as the only show in town. The ideologists of empire are not averse to providing an occasional platform for the pessimists, hoping that their critical posture can attract an audience among young rebels and that their pessimism can demoralize, disorient and disarm them.

Critical intellectuals with a bended knee have achieved certain notoriety among the educated classes. The flaunting of wealth in the midst of poverty horrifies these intellectuals. The horror of neo-liberalism evokes indignation at the barbaric practices of empire. This indignation, however, is accompanied by a whimper when it comes to articulating an alternative. After all the indignant cries they appeal to the elites to change their ways. The rhetorical flourishes, the exposé of the lies of empire are replaced by new deceptions. The idea that someone, somewhere in the power structure will transform barbarism into a generous welfare state. This combination of violent indignation and appeal to the bad conscience of imperial power brokers is nothing more than a bee in the bonnet of low-level policymakers, an excellent formula for a best seller. It vents indignation that resonates with the educated classes without asking them to sacrifice anything.

In sharp contrast to the above-mentioned intellectual postures, there is the irreverent intellectual, on the one hand, irreverent toward academic protocols and unimpressed by the prestigious titles and prizes, on the other, respectful of the militants on the front lines of the anti-capitalist and anti-imperialist struggles. They are steady and productive in their intellectual work that is in large part motivated by the big questions facing movement struggles; they are self-ironic anti-heroes, whose work is respected by the people who are actively working for a basic social transformation; they are objectively partisan, and partisan objective. The irreverent intellectuals discuss and listen to the pessimists and other intellectuals, despite their titles and preteens, to see if they have anything worthwhile to say.

For the irreverent and committed intellectual, prestige and recognition comes from the activists and movement intellectuals who are involved in popular struggles; they work with those intellectuals and activists. They conduct research looking for original sources of data; they create their own indicators and concepts, for example, to identify the real depths of poverty, exploitation and exclusion. They recognize that there are a few intellectuals in prestigious institutions and award recipients who are clearly committed to popular struggles and they acknowledge that these exceptions should be noted, while recognizing the many others who, in climbing the academic ladder, succumb to the blandishments of bourgeois certification. The irreverent intellectuals admire a Jean-Paul Sartre who rejected a Nobel Prize in the midst of the Vietnam War. Most of all, the irreverent intellectuals fight against bourgeois hegemony within the left by integrating their writing and teaching with practice, avoiding divided loyalties.

Euro-American imperialism combines violence and threats of violence against mass movements and regimes that oppose its world order and dissuasion and neutralization of Western Marxist intellectual grouplets. The latter typically universalize their condition, treating the Empire as one big debating society. As Perry Anderson stated: 'The force of this (hegemonic) order is not in repression but in dissuasion and neutralization.'[28] This should be news to the hundreds of dead Palestinians, several thousand dead Yugoslavs, tens of thousands of Colombians and hundreds of thousands of Iraqis (Anderson, 2000: 16).[29]

Objectively, US imperial power is built on very fragile foundations: a bubble economy which is collapsing, a quasi-tributary economy dependent on large-scale external flows of speculative capital to compensate for unsustainable huge merchandise trade deficits, a consumer-fuelled domestic economy in which households are already over-indebted and with negative savings, an empire without public backing for overseas ground wars, and a Ponzi-like New Economy based on firms with no products, no profits and, many, without revenues. Equally important, the class polarization between the billionaire owners of the means of finance, production and speculation and the great majority of the population has widened; as already seen, the ratio of income between CEOs and workers has widened from 80:1 to 470:1 in three decades; over 80 per cent of the US public do not believe their votes matter and that big business dominates the political sphere – what some political analysts might call a legitimacy crises. Social benefits across generations, skill levels and occupations have been savaged. Deregulation has led to unrestrained price gouging of consumers in public utilities.

Present-day imperialism has not created a 'workers' aristocracy'. A proletarianized middle class has been stripped of job security and rewarded with privileged but worthless benefits (stock options in NASDAQ are used to paper walls or, for the most resourceful, recycled as toilet paper). Old guard leaders of race, gender and ecology movements from the 1960s and 1970s and middle-aged prostrated intellectuals who have jumped on the bandwagon of the Third Way have been replaced by new leadership which is more militant, anti-corporate, anti-neoliberal and by a growing number of extra-parliamentary anti-capitalist activists.

True there is no consensus on the alternatives which run the gamut from community-based and -controlled economies to consumer–worker-based socialism, from changes in property regimes to a return of public regulation. It is sheer shortsightedness to argue that sectoral movements do not add up to some idealized collective movement made to order for the coffee-sipping intellectuals of Soho. The emergence of workable coalitions and joint actions, the common forums and dialogues do not add up to a new version of Lenin or Keir Hardy's working class party, but it is a beginning. The growing internationalism (without overseas oracles or revolutionary centres) evidenced in the North-South joint actions of peasants from the Third World and farmers from Europe is promising. There are enormous challenges in creating a new revolutionary socialist consciousness, generalizing it to reach the millions in motion, organizing and providing a new inclusive theory to provide diagnosis and strategic direction. One thing is very clear, intellectual progress of this burgeoning left will not depend on the intellectual fads and foibles of prostrate intellectuals who throw pebbles from the command pots of leftist journals that have lost touch with reality. Struggle for reforms in this movement are linked to structural challenges to empire and, in some cases, to the property regime. Multiple collective agencies of greater or lesser strength have emerged to call into question, the New Imperial Order, in a few instances struggling for state power.

While the public relations hucksters mount a propaganda campaign, even borrowing the language of the left, to promote science linked to control and exploitation of genes, plant, and so on, the left has counter-attacked by exposing the manipulative and thoughtless nature of corporate genetic engineering. Against the mindless embrace by the corporate hucksters (and a handful of leftists) of the development of the productive forces (or destructive forces), the left has brought to the fore the centrality of the social relations of production as defining the meaning, content and consequences of scientific work and advanced research. In this, the emerging left continues and deepens the intellectual work and practice of the last half century. A lot of work remains to be done, particularly in the field of ideological clarification, but much has already been accomplished in diagnosing the empire, discovering its fault lines and in creating the new radical movements.

Notes

1   Perry Anderson, one of the most influential left intellectuals in the Anglo-American world, has written the most succinct and polemical essay defining a new direction for *The New Left Review* (Anderson, 2000). In this essay, he defends the thesis of the complete dominance of the US Empire (what he dubs 'US hegemony') and the utter defeat and disintegration of the left. His thesis, however, is deeply flawed, in method,

theory and analysis, leading him to an unwarranted retreat toward a kind of apolitical centrist politics. This chapter, in part, is a refutation of his arguments as well as an advance on an alternative theoretical approach.

2   While Anderson's essay is largely concerned with defining a new direction for his journal (NLR) in the course of doing so he attempts to provide a historical–political context for its form and content over the last four decades.

3   Anderson's attack on theoretical or cultural writing which is committed to class-struggle politics and defence of arcane and 'art for art's sake' reactionary posturing comes out in the following 'Attempts to conscript [sic] any theoretical or cultural field for instrumental purposes [sic] will always be futile or counter-productive ... NLR will publish articles regardless of their immediate relationship, or lack of it, to familiar [sic] radical agendas'. Anderson's use of pejorative terms to caricature activist intellectuals and distort the issues in debate is a constant throughout the essay and suggests that what the essay lacks in substance it makes up in polemical zeal.

4   Anderson, in one of his less than lucid forays into the world of science, to bolster his passive ideological posture writes 'no collective agency able to match the power of capital is yet on the horizon. We are in a time, as genetic engineering looms [sic], when the only revolutionary force at present capable of disturbing its equilibrium appears to be scientific progress itself – the forces of production, so unpopular with Marxists convinced of the primacy of relations of production when a socialist movement was still alive. But if the human energies for a change of system are ever released again, it will be from within the metabolism [sic] of capitalism itself'. Quoting these theoretical ruminations is worthwhile in highlighting Anderson's retreat toward the kind of sloganeering General Electric made popular in the 1950s ('science is our principal product') and his uninformed use of science metaphors to cover up the shortcomings of his attempt to devise a theory of social change.

5   Throughout the essay Anderson has a tendency to ignore writers outside of his narrow circle of collaborators who have greater competence and depth. For example, in the field of media studies, Schiller, Parenti, Chomsky and Herman have produced far more significant work in the mass media than Debray, yet only the latter is cited.

6   Among the most virulent critics of the renewal of the left in the 1960s, and opponent of the Indo-Chinese revolution, was US writer Irving Howe and his quarterly *Dissent*.

7   On the revolutionary significance of rock, Anderson (2000: 7) writes: 'The two dominant markers of the period (1960s) was the emergence of rock music as a pervasive sound wave [sic] of youth revolt ... a popular form laying claim to both aesthetic breakthrough and social upsurge.' From pop rock in the 1960s to pop science in the 1990s, Anderson follows a well-worn path of the counter-cultural gurus of the earlier period to market populists of the 1990s.

8   The writers in this genre include Samir Amin, Gunder Frank, and Wallerstein, ex-theorists of 'dependency' and advocates of what has been termed (by Wallerstein) 'world systems theory'.

9   Bob Brenner, on the editorial board of *New Left Review* in a private conversation.

10   Perry Anderson (2000: 10), in his usual hyperbolic style, writes: 'American capitalism has resoundingly reasserted its primacy in all fields – economic, political, military, cultural – with an unprecedented eight year boom ... there is little doubt that the underlying competitive position of US business has been critically strengthened.'

11   Anderson repeatedly affirms his categorical denials of significant left opposition, as if to assure himself of their veracity. He asks and answers his own question: 'What is the principle aspect of the past decade? Put briefly, it can be defined as the virtually

uncontested consolidation and universal diffusion of neo-liberalism' (2000: 10). A few pages later, he repeats: 'In general what is strong is not democratic aspiration from below but the asphyxiation of public debate and political difference by capital from above' (p. 16). On the following page he makes even more exuberant claims in a fit akin to manic defeatism: 'For the first time since the Reformation, there are no longer any significant oppositions – that is systematic rival outlooks – within the thought-world of the West: and scarcely any on a world scale' (2000: 17).

12   Anderson's attraction to rightist ideologues and their writing is evident in several of his sweeping generalizations. 'By contrast (to the Left) commanding the field of direct political constructions of the time, the Right has provided one fluent vision of where the world is going, or has stopped, after another – Fukuijama, Brzezinski, Huntington, Yergin, Luttwak, Friedman. These are writers that unite a single powerful thesis with a fluent popular style. This confident genre ... finds no equivalent on the Left' (2000: 19). Carried away by his fervour for hard-right ideologues, Anderson later finds 'The most devastating criticism of the expansion of NATO and the war in the Balkans often came from the Right. The (NLR) review should welcome interventions like these' (2000: 24). I doubt if Le Pen, Haidar, Buchanan have time or interest in writing for NLR. In any case, Anderson is clearly not referring to the respectable right when he refers to their 'devastating criticism' since the earlier-mentioned writers all support NATO expansion, and so on.

13   Anderson in the antiseptic language of academia writes about the left: '... most of the tension between deviant [sic] or insurgent impulses [sic] from below and the established order has been absorbed as the market has appropriated and institutionalised youth culture in much the same way it earlier encapsulated avant-garde practices: but ... much more thoroughly' (2000: 20). Anderson's uninformed excursions into psycho-babble in discussing left movements ('deviant and insurgent impulses') his preposterous amalgamation of major trade union, peasant and student movements with 'youth culture' to argue for general cooptation belies a sad decline in his analytical abilities.

14   Anderson provides a litany of defeats for the left, which strangely includes the economic stagnation of Japanese capitalism (2000: 10–12).

15   Anderson grossly understates the role of violence in sustaining what he dubs 'US hegemony'. 'The force of this (US) order lies not in repression but dilution and neutralization; and so far it has handled its newer challenges with equanimity' (2000: 16). One is struck again by Anderson's attempt to give profundity to banality by adopting pseudo-scientific terminology.

16   Anderson's abuse of the term 'hegemony' to cover all instances of imperial rule (he forgets to use the I-word once) is an egregious fault given the pervasiveness of violence, overt and covert, that characterizes the past decade of US world supremacy.

17   Prostrators are not necessarily supporters of US imperialist power; they include writers with an inability to recognize any reality other than imperial power, they are imbued with a sense of awe and impressionability before the scribes and publicists of this power and harbour a deep-seated hostility to those 'unbelievers' who are engaged in struggle against the empire.

18   A typical case of Anderson's polemical excesses in analyzing the deeply divided green and feminist movements is found in the following: 'The performance of feminists in the United States and the Greens in Germany, where each movement is strongest – in the service of Clinton's regimen in the White House and NATO's war in the Balkans speaks for itself' (2000: 16).

19   For a more detailed account of the new revolutionary tendencies in Latin America see Petras (1999: 11–57).

20 Perry Anderson's ill-advised prophecy presumably is based on his acquaintance with Cardoso 25 years earlier, or related to his belief in the superior intellectual capacity of right-wing ideologues.

21 On 19–21 January 2000, a general strike and broad coalition of Indians, peasants and middle-level military officials actually seized parliament and established a popular regime of very short duration. Similar displays of mass power that challenge US client regimes occurred in Bolivia resulting in dozens of deaths and the reversal of neo-liberal policies. Likewise in Paraguay, student–peasant–trade union alliances have blocked the return of dictatorial rule. To say that this has no importance, that it doesn't measure up to a 'real opposition', is to engage in real or unintended apologetics. Realism's first rule of order is to recognize power even if it comes from below and the Third World.

22 See Anderson's litany of the pitfalls of the activist left today (2000: 13–14). What Anderson lacks in perception of the burgeoning social–political movements he makes up with psychobabble, a version of old-fashioned ad hominum argumentation. Characterizing activist-left-intellectuals as engaging in a kind of politics of 'consolation' he writes: 'there is a natural human tendency to try and find silver linings in what would otherwise seem an overwhelmingly hostile environment. The need to have some message of hope induces a propensity to over-estimate the significance of contrary processes, to invest inappropriate agencies with disinterested potentials, to nourish illusions in imaginary forces. It is also true that no political movement can survive without offering some measure of emotional relief to its adherents, which in periods of defeat will inevitably involve elements of psychological compensation' (2000: 13). If we can excuse the excess cynicism and manipulative machinations that Professor Anderson imputes to popular mass leaders, we are obligated to repudiate a posture which substitutes psychobabble for honest debate and discussion of programs, theories and strategies with intellectual activists.

23 Anderson, while cavalierly dismissing millions of protestors in India and thousands in France, attacking genetic modification ('no collective agency able to match the power of capital is yet on the horizon') joins hands with the publicists of Monsanto: 'We are at a time, as genetic engineering looms, when the only revolutionary force at present capable of disturbing its equilibrium appears to be scientific progress itself ...' (2000: 17). Anderson's belief in science divorced from class and state power that defines the tasks and uses of scientific research and discoveries and uncritical embrace of genetic engineering is too bizarre to warrant much comment.

24 Gains and reforms by mass feminist and environmentalist movements in struggle have, according to Anderson, 'proven compatible with the routines [sic] of accumulation' (2000: 16).

25 Based on a flawed historical–theoretical approach, Arrighi argued 'the displacement of an "old" region (North America) by a "new" region (East Asia) as the most dynamic centre of the processes of capital accumulation on a world scale is already a reality' (2000: 322).

26 Perry Anderson describes these right-wing ideologues and their polemical publications as follows: 'The doctrines of the Right that have theorized capitalism as a systematic order retain their tough minded strength. Those who always believed in the overriding value of free markets and private ownership of the means of production include many figures of intellectual substance' (2000: 16). In contrast, left-intellectual activists are described as 'sterile' maximalists, full of 'piety' and euphemisms, who 'lend credence to illusions, sustaining conformist myths' and who 'confuse the desirable from the feasible' (p. 14). Anthony Giddens beware, Blair may find a new speech writer.

27 As Anderson argues: 'One might say that by definition TINA (There is no alternative) only acquires full force once an alternative (Third Way Social Democratic) regime demonstrates that there are truly no alternative policies' (2000: 11). To consider the Social Democrats an alternative and their right-wing policies a historical novelty is absurd.

28 Robert Brenner (2000) puts into question some of Anderson's exuberant enthusiasm for the US economy.

29 Any account of the challenges to the US empire and its clients and allies must include the Palestinians' heroic struggle against the Israeli settler-colonial regime. Despite thousands of casualties, assassinations and a murderous blockade inflicted by the Israeli military juggernaut, the intifada continues with virtually no support of any sort from the brilliant circle of Anglo-American writers who publish in Western Marxist literary–political journals.

Bibliography

Alden, Edward (2001), 'Manufacturers in Call to Bush on Strong Dollar', *Financial Times*, 8 June, London.

Alden, Edward and Christopher Bowe (2001), 'Bush Seeks Friends in Steel Industry', *Financial Times*, 8 June, London.

Alden, Edward and Richard McGregor (2001), 'White House Promises to Protect U.S. Steelworkers', *Financial Times*, 7 June, London.

Alden, Edward and Michael Peel (2001), 'U.S. May Ease Stance Over Money Laundering', *Financial Times*, 1 June, London.

Althusser, Louis (1970), *Reading Capital*, London: New Left Books.

Amalric, Frank (1998), 'Sustainable Livelihoods, Entrepreneurship, Political Strategies and Governance', *Development*, 41 (3): 31–44.

Anderson, Perry (2000), 'Renewals', *New Left Review*, 1 (Jan–Feb): 5–24.

Arrighi, Giovanni (1994), *The Long Twentieth Century,* London: Verso.

Baker, R. (1999), 'Private Banking and Money Laundering: A Case Study of Opportunities and Vulnerabilities', *Hearings before the Permanent Subcommittee of Investigations of the Committee on Governmental Affairs of the United States Senate*, November 9 and 10, testimony Raymond Baker, p.85.

Balakrishnan, G. (2000), 'Virgilian Visions', *New Left Review*, 5 (Sep–Oct).

Barkin, David (1998), *Riqueza, probeza y desarrollo sustentable*, Mexico City: Centro de Ecologia y Desarrollo.

Bartra, Roger (1993), *Agrarian Structure and Political Power in Mexico*, Baltimore: Johns Hopkins University Press.

Bartra, Roger (1976), 'Si los campesinos se extinguen', *Historia y Sociedad*, 8 (Winter): 71–83.

Bernstein, Henry (2001), 'The Peasantry in Global Capitalism: Who, Where and Why?' *Socialist Register*, London: Merlin.

Blackburn, Robin (2000), 'Cuba on the Block,' *New Left Review*, 4 (July–August).

Booth, David (1985), 'Marxism and Development Sociology: Interpreting the Impasse,' *World Development*, 13 (7).

Boulding, Kenneth and Tapan Mukerje (eds) (1972), *Economic Imperialism*, Ann Arbor, MI: The University of Michigan Press.

Brass, Tom (2000), *Peasants, Populism and Postmodernism: The Return of the Agrarian Myth*, London: Frank Cass Publishers.

Brass, Tom (1991), 'Moral Economists, Subalterns, New Social Movements and the (Re) Emergence of a (Post) Modernised (Middle) Peasant', *Journal of Peasant Studies*, 18 (2).

Brenner, Robert (2000), 'The Boom and the Bubble', *New Left Review*, 6 (Nov–Dec).

Brewer, Anthony (1980), *Marxist Theories of Imperialism: A Critical Survey*, London: Routledge & Kegan Paul.

Bukharin, Nicolai (1929), *Imperialism and the World Economy*, London: Martin Lawrence Limited.

Bulmer-Thomas, Victor (1996), *The New Economic Model in Latin America and its Impact on Income Distribution and Poverty*, New York: St. Martin's Press.

Burgwal, Gerrit (1990), 'An Introduction to the Literature on Urban Movements in Latin America,' in Willem Assies et al. (eds), *Structures of Power, Movements of Resistance: An Introduction to the Theories of Urban Movements in Latin America*, Amsterdam: Centre for Latin American Research and Documentation.

Burnham, James (1941), *Managerial Revolution: What is Happening in the World*, New York: John Day.

Caldart, Roseli Salete (2000), *Pedagogia do Movimiento Sem Terra*, Petropolis RJ: Vozes.

Caldart, Roseli Salete (1997), *Educação em Movimento. Formação de educadoras e educadores No MST*, Petrópolis RJ: Vozes.

Calderón, Fernando (1995), *Movimientos sociales y política*, México DF: Siglo XX1.

Calderón, Fernando and Elizabeth Jelín (1987), *Clases y movimientos sociales en America Latina. Perspectivas y realidades*, Buenos Aires: Cuadernos CEDES.

Camacho, D. and R. Menjivar (eds) (1989), *Los movimientos populares en América Latina*, México DF: Siglo XXI.

Cancian, Frank (1992), *The Decline of Community in Zinacantan*, Stanford: Stanford University Press.

Cancian, Frank (1987), 'Proletarianization in Zinacantan 1960–83', in Morgan Maclachan (ed.), *Household Economies and Their Transformation*, Lanham Md: University Press of America.

Cane, Alan (2001), 'Meltdown, But the Strongest Keep Their Cool', *Financial Times 500 – The World's Largest Companies*, 11 May, Supplement, London.

Castells, Manuel (1999a), *The Information Age – Economy, Society, Culture*: 1, Oxford: Blackwell.

Castells, Manuel (1999b), *The Information Age – Economy, Society, Culture, 3*, Oxford: Blackwell.

Castells, Manuel (1997), *The Information Age – Economy, Society, Culture, 2*, Oxford: Blackwell.

Castells, Manuel (1993), 'The Informational Economy and the New International Division of Labor', in Martin Carnoy et al., *The New Global Economy in the Information Age: Reflections on Our Changing World*, University Park: Penn State University Press.

Castells, Manuel (1983), *The City and the Grassroots: A Cross-Cultural Theory of Urban Social Movements*, London: Edward Arnold.

Casteñeda, Jorge (1993), *Utopia Unarmed: The Latin American Left After the Cold War*, New York: Random House.

Chambers, Robert and Gordon Conway (1998), 'Sustainable Rural Livelihoods: Some Working Definitions', *Development*, 41 (3).

Debray, Regis (1967), *Revolution in the Revolution*, New York: Monthly Review Press.

Deere, C.D., N. Pérez and E. Gonzales (1994), 'The View from Below: Cuban Agriculture in the Special Period in Peacetime', *Journal of Peasant Studies*, 21 (2).

De Janvry, Alain (1981), *The Agrarian Question and Reformism in Latin America*, Baltimore: Johns Hopkins University Press.

De Vylder, S. (1976), *Allende's Chile: The Political Economy of the Rise and Fall of the Unidad Popular*, Cambridge: Cambridge University Press.

Dialogos@Col1.Telecom.com.co.

Dominguez, Jorge (ed.) (1994), *Social Movements in Latin America The Experience of Peasants, Workers, the Urban Poor and the Middle Sectors*, New York: Garland Publishers.

Doremus, Paul, William Kelley, Louis Pauly and Simon Reich (1998), *The Myth of the Global Corporation*, Princeton: Princeton University Press.

Eckstein, Susan (1989), *Power and Popular Protest: Latin American Social Movements*, Berkeley: University of California Press.

Edelman, Marc (2000*), Peasants Against Globalization: Rural Social Movements in Costa Rica*, Stanford: Stanford University Press.

Escobar, Arturo and Sonia Alvarez (eds) (1992), *The Making of Social Movements in Latin America: Identity, Strategy, and Democracy*, Boulder CO: Westview Press.

Escobar, Arturo (1995), *Encountering Development: The Making and Unmaking of the Third World*, Princeton NJ: Princeton University Press.

Esteva, Gustavo and M.S. Prakash (1998), *Grassroots Postmodernism*, London: Zed Books.

Esteva, Gustavo (1983), *The Struggle for Rural Mexico*, South Hardy, MA: Bergin and Garvey.

Esteva, Gustavo (1978), '¿Y si los campesinos existen?', *Comercio Exterior* [Mexico City] 28 (June): 699–732.

FARC-EP (2000), *Historical Outline – International Commission Revolutionary Armed Forces of Colombia Peoples Army*, Toronto: FARC-EP, International Commission.

FARC website http://www.farcep.org/

Financial Times, 'FT 500: The World's Largest Companies', 11 May 2001.

Financial Times (2000), 1–2 July.

Ford, David (1989), 'Epilogue: Postmodernism and Postscript', in David Ford (ed.), *The Modern Theologians*, 2, Oxford: Basil Blackwell.

Foweraker, Joe (1995), *Theorizing Social Movements*, Boulder, CO: Pluto Press.

Frank, Thomas (2000), *One Market Under God*, New York: Doubleday.

Giddens, Anthony (1994), *Beyond Left and Right: The Future of Radical Politics*, Cambridge: Polity Press.

Giddens, Anthony (1990), *The Consequences of Modernity*, Cambridge: Polity Press.

Giddens, Anthony, with C. Pierson (1998), *Conversations with Anthony Giddens: Making Sense of Modernity*, Stanford CA: Stanford University Press.

Gitlin, Todd (1987), *Sixties: Years of Hope, Days of Rage*, New York: Bantam Books.

Gledhill, J. (1988), 'Agrarian Social Movements and Forms of Consciousness', *Bulletin of Latin American Research*, 7 (2).

Gordon, Robert (1999), 'U.S. Economic Growth Since 1870: One Big Wave?' *The American Economic Review*, May.

Gordon, Robert (1999), 'Has the New Economy Rendered the Productivity Slowdown Obsolete', June: http://faculty-web.at.nwu.edu/education/gordon/researchhome.htm

Green, Duncan (1995), *Silent Revolution: The Rise of Market Economics in Latin America*, London: Cassell.

Guattari, Felix and Antonio Negri (1990), *Communists Like Us*, New York: Semiotext(e).

Gulbenkian Commission (1996), *Open the Social Sciences: Report of the Gulbenkian Commission on the Restructuring of the Social Sciences*, Stanford CA: Stanford University Press.

Haber, Paul Lawrence (1996), 'Identity and Political Process: Recent Trends in the Study of Latin American Social Movements', *Latin American Research Review*, 31 (1): 171–87.

Haber, Stephen (1997), 'The Worst of Both Worlds: The New Cultural History of Mexico', *Mexican Studies /Estudios Mexicanos*, 13.

Halebsky, Sandor and Richard Harris (eds) (1995), *Capital, Power and Inequality in Latin America*, Boulder CO: Westview Press.

Hardt, Michael and Antonio Negri (2000), *Empire*, Cambridge MA: Harvard University Press.

Harvey Neil (1994), *Rebellion in Chiapas: Rural Reforms, Campesino Radicalism and the Limits to Salinismo*, San Diego: Center for US-Mexican Studies.

Hobsbawn, Eric (1994), *The Ages of extremes: The Short 20th Century, 1914–1991*, London: Michael Joseph.

Hobson, J.A. (1902, 1967), *Imperialism: A Study*, Ann Arbor MI: University of Michigan Press.

Howarth, David, J. Alettta and Yannis Slavrakakis (eds) (2000), *Discourse Theory and Political Analysis: Identities, Hegemonies and Social Change*, Manchester: Manchester University Press.

INCRA – Instituto Nacional de Colonização e Reforma Agrária (1999), *Balanço da Reforma Agraria e da Agricultura Familiar 1995–99*, Brasilia: Ministério do Desenvolvimiento Agrário.

Italy 79 Committee (1982), *The Italian Inquisition*, London: Red Notes.

Jameson, Fredric (2000), 'Globalization and Political Strategy', *New Left Review,* 4 (July–August).

Kay, Cristobal (1999), 'Rural Development: From Agrarian Reform to Neoliberalism and Beyond', in Robert Gwynne and Cristobal Kay (eds), *Latin America Transformed*, New York: Oxford University Press.

Kay, Cristobal (1998), 'Latin America's Agrarian Reform: Lights and Shadows', *Land Reform*, 2.

Kay, Cristobal (1982), 'Achievements and Contradictions of the Peruvian Agrarian Reform', *Journal of Development Studies*, 18 (2): 141–70.

Kay, Cristobal (1981), 'Political Economy, Class Alliances and Agrarian Change in Chile', *Journal of Peasant Studies*, 8 (4): 485–513.

Kearney, Michael (1996), *Reconceptualizing the Peasantry*, Boulder CO: Westview Press.

Kelly, Kevin (1998), *New Rules for the New Economy: Ten Radical Strategies for a Connected World*, New York: Viking.

Kitching, Gavin 1982), *Development and Underdevelopment in Historical Perspective*, London: Methuen.

Laclau, Ernesto and Chantal Mouffe (1985), *Hegemony and Socialist Strategy: Towards a Radical Democratic Politics*, London: Verso.

Latin American Perspectives (1994), 'Social Movements and Political Change in Latin America', *Latin American Perspectives*, 21 (5).

Lenin, V.I. (1950), 'Imperialism: The Highest Stage of Capitalism', *Selected Works*, I, Moscow: Foreign Languages Publishing House.

Liamzon, Tina et al. (eds) (1996), *Towards Sustainable Livelihoods*, Rome: Society for International Development.

Luard, Evan (1990), *The Globalization of Politics: The Changed Focus of Political Action in the Modern World*, New York: New York University Press.

Luxemburg, Rosa (1951), *The Accumulation of Capital*, New York: Monthly Review Press.

Luxemburg, Rosa and Nicolai Bukharin (1972), *Imperialism and the Accumulation of Capital*, London: Allen Lane.

Macas, Luis (2000a), 'Diez años del levantamiento del *Inti Raymi* de Junio de 1990: un balance provisional', *Boletín Mensual*, Instituto Científico de Culturas Indigenas, 15 June.

Macas, Luis (2000b), 'Movimiento indígena Ecuatoriano: Una evaluación necesaria', *Boletín ICCI RIMAY*, 3 (21).

Macas, Luis (1999), 'Los desafíos del movimiento indígena', *Boletín ICCI*, 1 (1).

Mallon, Florencia (1999), 'Time on the Wheel: Cycles of Revisionism and the New Cultural History', *Hispanic American Historical Review*, 79 (2): 331–51.

Mallon, Florencia (1995), *Peasant and Nation: The Making of Postcolonial Mexico and Peru*, Berkeley CA: University of California Press.

Mallon, Florencia (1994), 'The Promise and Dilemma of Subaltern Studies: Perspectives from Latin American History', *American Historical review*, 99 (5): 1491–1915.

Mallon, Florencia (1992), 'Indian Communities, Political Cultures and the State in Latin America, 1780–1990', *Journal of Latin American Studies*, 29, Supplement.

Marcos, Subcomandante (1994), 'A Tourist Guide to Chiapas', *Monthly Review*, 46 (May): 8–18.

Markoff, John (1996), *Waves of Democracy, Social Movements and Political Change*, Thousand Oaks CA: Pine Forge Press.

Matta Aldana, Luis Alberto (1999), *Colombia y las FARC-EP Origen de la Lucha Guerrillera*, Nafarroa: Txalaparta.

Bibliography

Max-Neef, Manfred (1989), 'Human Scale Development: An Option for the Future', *Development Dialogue*, 1.

McMichael, Philip (1996), *Development and Change: A Global Perspective*, Thousand Oaks CA: Pine Gorge Press.

Mills, C. Wright (1956), *The Power Elite*, New York: Oxford University Press.

Moore, David and Schmidz (eds) (1994), *Crisis and Renewal in Development Discourse*, London: MacMillan.

Munck, Gerardo (1997), 'Social Movements and Latin America: Conceptual Issues and Empirical Applications', Paper presented to the Latin American Studies Association, Guadalajara, 17–19 April.

Munck, Ronaldo and Denis O'Hearn (eds) (1999), *Critical Development Theory: Contributions to a New Paradigm*, London: Zed Books.

Negri, Antonio (2001), 'The Imperial System', *Brecha*, March 15–22.

Negri, Antonio (1989), *The Politics of Subversion*, Oxford: Polity Press.

Negri, Antonio (1988), *Revolution Retrieved: Writings on Marx, Keynes, Capitalist Crisis, and New Social Subjects 1967–83*, London: Red Notes.

Negri, Antonio (1984), *Marx Beyond Marx: Lessons on the Grundrisse*, Massachussets: Bergin & Garvey Publishers, Inc.

Norris, Christopher (1997), *Teoría acrítica. Posmodernismo: intelectuales y la Guerra del Golfo*, Madrid: Cátedra.

Nugent, Daniel (1995), 'Northern Intellectuals and the EZLN', *Monthly Review*, 47 (3).

Oman, Charles (1996), *The Policy Challenges of Globalization and Regionalization*, Paris: OECD Development Centre.

Overton, James (2001), 'Peasants on the Internet? Informalization in a Global Economy', *Journal of Peasant Studies*, 28 (4).

Owen, Roger, and Bob Sutcliffe (eds) (1972), *Studies in the Theory of Imperialism*, London: Longman.

Petras, James (2000), *Globaloney*, Buenos Aires: Antidote.

Petras, James (1999), *The Left Strikes Back: Class Conflict in the Age of Neoliberalism*, Boulder, CO: Westview.

Petras, James (1998), 'The Political and Social Bases of Regional Variation in Land Occupations in Brazil', *Journal of Peasant Studies*, 25 (4).

Petras, James (1997), 'Latin America: the Resurgence of the Left', *New Left Review*, 223 (May–June): 17–47.

Petras, James (1980), 'The Imperial State', *Review*, Fall.

Petras, James and Morris H. Morley (1983–84), 'The Errors of Edward Thompson', *End Papers*, 6 (Winter): 105–107.

Petras, James, and Morris H. Morley (1980), 'The US Imperial State', *Review*, IV (2).

Petras, James and Henry Veltmeyer (2001a), 'Are Latin American Peasant Movements Still a Force for Change?' *Journal of Peasant Studies*, 28 (2).

Petras, James and Henry Veltmeyer (2001b), *Unmasking Globalisation: The New Face of Imperialism*, London: Zed Books / Halifax: Fernwood Books.

Petras, James and Henry Veltmeyer (2000), *Brasil de Cardoso: Expropriação de un país*, Petrópolis: Editorial Vozes.

Petras, James and Henry Veltmeyer (1999), 'Latin America at the End of the Millennium', *Monthly Review*, (July–August): 31–52.

Rahnema, M. and V. Bawtree (eds) (1997), *The Post-Development Reader*, London: Zed Books.

Randall, L. (1996), *Reforming Mexico's Agrarian Reform*, New York: M.E. Sharpe.

Red Notes (1978), *Living With an Earthquake: Italy 1977–78*, London: CSE Books.

Red Notes (1979), *Working Class Autonomy and the Crisis: Italian Marxist Texts of the Theory and Practice of a Class Movement, 1964–79*, London: CSE Books.

Redfield, Robert (1956), *The Little Community, and Peasant Society and Culture*, Chicago: University of Chicago Press.

Reich, Robert (1992), *The Work of Nations*, New York: Vintage 1992.

Robles, Wilder (2000), 'The Rural Landless Workers Movement in Brazil', *Canadian Journal of Development Studies*, 22 (2).

Roman, Richard and Edur Velasco Arregui (1997), 'Zapatismo and the Workers' Movement in Mexico', *Monthly Review*, 49 (July–August): 98–116.

Roseberry, William (1989), *Anthropologies and Histories: Essays in Culture, History and Political Economy*, New Brunswick: Rutgers University Press.

Sachs, Wolfgang (1999), *Planetary Dialectics*, London: Zed Books.

Sachs, Wolfgang (ed.) (1992), *The Development Dictionary: A Guide to Knowledge and Power*, London: Zed Books.

Sartre, Jean-Paul (1961), *Sartre on Cuba*, New York: Ballantine.

Schumpeter, Joseph A. (1951), *Imperialism and Social Classes*, New York: Augustus M. Kelley, Inc.

Schuurman, Frans (ed.) (1993), *Beyond the Impasse: New Directions in Development Theory*, London: Zed Books.

Scott, James (1990), *Domination and the Arts of Resistance: Hidden Transcripts*, London and New Haven: Yale University Press.

Seligson, M.E. (1995), 'Thirty Years of Transformation in the Agrarian Structure of El Salvador', *Latin American Research Review*, 30 (3): 33–74.

Slater, David (1985), *New Social Movements and the State in Latin America*, Amsterdam: CEDLA.

Spiegel, Peter (2001), 'Hawk to Head Pentagon Group Advising Bush on Defence Policy', *Financial Times*, 5 June, London.

Stedile, Joao Pedro (2000), Interview, 14 May.

Stedile, Joao Pedro and Sergio Frei (1993), *A luta pela terra no Brasil*, Sao Paulo: Scritta.

Stiglitz, J. (2002), *Globalization and its Discontents*, New York: W.W. Norton.

Sweezy, Paul and Leo Huberman (1960), *Cuba: Anatomy of a Revolution*, New York: Monthly Review Press.

Thompson, E.P. (1983), *The Nation*, 26 February and 16 April.

UNRISD-United Nations Research Institute for Social Development (2000), 'Civil Society Strategies and Movements for Rural Asset Redistribution and Improved Livelihoods', UNRISD – Civil Society and Social Movements Programme. Geneva: UNRISD.

Veltmeyer, Henry (2001a), 'Civil Society and Social Movements in Latin America: the Dynamics of Intersectoral Linkages and Alliances', Thematic Paper. Geneva: UNRISD.

Veltmeyer, Henry (2001b), 'The Politics of Language: Deconstructing Postdevelopment Discourse', Paper presented as keynote address at meeting of the Canadian Association for the Study of International Development (CASID), 27 May, Quebec City.

Veltmeyer, Henry (2000a), 'The Dynamics of Social Change in Mexico and the EZLN', *Latin American Perspectives*, 27 (5): 88–110.

Veltmeyer, Henry (2000b), 'The Post-Marxist Project: an Assessment and Critique of Ernesto Laclau', *Sociological Inquiry*, 70 (4).

Veltmeyer, Henry (1997), 'New Social Movements in Latin America: The Dynamics of Class and Identity', *Journal of Peasant Studies*, 25 (1): 139–69.

Veltmeyer, Henry (1993), 'The Landless Workers Movement in Contemporary Brazil', *Labour, Capital and Society*, 26 (2): 204–25.

Veltmeyer, Henry (1983), 'Surplus Labour and Class Formation on the Latin American Periphery', in Ron Chilcote and Dale Johnston (eds), *Theories of Development*, Beverly Hills, CA: SAGE Publications.

Veltmeyer, Henry and Anthony O'Malley (2001), *The Dynamics of Community Development in Latin America*, West Hartford, Conn: Kumarian Press.

Veltmeyer, Henry, and James Petras (2000), *The Dynamics of Social Change in Latin America*, London: Macmillan Press.

Veltmeyer, Henry, and James Petras (1997), *Neoliberalism and Class Conflict in Latin America*, London: Macmillan Press.

Veltmeyer, H., Petras, J. and Vieux, S. (1997), *Neoliberalism and Class Conflict in Latin America*, London: Macmillan Press.

Vilas, Carlos (1995), *Between Earthquakes and Volcanoes: Market, State, and the Revolution in Central America*, New York: Monthly Review Press.

Warren, Bill (1990), *Imperialism: Pioneer of Capitalism*, London: NLB.

Wickham-Crowley, Timothy (ed.) (1991), *Exploring Revolution: Essays on Latin American Insurgency and Revolutionary Theory*, Armonk: ME Sharpe.

Wolf, Martin (1999), 'Not So New Economy', *Financial Times*, 1 August, London.

Wolfe, Eric (1969), *Peasant Wars in the Twentieth Century*, New York: Harper and Row.

Zamora, Ruben (1995), 'Foreword', in Fred Rosen and Deirdre McFadyen (eds), *Free Trade and Economic Restructuring in Latin America*, New York: Monthly Review Press.

Zamosc, León (1986), *The Agrarian Question and the Peasant Movement in Colombia*, Cambridge and New York: Cambridge University Press.

Zapata, Francisco (1987), 'El nuevo carácter de los movimientos sociales en América Latina', *Estado y Sociedad*, 3 (Diciembre).

Index

n/ns indicates note/s.

academic-apolitical intellectuals
156–7
activism, NGOs 147–8
activist-intellectuals 156
adjudication 45–6
Afganistan 144, 145, 146, 147, 148
agrarian reform
impact of IFIs 116
and peasant movements 90–92, 93–4
agriculture
EU 7, 44, 45
US 5, 7, 44, 45
ALCA *see* Latin American Free Trade
Area
Alden, E. 64
and McGregor, R. 63, 64
Anderson, P. 151, 152, 153, 154, 156, 172,
173–5*ns*
Another Development (AD) approach
83–4, 105*ns*
'anti-dumping' regulations 6, 45, 64, 78
anti-globalization activities, NGOs 142,
143
Argentina 21–2, 25–6, 27, 30
economic crisis 5, 21, 26, 30, 44
–US relations 80
see also unemployed workers'
movement
Asia 46, 47
economic crisis 5, 43–4, 58

Baker, R. 33, 34
Balkan states 72, 75, 144
Bartra, R. 88, 107*n*
Bell, D. 154
bin Laden, Osama 144, 146, 147
biotechnology industry 61–2, 71

Brazil 26–7, 28–9, 30–31
economic crisis 44
mass media 23
steel exports 6, 45, 78
–US relations 80
Worker's Party (PT) 23, 26–7, 28–9
see also Rural Landless Workers'
Movement (MST)
Bush Administration 19–20, 22
anti-terrorism campaign 139–41, 144,
145–6, 147–9
crisis management 70–73
unilateralism 75–7
vs Clinton Administration 74–5, 77

capitalist business cycle 42, 59, 60
Cardoso, F.H. 23, 26, 45, 78, 80, 161–2
Casteñeda, J. 22
Cavallo, D. 80
CB *see* correspondent banks
central banks 5, 50
Chavez, H. 18–20, 25, 30
Cheney, D. 75, 76
Chile 89
China 76, 164–5
Citibank 34, 35–6
class
new peasantry/social movements
87–97
new proletariat/subaltern 14–16
political organization/leadership
118–19, 123*n*
transnationalist capitalist (TCC) 47, 48,
49, 50
unemployed 129, 132
world system approach 43
see also Marxist perspectives

187